The End of
Superpower Conflict
in the Third World

The End of
Superpower Conflict
in the Third World

EDITED BY

Melvin A. Goodman

Westview Press
BOULDER • SAN FRANCISCO • OXFORD

This Westview softcover edition is printed on acid-free paper and bound in library-quality, coated covers that carry the highest rating of the National Association of State Textbook Administrators, in consultation with the Association of American Publishers and the Book Manufacturers' Institute.

Copyright © 1992 by Westview Press, Inc.

Published in 1992 in the United States of America by Westview Press, Inc., 5500 Central Avenue, Boulder, Colorado 80301–2877, and in the United Kingdom by Westview Press, 36 Lonsdale Road, Summertown, Oxford OX2 7EW

Library of Congress Cataloging-in-Publication Data
The end of superpower conflict in the Third World / edited by Melvin
A. Goodman.
    p. cm.
Includes bibliographical references and index.
ISBN 0-8133-8046-4
    1. World politics—1989– 2. Security, International.
3. Developing countries—Foreign relations. I. Goodman, Melvin A.
(Melvin Allan), 1938–   .
D860.E54 1992
327'.09'045—dc20   92-6659
                                                                         CIP

Printed and bound in the United States of America

The paper used in this publication meets the requirements
of the American National Standard for Permanence of Paper
for Printed Library Materials Z39.48-1984.

10   9   8   7   6   5   4   3   2   1

For Suzy and Michael

Contents

Preface

This study describes and analyzes the efforts of the United States and the former Soviet Union to resolve regional confrontations. U.S. Presidents Ronald Reagan and George Bush worked closely with former President Mikhail Gorbachev to resolve crises in Afghanistan, Angola, Cambodia, El Salvador, Nicaragua, and the Persian Gulf. The United States took steps to improve bilateral relations with former enemies in Southeast Asia, and Russia continued Soviet policies to develop ties with Israel, South Korea, and South Africa. New U.S.-Soviet strategies in turn encouraged negotiations to resolve conflicts in the Middle East, the Korean peninsula, and southern Africa. In addition, North and South Korea, Argentina and Brazil, and India and Pakistan entered agreements designed to end the risk of nuclear deployment and reduce the risk of nuclear war.

The replacement of the Soviet Union by a new Commonwealth of Independent States (CIS) generated a major debate about the future of international relations, including the impact of the CIS on conflict resolution. The debate turned in part on perceptions of the commonwealth, which is not a state but a fig leaf for an unwieldy grouping of republics, designed to determine responsibility for borders and military assets. The debate also focused on whether Russia and its president, Boris Yeltsin, would continue to concern itself with resolving problems that have burdened the international arena over the past several decades. Despite the confusion and uncertainty introduced by the coup in Moscow in August 1991 and the differences between Slavic and non-Slavic foreign ministries since the formation of the commonwealth in December, there has been remarkable continuity in Moscow's foreign policy.

The international community, recognizing the importance of a stable commonwealth, extended billions of dollars in loans, credits, and even grants to the CIS. Most of this aid came from the European Community, but the United States and Japan also extended $5 billion in credits. Russia, anxious to receive Western support, moved quickly to remove tactical nuclear weapons from Ukraine, Kazakhstan, and Belarus; withdraw former Soviet forces from eastern Germany and Poland; and support conflict resolution in the Third World. Following the formation of the commonwealth in December, Moscow encouraged the dismantling of the guerrilla military apparatus in El Salvador, hosted the third phase of the Middle East peace process for discussion of arms control and refugee problems, and ended military deliveries to the Najibullah government in Afghanistan.

The states of the commonwealth also continued to reduce arms deliveries to the Third World, including such hard-currency customers as Libya and Syria. Third World states, moreover, are showing signs of losing interest in Russian weapons systems because of the withdrawal of Russian military advisers, who would maintain these systems, and production problems in the commonwealth that will compromise the distribution of spare parts. The Russian deputy minister for the economy believes that earnings for arms transfers in 1992 will be less than $1.5 billion.

Yeltsin has indicated that Russia will continue efforts to resolve regional differences in order to qualify for international assistance. He has told visiting delegations that Moscow will discuss with Japan the return of the four Kurile islands, the Northern territories that Stalin seized at the end of World War II. Gorbachev was willing to consider "joint administration" of the islands, but Yeltsin presumably realizes that the issue of the return of the islands must be placed on the negotiating table in order to get Japanese financial assistance in developing Russian resources in Siberia, particularly timber, natural gas, and oil.

Yeltsin wants to move quickly to take advantage of Gorbachev's announcement in September that Soviet troops would be withdrawn from Cuba, realizing that the Cuban connection has been a major obstacle to obtaining economic assistance from the United States. It is not certain that the Russians will evacuate Lourdes, an electronic monitoring facility near Havana that is Moscow's largest and most sophisticated spy station outside its border, but the Soviet 2,800-man combat brigade presumably will depart by 1993. Russian officials have been meeting with members of the Cuban opposition, based in Miami, and Yeltsin's foreign minister has informed Cuban exiles that Russian subsidies to Havana have ended.

For the next several years, the Russians will be preoccupied with their internal crises and will play only a supporting role in most efforts to resolve conflicts. As a result, Russia and the commonwealth will be more than willing to follow Washington's lead in resolving disputes in the Third World. The grim realities of the Russian economy, including chronic shortages of economic goods, inefficient use of natural resources, and backward industries, will compel the commonwealth to insinuate itself with the West. For the first time since the end of World War II, Moscow will have to limit its interests abroad to meet domestic requirements and diminish and democratize a military force that formerly had international objectives. The former Soviet navy has left the Indian Ocean and the Mediterranean Sea, and the former Soviet army will have to worry more about paying its personnel than procuring sophisticated weaponry. Third

World states will have to look elsewhere for military and economic assistance.

Russia will remain actively engaged in proliferation issues in view of the fact that many nations with missiles or missile programs (e.g., China, Iran, Israel, India, and Pakistan) could target the nations of the commonwealth, including the Russian republic. Russia also will be concerned with its "sensitive southern frontier," particularly Afghanistan, China, Iran, and Turkey, and will make special efforts to stabilize those relationships. With millions of ethnic Russians living in non-Russian republics, Moscow will become more interested in using the human rights provisions of the United Nations and the Council for Security and Cooperation in Europe (CSCE) as a way to protect Slavic minorities.

The end of superpower conflict in the Third World raises many questions for readers of this book. Will the dissolution of the Soviet Union and possible retrenchment in the United States increase the role of the UN and the Security Council in conflict resolution? Will the "civil crisis" in the commonwealth threaten the continuity of Moscow's role as a stabilizing force in the international arena? Will the new government in Moscow continue to support UN peace efforts in Afghanistan, Cambodia, and Yugoslavia? Is the United States, which formerly exaggerated Soviet influence and power in the Third World, now exaggerating the threat of Moscow's contribution to nuclear proliferation? What is the legitimate role of Russia and the United States in halting or at least retarding nuclear proliferation? Finally, will Moscow's experience in conflict resolution provide experience and lessons for resolving crises within the commonwealth, particularly in the Caucasus? This book suggests answers to some, but not all, of these questions and attempts to shed new light on the field of conflict resolution.

The authors are from both academic and government communities and have received assistance from many people in writing this book. Special thanks must go to Ms. Angelique Crumbly of the National War College, who solved many problems in melding the texts from the contributors.

Melvin A. Goodman
Washington, D.C.

1

Introduction: Moscow's Plan for Conflict Resolution in the Third World

Melvin A. Goodman

The failure of the reactionary coup in Moscow in August 1991 launched political shock waves in Russia that will bring radical changes in global politics. The collapse of the Communist party in the Kremlin will have a powerful ideological impact, isolating China, Cuba, North Korea, and Vietnam. The decline in Soviet power will be felt in Africa and the Middle East, where erstwhile Soviet clients will have to look elsewhere for political and diplomatic support. The disastrous Russian economy will limit Moscow's influence throughout the Third World and increase dependence on Western economic and technical assistance. As a result, Boris Yeltsin and his immediate successors presumably will remain interested in arms control with the United States and conflict resolution in the Third World.

There can be no doubt that former President Gorbachev has made extraordinary changes in policy toward the Third World. Nothing, surely, resembles the crude behavior of his predecessors. Everything seems in flux, with changes in domestic and foreign policy almost daily. Western observers, and especially American officials, can be truly grateful for the reductions in the Russian defense budget, unilateral cuts in Russian ground troops, and the end to Communist regimes in Eastern Europe. Under Gorbachev, Moscow cut military and economic assistance to the Third World and concluded a series of arms control measures favorable to interests of the United States.

Consider what has happened within a bare few years. The USSR's withdrawal from Afghanistan decreased the possibility of military operations in Southwest Asia and possible Soviet-American confrontation. Soviet policies were central to Cuban withdrawal from Angola and Vietnamese withdrawal from Cambodia. Now political solutions to regional problems are at the top of the Russian agenda, including the unprecedented Soviet-

American cooperation to end the conflict in the Persian Gulf and limit Saddam Hussein's military power.

Presidents George Bush and Gorbachev served notice at their summit meeting in September 1990 that Iraq would not benefit from its aggression in Kuwait. The Soviet stance came despite the existence of a treaty of friendship and cooperation with Iraq since 1972 and the Soviet role as Iraq's main weapons supplier. Presumably Gorbachev's predecessors would have shielded Iraq from Western criticism and continued arms shipments; Gorbachev, however, supported the first joint crisis management exercise with the United States and, in doing so, used a Third World crisis to establish a firmer basis for detente with Washington.

All in all, the failure of the coup will reinforce the changes in Soviet foreign policy during the Gorbachev era. Since 1985, the Soviets have been conducting a strategic retreat from the gains of the Brezhnev era. The disappearance of Soviet presence in many client states, the turning of these nations to other sources and, for the most part, the limited availability of alternative sources for military and economic largesse, constitutes one of the minor miracles of recent history. The achievement of a superpower consensus has brought stability and conciliation to long-standing trouble spots in Angola, Cambodia, and Nicaragua and secured the resolution of the crisis in the Persian Gulf. It is a most gratifying change from what has been one of the most worrisome developments of the past generation and more.

The Effect of Gorbachev

Reexamination of Soviet policy began with Gorbachev's accession and the decision to withdraw from Afghanistan. From the outset, Gorbachev had expressed his intention to change policy, particularly in the Third World. Recognizing that his ability to do so required sweeping personnel and organizational change, he replaced the top decision-makers in the field of foreign policy and reorganized party and government institutions dealing with national security. He changed leadership of the foreign ministry and the central committee's International Department and created a new foreign affairs department under Aleksandr Yakovlev to report directly to the Politburo.[1] The changes indicated that Gorbachev was giving high priority to improved relations with the United States and the West, and political rather than military solutions to Third World problems. The Soviets no longer brusquely dismissed U.S. demands that more conciliatory behavior in the Third World was a condition to more stable Soviet-American relations.

Gorbachev's interest in diminishing the Soviet military position in the Third World was part of another interest of the Soviet leader—demilitarization. Since 1985 there has been a decline in the status of the military, a reduced role in decisionmaking, and a reduction in defense spending and modernization. Top military leaders were reshuffled—the defense minister, first deputy defense ministers, commanders of theater forces, chiefs of military districts, and the chief of the Main Political Directorate of the Army and Navy. The latter position was particularly important because it was within the defense ministry but subordinate to the central committee of the party.

Gorbachev maintained that the Soviet Union had no interest in contesting U.S. superiority in power projection. Michael MccGwire may be correct in arguing that the Soviets once sought use of the political and physical infrastructure in the Third World to meet their requirements in case of world-wide war, but the current leadership surely is reducing any military role for forces in South Asia and the Middle East.[2] The Russians are showing no interest in extended deployments in distant areas and appear to favor reducing the size of their Navy and limiting the mission in out-of-area waters to reconnaissance. Older ships are being scrapped and modernization curtailed, which supports Moscow's declared interest in naval arms limitation and creation of nuclear-free zones in the Pacific.

All this is consistent with Gorbachev's position at the 27th Soviet Party Congress in 1986 rationalizing a closer relationship with the United States and encouraging greater attention to regional security in the Third World. Gorbachev repeatedly stated afterward that a resolution of the war in Afghanistan might bring increased effort to settle regional conflicts and defuse sources of tension with the United States. Former Foreign Minister Shevardnadze was openly critical of Brezhnev's "confrontational spirit."[3] At the United Nations General Assembly in December 1988, on the anniversary of Pearl Harbor, Gorbachev made an unexpected announcement of a unilateral troop reduction and reminded his audience that the "bell of every regional conflict tolls for all of us."[4] He used the occasion to gather support for cooperation with the United States and progress toward regional settlements. He advocated such settlements in Angola, Cambodia, Ethiopia, and Mozambique.

The Need for Economic Savings

The reason for this change is in the main economic: Moscow can no longer afford to pay the bill. The Soviet economy was sinking and could not support the cost of regional crisis. According to the Central Intelligence Agency, economic problems in the USSR reached "near crisis proportions" in 1989–1990 after a disappointing performance in 1987–1988.[5]

The economy is plagued by unfinished construction projects. Oil production has fallen, for the first time since the end of the Second World

War. In this respect it resembled the United States, which once—in the far-off 1920s—dominated world oil markets. Transportation, too, has suffered, with widespread breakdowns interfering with deliveries of raw materials to factories, of finished goods to consumers. Production of consumer goods is one of the sorest points in all of the much-discussed failures of the Soviet economy: it has increased at most—figures are uncertain—by a mere one percent, which hardly equals the rate of population growth. Machinery production—usually the fastest growing category of industrial output—registered no growth in 1990–1991.

The dissatisfaction of Russian consumers has helped increase such evidence of social tension as strikes and ethnic clashes. Russian researchers believe that strikes in the USSR rose from two dozen, involving a few thousand workers, in 1987–1988 to more than 55, involving several hundred thousand, in 1989.[6] Erosion of labor discipline and losses in work time due to strikes and ethnic unrest contributed to the economy's poor showing. Ethnic tension in the Caucasus and Central Asia continues to disrupt production and transportation. Price increases and rationing are worsening a situation that already finds 43 million people, or fifteen percent of the population, living in poverty, according to former Prime Minister Nikolai Ryzhkov.

Moscow's international financial position has deteriorated, with the USSR borrowing heavily to finance increased imports. The hard-currency trade balance went from a surplus of $2.6 billion in 1988 to a deficit of $1.8 billion in 1989. Oil exports fell because of decline in production, labor unrest, and distribution bottlenecks. Increased borrowing raised hard-currency debt to $47 billion in 1989, more than doubling the total of $22 billion in 1984, the last year before Gorbachev's accession. For the first time in decades the Soviets failed to pay for imports on time, and as a result Western bankers have tightened credit to the USSR.

To stabilize the economy, the Soviets must cut the deficit, attract Western technology and expertise, break up state monopolies, and create a safety net for their people. Moscow is obtaining membership in such international economic organizations as the World Bank, International Monetary Fund, and General Agreement for Tariffs and Trade, which would not have happened if Moscow pursued an expansionist policy in the Third World. Joint ventures with the United States, Japan, and key states of Western Europe could end should Moscow return to policies of the Brezhnev era. Only stable relations with the United States can provide the international predictability that Moscow requires to concentrate on domestic problems.

In addition to the reduction in Russian military deliveries to the Third World and Moscow's own military activity in noncontiguous areas, the Russians are warning Third World clients to expect less economic assistance. The escalating costs of aid to Third World economies as well as the large foreign debts of Third World states have caused the Russians to become increasingly impatient with poor economic performance. The Russians, as a result, have been particularly critical of Third World leaders for expecting socialist states to finance "dubious efforts to force change" through rapid industrialization.[7] More recently, a Russian economist with ties to the leadership, Nikolai P. Shmelyov, told the Congress of People's Deputies that it was becoming necessary to cut assistance to such states as Cuba and Nicaragua in order to balance the Russian budget.[8] Shmelyov's speech, which was one of the more radical addresses to the Congress in the summer of 1989, argued that cutting aid to Latin America would "suffice to maintain the balance of the consumer market" in Russia.

For the first time, the Russians have even published an official list of their debtors in the Third World, presumably as a warning that assistance will be cut. The list, which appeared in the official government newspaper in March 1990, reported the foreign debt to the Soviet Union as greater than 85 billion rubles, with Cuba and Vietnam as the greatest "socialist" debtors in the Third World, and India and Syria the leaders among the "developing" countries. The article supported the view that "effective trade" should replace aid and that Russian generosity had to be curtailed. In addition to warning Third World states to expect less largesse, it reminded Russian readers "not to count seriously on these debts being repaid soon."[9]

Military and economic assistance declined in 1989 and 1990, and will continue to do so. Russia's radical plan for transition to a market economy by 1992 calls for a 75 percent cut in all forms of economic assistance, a move that is likely to have a significant effect on client states such as Cuba, Ethiopia, and Vietnam. A Soviet party official remarked in May 1990 that Moscow is placing less emphasis on the Third World and will undertake a "radical review in the near future" of its military assistance program.[10] Those states with the greatest debts to the Soviet Union, such as Cuba, Vietnam, and Syria, are probably most vulnerable to future cuts; reductions in assistance in 1990–1991 hit the Middle East harder than any other region, with Iraq taking the deepest cut.[11] Arab government officials and intellectuals already believe that thay have "lost an ally of the kind that stood by them at times of crisis."[12] Not even Afghanistan could be protected from cuts in aid and the government in Kabul collapsed in April 1992.

A special warning was given to Cuba as Russia's largest debtor, which presumably will become a major item in the current debate in Moscow on appropriate assistance levels to Third World states. Opponents of foreign assistance are arguing that, because of Russia's economic problems, it is no longer possible to extend large amounts of aid to the Third World. Russian commentary has supported reductions in aid to Cuba in view of the fact that, "in certain social indicators" such as life expectancy and infant mortality, Cuba is "better off than certain regions of the Soviet Union."[13]

A former senior Cuban official involved in recent negotiations with the Russians remarked that Moscow is no longer supplying Cuba with oil to be sold for hard currency, which deprives Havana of $500 million from such sales.[14] Moscow informed the Cubans to expect reductions in every aspect of economic assistance, including subsidized prices for Cuban products and low-interest debt financing. Former Deputy Prime Minister Leonid Abalkin announced in Havana in April 1990 that Cuba's debt to Russia, approximately 15 billion rubles, would be payable in dollars beginning in 1995.

The Need for Military Savings

Economic problems have helped trigger the current malaise within the Red Army, which is showing some of the turmoil afflicting Russian society. Leon Trotsky had predicted as much when he wrote from exile that the army was a "copy of society and suffers from all its ills, usually at a higher temperature."[15] The declining power and status of the military has intensified ethnic and political dissent, the deterioration of living conditions, and separatism. Soldiers in the Caucasus are deserting their units and joining unofficial "national armies" that resist Russian security forces. The Baltics have seceded from the union and numerous republic legislatures have called for the establishment of their own armies. Reservists are not reporting, and protests forced the General Staff to cancel a call for reservists in 1990 during riots in Baku.

Draft resistance increased sharply in 1989 and probably will continue to rise due to the collapse of the USSR. When the Russian Army newspaper (*Krasnaya Zvezda*) published the results of the spring draft in 1990, it showed a lack of response by non-Russians, particularly in Armenia and the Baltics.[16] There have been large drops in republics with heavy populations of Muslims. All this affects any assessment of Russian military capabilities; the Red Army could reconstitute itself if faced with invasion, but deployment outside Russian borders, particularly in the Third World, would be difficult.

Military and economic problems not only reduce the Russian threat but add an element of irreversibility to retreat in the Third World. Another Afghan adventure appears remote, and dispatch of large numbers of advisers and technicians to Third World states is not likely. Naval deployments in out-of-area waters will continue to decline, and the virtual evacuation of Cam Ranh Bay suggests that Moscow is losing interest in access to facilities overseas. Intelligence from satellite reconnaissance vehicles could make collection facilities in Cuba and Vietnam unnecessary.

In addition to signalling that the USSR planned to look for regional solutions to military problems in the Third World, Gorbachev used the party congress in 1986 to indicate that Moscow was not willing to assign greater amounts of military resources for priority missions abroad. He suggested, for example, that the costs of substantial increases in forward-deployed forces may not be justified by potential benefits in the Third World. In the wake of these remarks, there was a lower operational tempo to Soviet naval activity in support of out-of-area missions and Third World client states.

The USSR sent no naval task force to the Caribbean in 1986 and 1987, and the task force that arrived in the Caribbean in 1988 stayed for a shorter period of time than usual and did not enter the Gulf of Mexico. The Soviets reduced the number of reconnaissance flights out of Cuba and Angola with a particular decline in TU-95 Bear deployments to Cuba.[17] Naval operations are being conducted closer to the Soviet mainland and out-of-area deployment of Soviet ships has dropped everywhere, including in the South China Sea off the coast of Vietnam.

Demilitarization and the Third World

Moscow's unwillingness to compete with the United States in the Third World indicates that reducing forces for power projection are just as important as strategic and conventional force limits. Gorbachev was willing to pursue arms control agreements along the lines of U.S. negotiating positions as in INF and START, and recognized the Soviet industrial base could not afford competition in the Third World. Military and conservative opposition to these agreements, however, probably contributed to the coup against Gorbachev in 1991.

Unlike the United States, the importance of power projection was never apparent to Soviet strategists, who have a more linear view of their geopolitical situation. Soviet conventional forces had been developed to defend their borders and introduce power into contiguous areas, not to apply pressure against U.S. interests far from the USSR.[18] Brezhnev looked for opportunities to expand military presence in the 1970s, increasing aid and advisors in Africa, Asia, Latin America, and the Middle East. Gorbachev reduced the Soviet presence and pursued solutions to regional confrontation. He called for greater activism by the United Nations in settling interethnic disputes, handling early warning in explosive areas, arranging naval forces for joint actions, supervising national elections, and combatting international terrorism and drug trafficking.

Gorbachev demonstrated that he was aware of the difficult resource constraints that faced the USSR and that he was capable of adjusting his commitments in the Third World in order to limit activities abroad. The reduced Russian presence in terms of military and economic assistance and advisors and technicians indicates that Yeltsin will not allow Russia to pursue international commitments that cannot be supported by the current level of Moscow's economic and military strength. Although the historian Paul Kennedy has demonstrated that, in certain cases, defense spending can stimulate economic growth (e.g., Britain in the 19th century and Japan in the 1930s), it appears that Yeltsin, like Gorbachev before him, recognizes a negative relationship between defense spending and economic performance in the USSR over the past two decades.[19] In other words, Gorbachev's "new thinking" in foreign policy was designed to reduce competition and spending in the Third World so that economic resources can be channeled to Moscow's industrial and technological base. This strategy was just one aspect of Gorbachev's overall effort to gain control of the national security agenda and to demilitarize the Russian decisionmaking process.

In the Third World, there has been a decline in the operational tempo and presence of Russian naval and naval aviation forces. Naval exercises have been cut and joint exercises with Third World navies have become extremely rare. Naval reconnaissance from Third World airfields has ended and military advisers have been withdrawn from Mozambique and Ethiopia. Political agreements in Angola and Cambodia will mean a reduction in the Russian advisory presence in southern Africa and Southeast Asia as well. Soviet military assistance to the Third World dropped sharply from 1988 to 1991, in part due to the decline in Third World purchases of new weapons systems and the emphasis in the Third World on less expensive spare parts, ammunition, and support services.[20] The increase in Third World debt and the cease-fire between Iran and Iraq are also factors in the decline of Soviet weapons agreements with Moscow's client states; the Soviets did not resume deliveries of arms to Iran until 1990.[21] In 1989, the Soviets stopped direct military assistance to Nicaragua.[22]

Linkage in the Third World

Under Gorbachev there was a new willingness to recognize linkage between the larger East-West relationship and the problem of regional conflict. Leonid Brezhnev believed that the six-day war in 1967 between Arabs and Israelis required the establishment of hotline communications between Moscow and Washington and that the October war in 1973 (and particularly the U.S. nuclear alert during the hostilities) threatened Moscow's relations with its clients in the region. Nevertheless, Brezhnev never seemed to appreciate the effect on relations with the United States of Moscow's actions on behalf of its clients, particularly the threats to "intervene" during the wars in 1967 and 1973 and the assumption of air defense in Egypt during the "war of attrition" in 1970.

Unlike his predecessors, Gorbachev explored ways to reduce the level of competition in the Third World in order to protect the larger Soviet-American bilateral relationship. His reinvigoration of the national security apparatus and foreign policy bureaucracy was designed to support such an objective. Gorbachev recognized, in other words, that linkage was a viable strategy and that regional conflicts had the potential to complicate relations with the United States.

The sudden invigoration of Russian policy towards the United Nations is part of a broad effort to demonstrate Moscow's desire for constructive, political solutions to regional conflicts. Moscow laid the groundwork for this policy in 1986, when it unexpectedly agreed to pay its assessment for the United Nations Interim Force in Lebanon that had been present in southern Lebanon since 1978 without Soviet support. The following year, the Soviets announced they would pay $225 million to the U.N. to cover the USSR's dues for the year as well as Moscow's assessment for past U.N. peacekeeping operations—including those in the Golan Heights. Then, in a major statement of policy, which appeared in *Pravda* in September 1987, Gorbachev made an eleven-point proposal for strengthening the status and scope of the United Nations, including the creation of multilateral center to manage conflicts that would incorporate a UN hotline to the capitals of the five permanent members of the Security Council.[23]

Official Soviet statements over the past several years strongly indicate that measures will continue to be taken to reduce Russian assets and commitments in the Third World and arrange regional solutions to crisis situations, preferably in conjunction with the United States. The Soviets completed their withdrawal from Afghanistan and encouraged such clients as Cuba and Vietnam to reduce military involvements in Angola and Cambodia, respectively. Libya was pressed to end its political isolation in the Middle East, and Ethiopia was pushed to find a political solution to its differences with Eritrea that have produced hostilities over the past two decades.

Gorbachev's meeting with South Korean President Roh Tae Woo in June 1990 led to the establishment of diplomatic relations between Moscow and Seoul and to the visit of the highest-level North Korean delegation to view Seoul since the end of the Second World War. The meeting between North and South Korean prime ministers took place in September 1990, marking Pyongyang's recognition of the changing global environment. Moscow has been demanding hard currency for its oil deliveries to North Korea and, as a result, Pyongyang is making commercial contacts with China and the United States as well as South Korea. The dialogue between the two Koreas offers the first promise of genuine stability in Northeast Asia since the Korean War.

Gorbachev clearly signalled that the USSR wanted to disengage itself from the political risks and military costs of involvement in the Third World on behalf of the progressive states and would seek ties to nonsocialist and noncommunist states in order to expand Moscow's international presence. The Russians are looking for ways to deemphasize ideology in their ties to Third World states and the ideological competition with the United States in the Third World. As part of a more pragmatic approach, they are emphasizing the importance of regional settlements and indicating that Russian-American cooperation is the key to regional stability.

All these actions in the Third World are consistent with Gorbachev's recognition of the linkage between the Soviet-American bilateral relationship and the behavior of the superpowers in the Third World as well as of the need to defuse regional conflicts that carry the risk of compromising those relations. In an article in the authoritative party journal *Kommunist,* three members of the Soviet Union's Institute for the Study of the USA and Canada (Deputy Director Vitaly Zhurkin, section head Sergey Karaganov, and senior researcher Andrey Kortunov) argued that, while the threat of premeditated nuclear aggression is decreasing, "the threat of war may be increasing in part due to the struggle in regional sectors."[24] The three officials contended that any state that relies exclusively on military means "sets its own security against international security" and that the search for security requires negotiations with adversaries as well as concessions and compromises that accommodate the interests of those adversaries.

These views are consistent with the positions taken by Gorbachev since the 27th Soviet Party Congress in 1986 and provide the rationalization not only for Moscow's arms control agreements with the United States but also for its current approach to regional security matters in the Middle East, Southwest Asia, and Africa. For the past several years, Gorbachev repeatedly has stated that a resolution of the war in Afghanistan might pave the way for increased efforts to settle other regional conflicts, an approach that was argued strongly in an *Izvestia* article of April 22, 1988, by Konstantin Geyvandov.[25] He stated that the Geneva agreements on Afghanistan "can be seen as the first model for peaceful solution of regional conflicts on the basis of the principles of new political thinking" and that the Soviet Union and the United States, "as mediators and official guarantors of the settlement of the Afghan problem, have set a precedent for the constructive collaboration which is extremely necessary for the improvement of international relations as a whole."

In May 1988, when the Soviets began their actual troop withdrawal from Afghanistan, Vyacheslav Dashichev of the Institute of Economics of the World Socialist System, wrote in *Literaturnaya Gazeta* that Moscow's aggressive policies during the post-war era had undermined its security interests and provoked the formation of rival coalitions seeking to counter perceived Soviet expansionism.[26] He charged that Moscow had created the impression that the USSR was a dangerous power, seeking to eliminate bourgeois democracies and establish communism throughout the world. He accused Brezhnev of squandering opportunities created by the attainment of strategic parity with the United States. Dashichev also condemned past Soviet policy in the Third World, arguing that the Soviet leadership had no clear ideas about the USSR's state interests when it embarked on its Third World policy of the 1970s and that it had squandered material resources in the "pursuit of petty gains."

In the summer of 1988, the deputy chief of the foreign ministry's International Organizations Administration, Andrey V. Kozyrev, wrote a serious critique of recent Soviet foreign policy, again emphasizing Soviet errors in the Third World.[27] Kozyrev argued that Moscow's "direct and indirect involvement in regional conflicts" had led to "colossal losses by increasing international tension, justifying the arms race and hindering the establishment of mutually advantageous ties with the West." He also argued that Soviet military aid to various Third World regimes contributed to "protracted conflicts with an opposition that in turn depends on outside support." He concluded that the Soviets themselves gained no returns from extending large amounts of economic assistance and that it made no sense to build Soviet relations with Third World regimes on the basis of their "opposition to Western influence." Along with other Soviet officials, Kozyrev called for cooperation with Third World states on the basis of "mutually advantageous economic and technological cooperation."[28]

Much of Kozyrev's message was repeated in July 1988 at a foreign ministry meeting, when Shevardnadze stated that in the past the "Soviet confrontational spirit had been too strong."[29] The former Soviet foreign minister indicated that Moscow's withdrawal from Afghanistan could provide a model for the resolution of differences in Cambodia, southern Africa, Cyprus, and the Koreas. Shevardnadze even asked if "everything had been done to prevent the confrontation with China" and admonished his audience for failing to warn the Soviet political leadership that a prolonged war between Iran and Iraq could lead to a "massive U.S. presence in the Persian Gulf."[30]

These arguments from the Soviet foreign minister and other foreign ministry officials presumably framed the discussion that took place in Moscow in preparing Gorbachev's speech to the United Nations General Assembly on December 7, 1988, which turned out to be a seminal statement of Soviet foreign policy and one of the most important Soviet statements ever presented to the UN. In addition to calling for a unilateral troop reduction from Europe on the anniversary of the attack on Pearl

Harbor, Gorbachev reminded his audience that the "bell of every regional conflict tolls for all of us" and reaffirmed Moscow's commitment to remove its forces from Afghanistan.[31] His call for ending the deliveries of all military supplies to the belligerents in Afghanistan, which Gorbachev hitherto had opposed, seemed to indicate that a cease-fire and a halt to military deliveries were needed to protect the withdrawal of Soviet forces. Soviet withdrawal, in other words, had become more important that the staying power of the Afghan military. The Soviet general secretary used the occasion at the United Nations to gather additional support for his policy of increased cooperation with the West, particularly with the United States, and a search for regional settlements in the Third World. Once again, the signal to Moscow's clients in the Third World was the reduced role for Soviet military power in noncontiguous areas.

Shevardnadze reinforced this message in his plenary speech to the USSR Supreme Soviet in October 1989, when he referred to the decision to invade Afghanistan as "gross violation of our own legislation and of our own intraparty and civic norms and ethics."[32] Shevardnadze and Gorbachev, who were non-voting members of the Politburo in 1979 when the decision was made, apparently learned of the invasion from Soviet media accounts. In his speech, the Soviet foreign minister castigated the decision-making as taking place "behind the party's and the people's back . . . a *fait accompli*." As Gorbachev's point man on foreign policy in general, Shevardnadze thus made the case for extending glasnost to such sensitive international and military issues as the invasion of Afghanistan by vetting such decisions with the Supreme Soviet. At the very least, Shevardnadze was inviting *ex post facto* debate of such decisions in order to make it more difficult to use military forces in such scenarios.

Shevardnadze's implicit call for legislative oversight eroded the cult of secrecy in the Soviet Union, which was one of Gorbachev's goals, and placed pressure on the highly secretive Soviet defense establishment in areas of defense spending, weapons procurement, and power projection. Aleksey Arbatov, the son of the director of the USA Institute and the chief of a department at the Institute of World Economy and International Relations (IMEMO), had complained that the tradition of military secrecy inhibited the ability of disarmament experts to provide useful analyses for policymakers, especially with regard to calculating the kinds of military cutbacks needed to meet the requirements of Gorbachev's "reasonable sufficiency."[33]

The efforts of Gorbachev and Shevardnadze to erode the cult of secrecy and to end controls over the media made a major contribution to the defeat of the coup in 1991. The leaders of the coup were never able to control the media and, not until the second day of the coup, was an unsuccessful effort made to tighten controls over the media. By that time, however, the central press was carrying reports of resistance against the coup and the condemnation of the coup by chiefs of state in the United States, Britain, and Germany. The poorly organized coup quickly proved that Gorbachev had ended traditional censorship in the Soviet Union and that it could not be easily reestablished.

Crisis Prevention in the Third World

The Russians appear to believe that a greater military presence in the Third World does not assure greater political security for either Moscow or its clients, a belief that calls for a level of retrenchment in non-essential areas. In 1987, Gorbachev supported the idea of collective efforts to "defuse conflicts in all the planet's hot spots" and a greater United Nations role in this regard.[34] He announced the decision to withdraw from Afghanistan the following year and, since then, has cited the Afghan settlement as an "important international landmark."[35] Gorbachev's support for regional settlements through the auspices of the United Nations (e.g., Afghanistan) or American mediation (e.g., Angola) had been justified as a means to make sure that local conflicts do not "engender confrontation" between the superpowers.[36] And at the United Nations on the anniversary of Pearl Harbor, Gorbachev reminded his audience that:

> The bell of each regional conflict tolls for all of us. This is particularly true because these conflicts are occurring in the Third World which even without this has many troubles and problems on a scale which cannot fail to concern all of us.[37]

In addition to the pursuit of regional settlements and the reassessment of Soviet prospects in the Third World, Gorbachev abandoned the "zero-sum" thinking that drove previous Soviet leaders to exploit U.S. vulnerabilities in the Middle East and Africa. In the 1970s, Brezhnev took advantage of every opportunity to benefit from constraints upon U.S. actions in the wake of Watergate and the evacuation from Vietnam. Brezhnev appeared to believe that the ideological competition with the United States required Soviet assistance to national liberation struggles. Gorbachev, on the other hand, recognized the effect of such competition on the balance of power between the superpowers and has cited Soviet military involvement in regional conflicts as a cause for the collapse of detente. The deputy director of the African Institute wrote in 1989 that military assistance did not create reliable allies and regional conflicts did not end in clear victories.[38]

Among the various issues confronting the United States and Russia in the Third World, the most difficult are resolving the longstanding civil wars fought by their clients in Afghanistan, Angola, and Cambodia. The Afghan civil war, which compromised Soviet-American relations in 1979 when Moscow invaded, is the regional conflict the two superpowers most wanted to resolve. Moscow and Washington made the most dramatic progress in their attempts to negotiate an end to the civil war in Angola; Soviet and American officials participated directly in the peace talks for the first time and agreed in principle to lead an international monitoring group to supervise a cease-fire and elections. The two powers share similar goals in Cambodia, where both are trying to prevent a return to power by the Khmer Rouge, a group responsible for the deaths of more than a million people in the late 1970s. They have persuaded the Hun Sen government, the Khmer Rouge, and two other guerrilla groups to establish a council that would share power with the United Nations until elections could be held. And for the first time, the United States has opened talks with Hanoi and Phnom Penh.

Regional conflicts also increase the possibility of the use of weapons of mass destruction. Iraq's invasion of Kuwait raised serious questions about nuclear, chemical, and even biological weapons programs in Baghdad. Both India and Pakistan pursue a nuclear weapons capability, which would have to taken into account in any struggle over Kashmir. According to experts in the field of nonproliferation, at least ten nations are supplying nuclear technology to more than forty recipient states.[39] Any Russian-American dialogue on Third World issues will have to include these matters, including the establishment of regional security measures.

The Bell of Regional Conflict

Gorbachev acknowledged that security concerns would be limited by domestic political and economic problems and the importance of relations with the United States and Western Europe. His objectives were political in the Middle East, where the Soviets reduced military sales to Iraq, Libya, and Syria, while improving relations with Egypt and Israel. He did nothing to defend Libya from U.S. raids in 1986 or help Qadhafi in Chad in 1987; he warned Libya and Syria that terrorism was counterproductive and could lead to another round of hostilities. He reduced commitments to Marxist and radical states in Africa and brokered an Ethiopian-Somali agreement against further hostilities. In 1990, Gorbachev supported U.S. efforts to condemn the Iraqi attack against Kuwait and issued an unprecedented joint statement with Washington to rally international support. Future Russian efforts for regional security in the Persian Gulf probably will include limits on arms transfers, particularly nuclear and chemical weapons technology.

The Soviets played a major role in orchestrating the Cuban withdrawal from Angola and the Vietnamese withdrawal from Cambodia in 1989–

1990.[40] The end to military shipments to Nicaragua in 1989 indicated that the Soviets were not going to allow events in Central America to become an obstacle in Soviet-American relations. The following year, the Soviets encouraged the election in Nicaragua that led to the stunning defeat of the Sandinistas. The Soviets also encouraged the PLO dialogue with the United States and have been supportive of U.S. efforts to arrange a dialogue between Israel and the Palestinians over the occupied territories.

A Soviet official conceded in 1990 that Moscow did not have vital interests in the Third World and that "large-scale arms deliveries are in no way a guarantee of firm influence, as shown by the example of Egypt and other countries."[41] Unlike Czechoslovakia, the Soviets cannot be expected to renounce the export of weapons in principle. Economic and military factors will demand a Russian role in weapons transfers. But it is likely that Moscow will be more willing to limit weaponry in areas of conflict, apply the test of "reasonable sufficiency" to arms agreements, and reduce transfers of sophisticated weapons.

The Russians appear willing to negotiate such limits with the United States and, on their own, may apply limits to states not solvent or in debt to Moscow. For the first time in nearly a decade, the United States has surpassed Russia as the biggest supplier of weapons to the Third World, with Russian arms transfers declining from 1988 to 1991. The winding down of regional conflicts and the inability of many client states to pay hard currency have contributed to the Russian decline in arms sales. The major losers have been Iraq, Libya, and Syria, which means that Moscow has lost hard currency and transfers of petroleum.

A Soviet general officer conceded several weeks after the Iraqi invasion of Kuwait that Moscow had made a major mistake in selling and giving "state-of-the-art devastating weapons" to countries on its southern border.[42] He argued that, in order to settle regional conflicts, it was necessary to "stem the mighty flow of weapons to the Third World." In doing so, he made a case for establishing an international covenant on arms trade similar to the Nonproliferation Treaty of the 1960s to control nuclear technology.

On balance, new thinking has produced success in Afghanistan, Angola, Cambodia, and Ethiopia and the possibility of greater stability for the Middle East and the Persian Gulf. Gorbachev promoted an expanded role for the United Nations in peacekeeping for the Third World and, unlike his predecessors, no longer used the Security Council merely to take rhetorical swipes at the United States. He called for revival of the UN Military Staff Committee and suggested stationing of UN observation points in explosive areas and UN naval forces in the Persian Gulf.[43] For the first time since the end of the Second World War, the Soviet Union and the United States entered a genuine dialogue on the Third World, with vast implications for nuclear nonproliferation, arms limitation, and conflict resolution. Continued cooperation between the United States and Russia in Cambodia, El Salvador, Ethiopia, and Iraq in the wake of the failed coup attempt strongly indicates that conflict resolution in the Third World will maintain a high priority in Russian foreign policy.

Notes

1. *The New York Times,* October 21, 1988, p. 3.

2. Michael MccGwire, *Military Objectives in Soviet Foreign Policy,* Washington, D.C.: Brookings Institution, 1987, p. 220. MccGwire's book usefully identifies key decision points in Soviet strategic thinking but, in general, exaggerates the importance of the Third World to Soviet military and geopolitical interests.

3. *Pravda,* August 17, 1988, p. 3. Speech by Foreign Minister Shevardnadze to the USSR Ministry of Foreign Affairs.

4. *The New York Times,* December 8, 1988, p. 1. General Secretary Gorbachev speech to the UNGA.

5. See "The Soviet Economy Stumbles Badly," Central Intelligence Agency paper presented to the Technology and National Security Subcommittee of the Joint Economic Committee, Congress of the United States, June 1991.

6. "The Soviet Economy Stumbles Badly," CIA paper, p. 22.

7. Joseph Whelan, *The Soviet Union in the Third World, 1980–1982: An Imperial Burden or Political Asset,* Washington, D.C., US Government Printing Office, 1984, pp. 295–296.

8. *The New York Times,* June 9, 1989, p. 3, "Radical Plan to Balance Soviet Budget" by Bill Keller.

9. *Izvestia,* March 2, 1990, p. 3, "Unique Document: Who Owes Us 85.5 Billion Rubles." The article was addressed to Premier N. I. Ryzhkov, Chairman of the USSR Council of Ministers.

10. *The Washington Post,* May 27, 1990, p. 23, "Soviets Plan to Review Military Aid."

11. In March 1990, *Izvestia* published the first detailed breakdown of debts owed to the Soviet Union: Cuba ($24 billion), Vietnam ($15 billion), Mongolia ($15 billion), India ($14 billion), Syria ($10 billion), Iraq ($6 billion), Afghanistan ($5 billion), and Algeria ($4 billion).

12. *The New York Times,* March 6, 1990, p. 1, "Arabs Fear End of Cold War Means a Loss of Aid and Allies" by Youssef M. Ibrahim.

13. *New Times,* February 20–26, 1990, p. 7.

14. *The New York Times,* September 13, 1990, p. 3, "Cuban Defector Tells of Soviet Cuts" by Howard W. French.

15. L. D. Trotsky, *The Revolution Betrayed,* London: New Park Publishers, 1967, p. 222 (first published in 1936).

16. *The Washington Post,* August 19, 1990, p. C4, "The Soviet Military's Recruitment Nightmare" by Murray Feshbach.

17. *The New York Times,* July 17, 1988, p. 1. See unpublished paper by Wayne P. Limberg, "Moscow and Regional Conflicts: Linkage Revisited," American Political Science Association, Washington, D.C., 1988.

18. Western military writings have exaggerated the importance of power projection to Soviet military planning See writings of Michael MccGwire, particularly *Military Objectives in Soviet Foreign Policy,* Washington, D.C.: Brookings Institution, 1987; and John Hines, Phillip Petersen, and Notra Trulock III, particularly their "Soviet Military Theory from 1945–2000: Implications for NATO," *The Washington Quarterly,* Vol. 9, No. 4, Fall 1986, pp. 122–129.

19. See Paul Kennedy, *The Rise and Fall of the Great Powers,* New York: Random House, 1987.

20. The Soviet Union registered a substantial decrease in its share of Third World arms transfer agreements, falling from 50.3% in 1987 to 33.4% in 1988. The total value of the Soviet Union's agreements also fell dramatically in 1988—from $19.4 billion in 1987 to $9.9 billion. See Richard F. Grimmett, "Trends in Conventional Arms Transfers to the Third World by Major Supplier, 1981–1988," Washington, D.C.: Congressional Research Service, 1989.

21. The Soviets have supplied no arms to Iran since 1985 and delivered more than $10 billion in arms to Iraq during the same period; the USSR was responsible for nearly one-third of the arms delivered to the principals in the Iran-Iraq war since the start of fighting in 1980. West Europe's share of deliveries to Baghdad and Tehran is nearly 25% and China's share is more than 15%.

22. Although the Soviets have at least temporarily ended direct military deliveries to Nicaragua, they remain Cuba's principal supplier, making more than $12 billion in weapons deliveries. Cuba, of course, is Nicaragua's major supplier of military weapons systems.

23. *Pravda,* September 17, 1990, p. 1.

24. V. Zhurkin, S. Karaganov, A. Kortunov, "Challenges of Security: Old and New," *Kommunist,* no. 1, January, 1988.

25. *Izvestia,* April 22, 1988, p. 5.

26. Vyacheslav Dashichev, *Literaturnaya Gazeta,* May 1988, p. 17. Vyacheslav Dashichev is from the Institute of the Economics of the World Socialist System. The head of the institute, Oleg Bogomolov, published a letter in *Literaturnaya Gazeta* on March 16, 1988, in which he stated that his institute guarded against the Soviet intervention in Afghanistan on the grounds that it would undermine detente and damage the USSR's international stature. In the first authoritative account of the high-level military debate surrounding the invasion of Afghanistan, General of the Army Valentin I. Varrenikov, a deputy defense minister, stated in an interview with the weekly magazine *Ogonyok* that the General Staff was opposed to the invasion but was overruled by Defense Minister Dmitri F. Ustinov. Varrenikov was the senior defense ministry official in Afghanistan for the last four years of the war and, after the Soviets completed the withdrawal of forces, was named commander of ground forces. Varrenikov added that Marshal Nikolai Ogarkov, then chief of the general staff, and Marshal Sergei F. Akhromeyev, who later became chief of the general staff, also opposed the intervention. (Article in *The New York Times,* March 19, 1989, p. 27, by Bill Keller. Also see *The Washington Post,* March 20, 1989, regarding the same topic.

27. *Mezhdunarodnaya Zhizn (International Affairs)*, Summer 1988, Andrey V. Kozyrev, pp. 17–21.

28. *Ibid.*,

29. *Vestnik Ministerstva Inostrannykh Sel SSR*, August 1988, Speech by Foreign Minister Shevardnadze to the USSR Ministry of Foreign Affairs, pp. 27–46.

30. *Ibid.*, p. 35.

31. *The New York Times*, December 8, 1988, p. 1, General Secretary Gorbachev speech to the United Nations General Assembly.

32. *Pravda*, October 24, 1989, pp. 2–4.

33. *Mezhdunarodnaya Zhizn*, March 1989, p. 121. My own discussions with Soviet military and civilian experts in Moscow and Leningrad indicated that Gorbachev's efforts to force the sharing of sensitive security information and to encourage debate on issues of national security has contributed to the current tension between party and military officials in the Soviet Union.

34. *Pravda*, September 17, 1987, p. 1.

35. TASS, January 18, 1989, Gorbachev speech to the Trilateral Commission; *Krasnaya Zvezda*, February 24, 1989, p. 5.

36. Gorbachev, *Perestroika*, p. 176.

37. *Pravda*, December 8, 1988, p. 1, Gorbachev speech at the 43rd UN General Assembly.

38. *Izvestia*, February 4, 1989.

39. See Leonard Spector, *Nuclear Ambitions*, Boulder, Colo.: Westview Press, 1990.

40. According to official Soviet sources, there were 23,000 Cuban forces remaining in Angola as of December 1989, with the last Cuban soldier scheduled to leave by July 1991. Fewer than two thousand Cuban soldiers remain in Ethiopia following a withdrawal agrrement that was negotiated in September 1989. A small Cuban contingent is present in the Congo. See *Pravda*, December 24, 1989, p. 4.

41. *Mezhdunarodnaya Zhizn (International Life)*, April 1990, no. 4, "Reexamining Policy in the Third World," Andrey Kolosov, pp. 37–45.

42. *New Times*, August 27, 1990. p. 12. "The Threat from the South" by Major General Vadim Makarevsky.

43. *Pravda*, September 17, 1989, p. 1.

2

Implications of "New Thinking" for Russian-American Cooperation in the Middle East and Persian Gulf

Carolyn McGiffert Ekedahl

Moscow's new approach to regional conflict situations was dramatically illustrated by its unprecedented cooperation with Washington in the wake of Iraq's invasion of Kuwait in August 1990. The Soviet Union's support for UN initiatives designed to force Saddam Hussein's compliance with international law and its acceptance of a major U.S. military buildup in the region stand in sharp contrast to its previous exploitation of regional tensions and its opposition to any U.S. military deployments. The desertion of Iraq, a key client and hard-currency purchaser of Soviet arms, demonstrated Moscow's commitment to the centrality of relations with the United States.

Gorbachev's new policies in the Middle East included improving relations with Israel and the moderate Arab states, pressing radical Arab clients toward moderation and compromise, and taking a flexible posture toward resolution of the Arab-Israeli conflict. These policies, as well as Soviet cooperation during the Gulf crisis, gained Moscow its long-coveted inclusion in the Arab-Israeli negotiating process as Secretary of State James Baker sought Soviet inclusion in his initiative of 1991.

In the Middle East and Persian Gulf, as elsewhere in the Third World, new thinking was based on the conviction that foreign policy must serve domestic policy, that economic and political restructuring (perestroika) is the highest Russian priority, that Moscow's previous Third World policies had served it poorly, and that international stability and improved relations with the United States must take precedence over regional interests and clients. Russian policies therefore have been designed to prevent military entanglement, avoid strains in relations with Washington, and enhance

Russia's image as a responsible superpower intent on resolving regional disputes peacefully.

The weakening of central authority in the wake of the abortive hard-line coup of August 1991 reinforced the foreign policy directions of new thinking. The focus of the emerging states and fragile central institutions is on political and economic reconstruction, and there appears to be little, if any, interest in pursuit of an aggressive foreign policy. Even more than before, the Russians are pursuing policies designed to gain them enhanced credibility in the international community in order to gain access to credits and assistance.

Gorbachev's Inheritance

During the pre-Gorbachev years, both Washington and Moscow viewed Middle East events in an East-West context. The Soviets sought to reach strategic parity with the United States by extending their own global reach and undermining that of the United States. The United States tried to prevent and, during the Reagan Administration, "roll back" what it saw as the steady expansion of Soviet power. Developments perceived as Soviet successes in the Third World in the 1970s (Angola, Mozambique, Nicaragua, Afghanistan) combined with U.S. setbacks (Vietnam, Iran) fed a perception that the "correlation of forces" in the world was indeed shifting in Moscow's favor, as the Soviets were then claiming.[1]

From the mid-1950s to the early 1970s, the USSR made significant gains in the Middle East, largely through the exploitation of regional tensions. The Arab-Israeli wars of 1956, 1967, 1973, and 1982 created openings for Moscow, which identified with the Arab cause and capitalized on U.S. support for Israel to strengthen ties in the Arab world. A number of Arab states turned to the Soviets for military assistance and political support. As a result, Moscow was able to improve its own power projection capabilities, political credibility, and hard currency earnings.[2]

Its strengthened position made Moscow a factor that had to be considered in any regional conflict or in any effort to resolve regional tensions. Soviet arms enabled Moscow's clients to play enhanced regional roles; they gave Egypt the capability to challenge Israel in the late 1960s and early 1970s; enabled Syria to pose a military threat to Israel and play an active role in Lebanon; bolstered Libyan leader Qadhafi's ability to pursue his regional ambitions, and allowed Iraq both to wage war against Iran for nearly eight years and to invade Kuwait in 1990.

When Gorbachev came to power in 1985, however, the Soviet position in the Middle East had been stagnant for over a decade. Soviet expansion elsewhere in the Third World had not been matched in the Middle East. The Soviets had been expelled from Egypt in the early 1970s, losing significant military access which they never regained. Their alienation from Egypt—still the key Arab actor in the region—weakened their efforts to counter Arab disunity and forge a pro-Soviet, anti-U.S. Arab concensus. Moscow found itself isolated with more radical actors—Syria, Libya, Iraq, South Yemen, the Palestine Liberation Organization (PLO)—and discovered that it had virtually no control over their sometimes unpredictable and, from the Soviet point of view, counterproductive actions.

The Soviets were frustrated by successful U.S. efforts to cut them out of a role in the Middle East peace process. In December 1973, after the war between Egypt and Israel, the United States and the Soviet Union acted as co-chairs of a Middle East peace conference in Geneva. The conferences lasted only a few days, however, and Secretary of State Henry Kissinger then pursued his unilateral step-by-step diplomacy between Israel and the Arabs, designed to prevent Soviet participation. The Soviets played no role in the Israeli-Egyptian or the Israeli-Syrian agreements of 1974.

President Jimmy Carter briefly tried to include Moscow in the negotiating process, seeking to reconvene an international conference and issuing a joint statement in 1977 that called for a comprehensive solution to the Middle East problem.[3] Neither the Egyptians nor the Israelis wanted Soviet participation, however, and peace efforts shifted to the U.S.-run Camp David process. The Soviets played no role in the Egyptian-Israeli negotiations and peace treaty that resulted. Following the Israeli invasion of Lebanon in 1982, the United States again played the central role in negotiations aimed at getting PLO fighters out of Beirut and both Syrian and Israeli forces out of Lebanon. Moscow has insisted on participating in Middle East peace processes in order to legitimize its role in the region and formalize its global status. Its exclusion demonstrated that, in spite of military gains in the region, it had remained politically irrelevant. Unable to join negotiations, Moscow focused on undermining them; if it could not be a peacemaker, it could be a spoiler. By bolstering those Arabs (primarily the Syrians) who, for their own reasons, opposed U.S.-sponsored peace talks, the Soviets helped derail negotiations and even kill an agreement—the Israeli-Lebanese withdrawal agreement of May 1983. Through such destabilizing tactics, the Soviets reinforced regional tensions and insured their own continued relevance.

The Soviets were careful to avoid potential superpower confrontation. While often fostering tension, they did not encourage conflicts which might precipitate direct U.S. involvement or cause their own embarrassment (because of the poor performance of weapons supplied by the Soviets to the Arabs compared to those supplied by the United States to the Israelis). Soviet air forces did participate in several regional conflicts (Yemen in the 1960s and Egypt in 1970), but these commitments were limited and contained. In 1970, when their pilots and planes were shot down by the Israelis, the Soviets quickly disengaged. The Soviets never intervened militarily in the Middle East to secure their own interests or those of their clients; their only direct threat to do so occurred at the end of the 1973 war, when they were confident the United States would restrain Israel.[4]

While avoiding direct participation and potential military confrontation, Moscow did provide political support to its clients in conflict situations and, on numerous occasions, carried out military resupply operations. Chronic Arab-Israeli tensions, U.S. commitment to Israel, Soviet support for Arab positions, and the inclination of both superpowers to view the region in zero-sum terms (i.e., a gain for one was considered a loss for the other) guaranteed persistent strains in U.S.-Soviet relations.

The Impact of New Thinking

With the advent of new thinking, the Third World, considered by Gorbachev's predecessors to be a safe battleground for superpower competition, was placed in the context of the USSR's broader interests. Linkage between Soviet-Third World activities and more pressing national security interests was now accepted; the new leadership recognized that adverse trends in Soviet-Third World relations had undermined Moscow's more important interests. In order to proceed with political and economic restructuring, Gorbachev sought improved relations with the West, particularly the United States. He emphasized Moscow's interest in cooperating with Washington to resolve regional conflicts, hoping to create a more relaxed international environment.[5]

Under Gorbachev, the Soviets tried to relieve tensions between Washington and Moscow generally. In the Middle East specifically, they reduced their reliance on military instruments of policy, sought regional stability rather than tension, pursued cooperation with the United States on a broad range of issues, and tried to use the United Nations to bolster their own policies. They pursued a flexible approach to a wide variety of regional issues, including relations with Israel and moderate Arab states and diplomatic solutions to the Arab-Israeli dispute. These steps were accompanied by the public airing of differences with Arab clients such as Iraq, Libya, Syria, and the PLO over the use of force, terrorism, military parity with Israel, and political relations with Israel.

Reduced Military and Economic Support

The Soviets reduced both their own military activities in the Third World and military support for their clients. There was a decline in the operational tempo and presence of Soviet naval forces and aviation in the

Third World. Naval exercises were cut, joint exercises with Third World navies reduced, and military advisers withdrawn. In December 1989, on the eve of the Malta summit, Gorbachev slashed naval deployments in the Mediterranean by more than half, leaving a handful of warships, one or two submarines, and a few auxiliaries.[6] The Soviets made no effort to expand or upgrade facilities in Yemen or Syria,[7] and they urged the gradual withdrawal of foreign bases and naval fleets from the region.[8]

The number of Soviet military personnel in the Middle East also declined. According to the London-based International Institute for Strategic Studies, Syria lost 1,000 Soviet military advisers in 1989 and experienced a further drawdown in 1990.[9] Soviet military and economic experts were gradually withdrawn from Iraq following the latter's invasion of Kuwait in August 1990. As the primary function of military experts is to train their counterparts in the use and maintenance of Soviet-built equipment, declining arms sales presumably meant continuing reductions in the Russian physical presence.

Soviet arms deliveries to the Third World declined in 1990 for the third straight year, according to a Congressional Research Service report,[10] and Soviet military assistance to the Middle East and Persian Gulf also decreased. The Soviets accounted for 32 percent of the arms sold to the Middle East and Persian Gulf from 1983–1986, but only 20 percent from 1987–1990.[11] The value of arms deliveries to Libya fell from $9 billion during 1982–1985 to $2.5 billion during 1986–1989. Arms deliveries to Syria fell from $10 billion to $5.5 billion and to Iraq from $28 billion to $18 billion during the same periods.[12]

In part, this decline reflected reduced Third World demand. Some states were having problems absorbing the military equipment they already had and were purchasing less expensive spare parts, ammunition, and support.[13] The ceasefire between Iran and Iraq in 1988 was also a factor, reducing Iraq's need for equipment. Declining sales also reflected Soviet reluctance to continue underwriting arms transfers. In a *Pravda* article in June 1990, then Soviet Foreign Minister Eduard Shevardnadze wrote that the weakness of the Soviet economy would "restrict" Moscow's efforts on behalf of Third World states.[14] The Soviet Ambassador to Syria predicted in 1989 that military assistance to the Syrians would be reduced, and the Soviets halted arms deliveries to Iraq after the latter's invasion of Kuwait in August 1990.[15]

As with other issues, the Soviets tried to make a virtue of reality, suggesting that other nations also reduce their arms sales to the Third World. In his dinner speech for visiting Egyptian President Mubarak in May 1990, Gorbachev announced that the USSR would be willing to "limit" its arms sales to the region on the basis of "reciprocity" (i.e., U.S. restraint) and listed arms reduction to the level of "defense sufficiency" as a major component of any Middle East settlement.[16] This marked the first time that any Soviet leader had explicitly offered to limit Moscow's arms sales to the region, although Shevardnadze had previously stated that the region's "military potential" far exceeded its "real economic and demographic weight."[17]

The Soviets expressed increasing concern about the spread of advanced weaponry to the Middle East and Persian Gulf. They argued that regional states, including Israel, possess ballistic missiles that can reach Soviet territory, but emphasized that the most pressing danger is possible escalation of regional conflicts. During his trip to Egypt in February 1989, Shevardnadze proposed the creation of a "military risk-reduction center" and a "nuclear-free and chemical-free zone" in the Middle East.[18]

Emphasis on United Nations

The Soviet party program, adopted at the 27th Party Congress, called for enhancement of the role of the United Nations. The Soviets gave credibility to their rhetoric by agreeing to pay their assessment for the UN's International Force in Lebanon (UNIFIL) and by paying their overdue assessments for UN peacekeeping forces, including those in the Golan Heights. In 1987, Gorbachev issued an 11-point proposal for strengthening the scope of the United Nations, including the creation of a multilateral center to manage conflicts. He called for new UN functions such as verifying arms control agreements, investigating acts of international terrorism, and establishing international standards for human rights.[19]

The Soviets became increasingly eager to involve the United Nations in conflict resolution; internationalizing negotiations reinforced their own policies and political relevance. Their endorsement in July 1987 of UN Resolution 598, designed to bring an end to the Iran-Iraq war; their efforts to use the UN framework to work toward a solution of the Arab-Israeli conflict; and their emphasis on the central role of the United Nations in efforts to force Iraq's withdrawal from Kuwait demonstrated the importance of the United Nations to new thinking. By enhancing the role of the Security Council, where the USSR holds one of the five permanent seats, Moscow hoped to compensate for its own declining strength.

The Arab-Israeli Conflict

Improved Relations with Israel and the Moderate Arabs

Gorbachev was the first Soviet General Secretary to pursue expanded ties with Israel and to offer concessions in order to enhance Moscow's regional flexibility and international credibility. Moscow broke diplomatic relations with Israel in 1967 during the Six-Day War, a move that put the Soviet Union at a disadvantage vis-a-vis the United States in terms of mediating the Arab-Israeli conflict and contributed to the stagnation of the USSR's political position in the region.

In an effort to strengthen Moscow's image in the United States, relieve domestic political pressures, and improve relations with Israel, the Soviets allowed Soviet Jewish emigration to increase dramatically. In spite of strong Arab objections, Jewish emigration rose from 1,000 in 1986 to close to 300,000 in 1991.[20] Gorbachev's approval of direct air flights between the Soviet Union and Israel in late September 1990 gave impetus to the movement of emigrants directly to Israel.[21]

Gorbachev revealed the new attitude toward Israel at a state dinner for visiting Syrian President Assad in April 1987, asserting that the absence of diplomatic relations between the Soviet Union and Israel "cannot be considered normal."[22] Three months later, a Soviet consular delegation arrived in Tel Aviv. A similar Israeli delegation went to the Soviet Union in 1988; its status was upgraded from de facto to official consular status in January 1991.

The groundwork for the restoration of full diplomatic relations had been laid by late 1991, and the only question remained that of timing. Some commentators argued that relations should be restored immediately and without preconditions,[23] but the official government position continued to tie restoration of relations to efforts to stimulate a just peace in the region. Former Soviet Foreign Minister Aleksandr Bessmertnykh's historic visit to Israel in May 1991 and movement toward a peace conference in the summer presaged the imminent re-establishment of full diplomatic relations.

Under Gorbachev, the Soviets also upgraded relations with moderate Arab regimes. Shortly after coming to power, Gorbachev expressed interest in improving relations with Egypt whose gradual move back into the Arab fold complemented Soviet efforts to be identified with moderate Arab positions. The Soviet agreement in 1987 to accept Egyptian terms for repayment of its debt to the USSR paved the way for expanded economic ties, renewed discussion of military resupply, and high-level official exchanges.

The Soviets used the visit of Egyptian President Mubarak to the USSR in May 1990—the first by an Egyptian head of state since that of Anwar Sadat in 1972—to assert their own importance to the peaceful resolution of regional tensions and to identify with Egyptian positions. The visit resulted in a joint USSR-Egyptian declaration calling for cooperation in handling international security problems, setting up zones free of weapons in the Middle East, and enhancing the role of the United Nations in efforts to resolve regional problems.[24]

The Soviets made no attempt to undermine President Mubarak's peace initiative of September 1989, designed to facilitate Israeli-Palestinian talks.[25] This attitude contrasted with Soviet efforts to scuttle the Jordanian-PLO accord of early 1985 as well as any other initiative in which Moscow played no role. Mubarak reciprocated by insisting that both superpowers must take part in resolving the Arab-Israeli conflict.[26]

Soviet support for the coalition arrayed against Saddam Hussein after the invasion of Kuwait led to further improvement in Soviet-Egyptian relations. In February 1991, agreement was reached for an exchange of military attaches and a Soviet naval vessel visited an Egyptian port for the first time in over 15 years. Mubarak hosted meetings between Secretary of State Baker and Foreign Minister Bessmertnykh in May 1991, giving credibility to both the Egyptian and Soviet roles in the search for a solution to the Arab-Israeli conflict.

Reduced Support for Arab Radicals

Under Gorbachev, the Soviets took a firmer line toward their radical Arab clients. They made it clear that Soviet, not Arab, interests would dictate Moscow's foreign policy agenda—even in areas where Moscow had previously deferred to its clients. In 1986, Gorbachev lectured visiting Libyan official Abd al-Salam Jallud about the need for "restraint" and avoidance of any pretext for "imperialist attacks," above all terrorism in all its forms.[27] In 1987, he urged Syrian President Assad to seek a political settlement to the Arab-Israeli impasse and indicated that Moscow would no longer support Syrian efforts to attain military parity with Israel.[28] The Soviets encouraged the modification of PLO positions in 1988 and welcomed the resulting opening of a dialogue between the United States and the PLO in Tunisia in early 1989.[29] In 1990, Moscow abandoned Iraq and distanced itself from the PLO, which supported Saddam Hussein.

This new Soviet approach created concern among those Arab leaders who had depended on Soviet support. These leaders expressed dissatisfaction with Moscow's flexibility on the peace process, its expansion of contacts with Israel, its policy with respect to Soviet Jewish emigration, and its reduced willingness to subsidize arms sales. Several modified their own policies and moved to bolster their regional positions, at least in part because of their shifting perceptions of Soviet reliability. Syria's decisions to restore relations with Egypt in 1990 and to cooperate in the U.S. peace initiative of 1991 were the most dramatic manifestations of this trend, but Libyan efforts to improve ties to Egypt and its Maghreb neighbors as well as South Yemen's merger with the North can also be seen in this context.

Several of Moscow's disappointed Arab clients expressed support for the short-lived, hard-line Soviet coup of August 1991. Iraq, Libya, and some PLO spokesmen indicated that their interests would be better served if Gorbachev were no longer in power. Gorbachev called attention to this fact upon his return to Moscow.[30]

Flexibility Toward the Arab-Israeli Peace Process

In the wake of conflict resolution in Afghanistan, Angola, and the Iran-Iraq war, the Soviets asserted that precedents had been established for a "multi-option approach" to preparations for an international conference on the Arab-Israel dispute.[31] In a significant shift from the policies of the Brezhnev era, when Moscow had focused on undermining proceedings from which it was excluded and encouraged regional tensions in order to force its inclusion in the negotiating process, the Gorbachev regime sought participation through cooperation, positioning Moscow to play a constructive role through improved relations with Israel and the moderate Arabs and willingness to press the Syrians and the PLO toward a diplomatic solution. Soviet policy changed little during the early Gorbachev years as the Soviets maintained their insistence that the only acceptable negotiating framework was an international conference in which they would play a central role. They argued that such a conference must be authoritative, that all participants, including the USSR, must have an opportunity to play an effective role, and that the conference must not serve merely as an umbrella for direct talks between the parties to the dispute. This reflected their concern that the United States might organize separate negotiations. Moscow also continued to support the undermining of negotiations from which it was excluded; throughout 1985 it backed Syrian efforts to kill the Jordanian-PLO Accord of February 1985, which was aimed at establishing a dialogue with Israel.

The USSR gradually became more flexible with respect to virtually every question relating to the peace process and the Palestinian issue. It modified its position on the modalities of the negotiating process and an eventual settlement; gave active support to moderate elements of the PLO (led by Yasir Arafat) in its power struggle with Syria and more radical Palestinian factions; and urged the PLO to adopt a conciliatory posture toward Israel and a negotiated settlement. These policies lent credibility to Moscow's long-expressed but previously disingenuous willingness to use its good offices to move the peace process forward.

The shift in Soviet policy began after the collapse of the Jordanian-PLO accord in early 1986. In 1986, Gorbachev suggested that an international conference might be preceded by preliminary talks among the five permanent members of the UN Security Council—thus indicating, for the first time, that talks could proceed without PLO participation. A senior Soviet diplomat indicated in late 1987 that the Soviet Union did not require that an international conference have the right of veto or the power to enforce a solution, thus suggesting that conference modalities might be flexible.[32]

Following the outbreak of the Palestinian uprising (intifada) in December 1987, the dynamics of the negotiating environment also changed. The PLO, with Soviet encouragement, modified its positions and entered a dialogue with the United States. U.S. Secretary of State George Shultz advanced his own initiative, aimed at achieving negotiations between Israel and a Jordanian-Palestinian delegation within the framework of an international conference in which Moscow would participate. This was a major concession by the United States, which acknowledged for the first time since 1977 that the USSR had a role to play in the negotiating process.[33]

The Israelis under the leadership of Prime Minister Shamir did not accept the Shultz approach and countered with their own "election plan." While the Soviet Union criticized the Shamir plan, it refrained from attacking either President Mubarak's 10-point follow-up in September 1989 or U.S. Secretary of State Baker's five-point proposal of October 1989. In a departure from past practice, the Soviets did not campaign actively against these proposals. While new thinking was largely responsible for the policy, the Soviets probably also believed that Israel would reject the initiatives—as it did.

In his major speech on the Middle East in Cairo in February 1989, Shevardnadze moved further away from insistence on an international conference, suggesting a series of negotiations mediated by the UN Secretary General.[34] Subsequent Soviet foreign ministry statements called for the appointment by the UN Secretary General of a special representative who could organize negotiations.[35] Finally, in 1991, following the Persian Gulf war, Moscow cooperated with Secretary Baker in his efforts to convene a conference that would provide a framework for direct talks between Israel and its Arab adversaries. Thus, new thinking had gained for Moscow what its policies of competition had failed to achieve.

Lebanon: A Case Study

Moscow has had differences with Damascus over Lebanon since Syria first moved troops into Lebanon in the mid-1970s. For the most part, it deferred to Syria, however, both because Lebanon was more important to Damascus than to the USSR and because ongoing tensions served Soviet interests. The Soviets publicly defended Syria's right to be in Lebanon, resupplied and reinforced Damascus after its humiliating defeat in 1982, and participated in the undermining of the 1983 Israeli-Lebanese withdrawal agreement of 1983.

During 1989, the situation in Lebanon deteriorated following abortive elections and the establishment of two governments (one Christian and one Muslim). There was ongoing conflict between Lebanese groups seeking to strengthen their positions, and there were recurring threats of escalation involving Syria and Iraq, Syria and the Lebanese Christians, and Syria and the French.

In the past, Moscow might have tried to exploit these tensions to strengthen its own position vis-a-vis the United States. In this instance, it acted in a more constructive manner, urging moderation on all parties, including Syria and Iraq,[36] and endorsing various mediation efforts.

In May 1989, the Soviet Union and the United States issued a joint statement on Lebanon—the first such statement issued by the two countries since Gorbachev took office. They urged adoption of a ceasefire, expressed support for Arab League efforts to build a framework for national reconciliation, offered their good offices, and expressed support for the sovereignty, territorial integrity, and independence of Lebanon.[37] In July, the Soviets and the French issued an almost identical statement, but added a call for an end to arms deliveries to all Lebanese groupings—a reference to the new problems created by Iraqi arms deliveries to the Christian forces of General Aoun.[38]

Secretary Baker and Foreign Minister Shevardnadze issued a second joint statement on Lebanon in late September, affirming that the problems of Lebanon did not have a military solution and welcoming Arab League efforts to resolve the crisis.[39] Combined U.S. and Soviet pressure may well have inhibited Syrian military action against General Michel Aoun in late 1989.

Ironically, U.S.-Soviet partnership, with Syrian collaboration, in the Persian Gulf in late 1990 may have freed Syrian President Assad to move against Aoun. Syrian military action in October 1990 ended Aoun's claim to power. Subsequent tacit cooperation between Syria and Israel enabled the Lebanese Army to move into southern Lebanon and to challenge PLO positions for the first time since 1975.

The Persian Gulf

Gorbachev inherited a weak position in the Persian Gulf; in 1985 Moscow had good relations with only two regional states (Iraq and Kuwait). Its relations with Iran were poor and it had no diplomatic relations at all with any of the conservative Arab Gulf states (except Kuwait). Its position had been adversely affected by its occupation of Afghanistan as well as by the Iran-Iraq war. As elsewhere in the Third World, Gorbachev tried to alter regional perceptions of the Soviet Union and modify the environment in which Moscow was operating.

In 1991, the Soviet position in the Gulf was significantly changed—although still relatively weak. The Soviets had withdrawn from Afghanistan and the Iran-Iraq war had ended. Moscow had abandoned Iraq; Kuwait had been liberated but was devastated. Soviet relations with Iran had improved considerably and Moscow had established diplomatic relations with all the conservative Arab states, including Saudi Arabia.[40] The policies of new thinking were in large part responsible for the changes although dramatic regional events were also important.

The Iran-Iraq War (1980–1988)

Moscow's policy toward the Iran-Iraq war changed only marginally under Gorbachev and for good reason; it had been a pragmatic policy designed to keep Moscow's options open. The conflict had not entailed the risk of confrontation with the United States, and it had not even caused particular strains in superpower relations. Throughout the war, the Soviets shared several common objectives with the United States. Both wanted to prevent a broader conflict and neither wanted Iran or Iraq to emerge strengthened from the war. These shared interests produced tacit cooperation to control tensions and prevent escalation. Within the parameters of these objectives, however, the Soviets remained intent on advancing their own position and undermining that of the United States.

Throughout the war, as Moscow sought to prevent a victory by either Iran or Iraq, it tilted from support for one side to support for the other. During the period from 1980 until 1982, when Iraq seemed on the verge of a military victory, the Soviets implemented an arms embargo against both parties to the conflict. This action was directed far more at Iraq, with which the USSR had an extensive arms supply relationship, than at Iran. After 1982, when Iran expelled the Iraqis from its territory and moved its own troops into Iraq, the Soviets resumed arms deliveries to Baghdad and supported the Iraqi position with respect to ending the war. Moscow's concern with new Iranian advances on the ground in Iraq in late 1986 and early 1987 led to increased Soviet support for Baghdad and increased Soviet and international pressure on Iran.

The Soviet agreement to lease three oil tankers to Kuwait in March 1987 marked the USSR's first participation in the Gulf in a security role. It precipitated the U.S. decision to reflag 11 Kuwaiti tankers and then to protect those vessels with U.S. naval forces. The major U.S. naval buildup in the Persian Gulf during the summer of 1987 was an event the Soviets opposed and had not anticipated. In 1988, Shevardnadze criticized his senior leadership for having failed to "predict the mass American presence in the Persian Gulf."[41]

With the U.S. buildup, the Soviets reverted to a primary tenet of old thinking—the prevention of a shift in the military balance in favor of the United States. They became preoccupied with trying to inhibit and control the U.S. buildup. They first tried to coordinate efforts with the United States, proposing the joint reflagging of Kuwaiti tankers to protect them against Iranian attack, but the Reagan Administration flatly rejected the proposal.[42]

At this point, the Soviets tried to internationalize the naval presence. In July 1987, they called for withdrawal of all foreign fleets from the Gulf and, in October, they proposed the creation of a UN naval force to replace the U.S., British, and French fleets in the region.[43] While the Soviets were never clear about the objectives, composition, or duties of the proposed UN force, it was clear that they wanted a reduction of the U.S. naval presence in the Gulf.

The Soviets supported UN Resolution 598, passed in late 1987 and designed to bring about a ceasefire. They equivocated, however, about imposing the agreed sanctions against Iran, which refused to accept the resolution and which shared their opposition to the U.S. naval presence in the Gulf. They presumably hoped that tacit cooperation with Iran might help bring about a reduction in the U.S. presence. This equivocation, which slowed Moscow's developing relations with the conservative Gulf states and raised U.S. suspicions, contrasts with its subsequent willingness to abide by sanctions imposed on Iraq in 1990.

Moscow's efforts to balance between Iran and Iraq finally paid off in improved relations with Iran during the late 1980s. Concerned by the U.S. naval buildup in the Gulf in 1987, seeking to end its international isolation, and appreciative of Soviet refusal to enforce UN sanctions, Iran reduced its antagonistic rhetoric with respect to the USSR and welcomed high-level exchanges.

Political and economic relations improved rapidly after Ayatollah Khomeini sent a conciliatory message to Gorbachev in January 1989, six months before his death.[44] Subsequently, Shevardnadze visited Tehran and Majles Speaker Rafsanjani visited Moscow. The result was a number of agreements providing for economic cooperation, tourist exchanges, expanded cultural ties, and cross-border travel. The most dramatic document signed was a Declaration of Principles that included a Soviet agreement to "cooperate with the Iranian side with regard to strengthening its defense capability."[45] Gorbachev subsequently confirmed that arms sales to Iran were part of the Soviet Union's overall arms policy and asserted that such sales did not conflict with efforts to secure a more peaceful international climate; by 1990, MIG 29s and other Soviet military equipment were being delivered to Iran.[46]

Soviet relations with Iraq, which tended to fluctuate in response to Soviet-Iranian relations, improved during the latter years of the war because of Soviet arms deliveries, credit extensions, and support for Iraqi efforts to end the war. The Iraqis were angered, however, by Soviet equivocation

on implementation of 598, by Soviet support for Iran's 1989 claims to
have withdrawn from Iraqi territory, and particularly by the Soviet decision
to sell arms to Iran.[47]

Iraq's Invasion of Kuwait: 1990

Moscow's adherence to elements of old thinking throughout the Iran-
Iraq war made its reaction to Iraq's invasion of Kuwait on August 2, 1990,
even more dramatic. The Soviets immediately condemned the invasion,
announced the suspension of military deliveries to Baghdad and demanded
that Iraq withdraw unconditionally.[48] *Izvestia* commentator Aleksandr
Bovin observed that, had this crisis occurred 5–10 years ago, the Soviets
would have adopted a position of friendly neutrality and reacted strongly
and negatively to the appearance of U.S. forces in Saudi Arabia. For its
part, he said, Washington would have accused the Soviets of supporting
aggression and indulging the terrorist regime in Baghdad.[49]

Moscow supported UN efforts to resolve the crisis. On August 2, it
voted for UN Resolution 660, which condemned the aggression and
demanded Iraq's withdrawal. It subsequently endorsed UN resolutions
imposing trade sanctions on Baghdad, declaring the annexation of Kuwait
null and void, disputing Iraq's holding of foreign hostages and closing of
foreign embassies in Kuwait, permitting the use of force to implement
sanctions, and adding air interdiction to other boycott measures.

Perhaps most important, Moscow moved immediately to coordinate
policy with Washington rather than to undermine U.S. actions. On August
3, following a meeting at the Moscow Airport, Secretary Baker and Foreign
Minister Shevardnadze issued a joint statement endorsing UN condemnation of Iraq's invasion and urging the suspension of all arms shipments to
Iraq.[50] Baker referred to the agreement's historic nature, noting that in the
past the two nations would have viewed such a conflict "through an East-
West prism."[51]

A Difficult Soviet Policy Choice

This Soviet approach could not have been easy. As Shevardnadze noted
at a press conference on August 3, the USSR had maintained good relations
with Iraq for decades. The two countries had a Friendship and Cooperation
Treaty, signed in 1972, and a mutually beneficial arms supply relationship.
In August 1990, the Iraqi debt to Moscow was an estimated $6 billion
and Moscow certainly knew it was risking default; in fact, Iraq stopped
payment shortly after the invasion.[52]

The Soviets had thousands of advisers in Iraq as well as numerous
dependents. Soviet reluctance to pull all these experts out immediately
created misunderstanding between Moscow and Washington as Western

press articles charged that the Soviet military was helping the Iraqi war machine. One Soviet commentator speculated that neither the Defense Ministry nor the Foreign Ministry had wanted to take responsibility for withdrawing the experts because of the potential financial loss.[53] By early 1991, virtually all Soviet advisers had been withdrawn, however.

Soviet domestic opinion with respect to policy was divided, and criticism of Moscow's support for U.S. policy increased as the military situation deteriorated. Various Soviet spokesmen expressed reservations about U.S. policies—its force buildup, its overwhelming military action against Iraq, and its long-term intentions. Appearing before a Soviet legislative committee in late August, the Commander in Chief of the Warsaw Pact, General Vladimir Lobov, portrayed the U.S. buildup as a potential threat to the USSR's southern borders that might jeopardize East-West talks on cutting conventional weapons in Europe.[54] Deputy Foreign Minister Aleksandr Belonogov told a parliamentary committee that there were "no guarantees that the United States will ever leave Saudi Arabia after the crisis is over."[55]

Soviet Foreign Ministry spokesman Gennadiy Gerasimov refuted these statements the following week, stating that he could see "no connection" between the military balance in Europe and U.S. actions in the Gulf. He argued that the United States had sent its forces to the Gulf not on its own initiative but because it was "provoked into it by Iraqi actions."[56]

Articles in the government newspaper *Izvestia* were consistently more supportive of U.S. actions and Soviet policy than those in the party paper *Pravda* and the Defense Ministry paper, *Krasnaya Zvezda,* which accused Washington of using the crisis to build political influence and strategic presence in the Middle East.[57] A *Newsweek* article in September 1990 cited conflicting Soviet statements to support its credible thesis that both the foreign and defense ministry bureaucracies were lagging behind the leadership in applying new thinking to the crisis in the Gulf.[58]

Justification for Policy Choice

The Soviet leadership justified its abandonment of Iraq on moral and security grounds. Gorbachev called the Iraqi invasion a "violation of everything the world community now pins its hopes on as it seeks to put civilization on the tracks of peaceful development." He said Moscow had "no other choice" than to join the West in condemning Iraq because the use of force to redraw borders could "set off a perilous chain reaction endangering the entire world community."[59]

Moscow's approach also demonstrated its now unequivocal commitment to the centrality of relations with the West, particularly the United States. *Izvestia* commentator Stanislav Kondrashov elaborated on the rationale:

By sacrificing relations with another dictatorship the Soviet Union once again confirms its adherence to the new path—the abandonment of confrontation with the West, which distorted priorities in the foreign and domestic policies of the Soviet leadership and was one of the deep-seated causes of our present historical crisis. The new relations of cooperation and interaction, particularly with the United States, are now seen as one of the chief levers capable of lifting us out of the crisis. The strategic advantage in this area (both political and practical) will more than make up for the loss of friendship with Saddam Hussein.[60]

Cooperation with the United States

The rapid, high-level coordination of U.S.-Soviet policy following the invasion was largely serendipitous, emerging from meetings in Irkutsk between Secretary Baker and Foreign Minister Shevardnadze on the eve of the invasion. The two men had agreed in Irkutsk to meet immediately if the Gulf situation deteriorated. This agreement set up their subsequent meeting at Moscow Airport and the issuance of the historic joint statement only a day after the invasion occurred.[61]

Washington and Moscow maintained frequent contact and emphasized areas of bilateral agreement. The Bush-Gorbachev summit in Helsinki in early September produced a second joint statement affirming the two countries' cooperation. The two leaders stressed that their preference was to resolve the crisis peacefully, but stated that, if current efforts failed, they would consider additional steps "consistent with the UN Charter."[62] Continuing the pattern of high-level contacts, Baker met with Gorbachev and Shevardnadze in Moscow on September 13 and laid the foundation for passage of a UN resolution banning passenger and cargo flights into Iraq.[63]

In early October, following Shevardnadze's meetings with Secretary Baker and President Bush at the United Nations, a third joint statement was released, stressing U.S.-Soviet determination to strengthen UN peace keeping functions and endorsing continued sanctions against Iraq.[64] Finally, in late January 1991, following a visit to the United States by the new Soviet Foreign Minister, Aleksandr Bessmertnykh, a fourth joint statement was issued calling for Iraqi withdrawal from Kuwait.

Underlying Differences

Beneath the public displays of cooperation, there were numerous differences between Moscow and Washington with respect to dealing with the crisis. Whereas the United States was prepared to engage Iraq militarily—sending troops to Saudi Arabia, intercepting ships that might be breaking the embargo, and forcibly expelling Iraqi forces from Kuwait—the Soviet Union emphasized negotiations and declined to send its own forces to the

Gulf. Whereas Washington was prepared to act unilaterally, Moscow wanted all action to be sanctioned and implemented by the United Nations. Whereas the United States insisted that Iraq comply with all demands, the Soviet Union preferred mediation and compromise.

Soviet Preference for Political Resolution. The Soviets made it clear from the beginning of the crisis that they preferred negotiation to military action and were concerned by Washington's "militant" approach and "impatience." The initial Soviet reaction to the U.S. decision to send troops to Saudi Arabia was negative. Even Shevardnadze, a leading proponent of cooperation with the United States, was reportedly angered when informed of the decision by Baker.[65] A Soviet Foreign Ministry statement of August 7 argued that a "buildup in military presence and naval muscle-flexing in such a very tense and very complex situation is not the best line of action."[66] The following day, the Soviet military paper *Krasnaya Zvezda* charged that a Western military presence could only exacerbate the crisis.[67] The Soviets also reacted negatively to the announcement on August 12 that the United States was prepared to act unilaterally to enforce the embargo.

Moscow had particular difficulty agreeing to UN Resolutions 665 and 678. The former gave UN member states with naval forces in the area (primarily the United States) the right to take action "as may be necessary" to implement the international trade embargo against Iraq.[68] Passage of the resolution on August 25 marked the first time in the UN's 45-year history that such sweeping military authority had been conferred without the umbrella of a UN flag or command. Resolution 678, passed in late November, approved military action to force Iraqi withdrawal from Kuwait.

Moscow's support for the two resolutions was a dramatic reversal of its consistent opposition to the deployment of U.S. military force to Third World regions. The decision was a clear personal victory for Shevardnadze, who reportedly had established a close working relationship with Secretary Baker, and for new political thinking in general. It signalled Moscow's commitment to the centrality of its U.S. relationship over its previous, virtually automatic, support for Third World clients and its exploitation of regional conflict situations to further its own local interests and undermine those of the United States.

Nonetheless, the Soviets continued to try to head off the use of force against Iraq. An hour before the allied military action began in mid-January, Secretary Baker informed Foreign Minister Bessmertnykh by telephone. The latter in turn conveyed Gorbachev's request that the United States not proceed immediately. Gorbachev made one last effort to communicate with Saddam in order to persuade him to withdraw—but could not get through.[69]

As the allied bombing of Iraq intensified, the Soviets expressed misgivings about the campaign, emphasizing that the destruction of Iraq was not called for in the UN resolutions. In a statement released in early November, Gorbachev warned that the war was assuming an alarming scope and might be exceeding the UN mandate. At the same time, he affirmed Soviet adherence to the UN resolutions.[70] Finally, in mid-February, on the eve of the ground war, Gorbachev wrote to President Bush, requesting that the United States postpone the operation until Moscow could determine if its mediation efforts with Saddam could be productive.[71]

While eventually approving the use of force against Iraq, the Soviets made it clear from the beginning that direct Soviet military involvement was not a consideration. Early in the crisis, Shevardnadze had indicated that, if the United Nations called for a multinational force, the Soviet Union might participate,[72] but even this position was gradually abandoned. Vitaliy Naumkin of the Oriental Institute expressed a frequently stated position:

> Just as you had a Vietnam syndrome in the United States, so are we now experiencing an Afghanistan syndrome. Gorbachev cannot afford to send troops abroad. The Soviet people would be completely against it. Pershaps we could send two or three ships to the gulf as a symbolic contribution to a multinational force. But that's all.[73]

Soviet Preference for Multilateral Enforcement. The Soviets consistently tried to give responsibility for the enforcement of UN resolutions to the United Nations itself, by reviving the UN's moribund Military Staff Committee.[74] In his speech to the United Nations on September 25, 1990, Shevardnadze emphasized that the Military Staff Committee was the appropriate body to coordinate and implement UN-imposed sanctions.[75] The Chief of the Soviet General Staff, Mikhail Moiseyev, visiting the United States in October 1990, argued that no force should be used in the Persian Gulf unless approved by the United Nations.[76]

While the Soviets consistently supported collective actions to force Iraqi compliance, the United States preferred to rely on its own strength. In part, the U.S. position was based on concern that the UN approach was time consuming and ineffective.[77] The primary reason, however, as President Bush indicated, was that, while the United Nations might be useful when it served U.S. interests, the United States was not willing to surrender any authority to it.[78]

Soviet Preference for Mediation. The Soviets may have hoped at the beginning of the crisis that their traditional relationship with Iraq would enable them to mediate an end to the dispute, and they maintained their contacts with Baghdad. In mid-October Presidential Council member Yevgeniy Primakov met with Saddam Hussein in Baghdad and purported to have received indications of Iraqi willingness to negotiate. In early

February, Gorbachev again sent Primakov to Baghdad in a last-minute effort to gain a compromise, Primakov again reported a "glimmer of hope."[79] For the next week and a half, the Soviets tried vigorously but unsuccessfully to obtain an agreement that would end the crisis. Iraq, for its part, tried to use its contacts with the USSR to create a rift between Moscow and Washington. In early September, Tariq Aziz told Gorbachev that Iraq would welcome a more active Soviet role in working out a compromise to the crisis.[80] He also held out the prospect that Soviet citizens would be treated differently than those of other nations, saying they they "can stay in our country or leave it."[81] In October, the Iraqis reverted to threats, charging that, if the Soviets gave military intelligence to the United States, Soviet citizens would not be allowed to leave Iraq.[82]

Soviet Preference for Compromise. Moscow was consistently more willing than Washington to consider a compromise solution to the crisis. Shevardnadze professed to see hope in the proposal made by Saddam Hussein on August 19, which linked resolution of the Kuwait situation to resolution of the Palestinian problem, and both he and Gorbachev pushed this approach in subsequent meetings with U.S. officials.[83] In a speech in Vladivostok in early September, Shevardnadze called for fresh UN efforts to resolve the Persian Gulf crisis, including the rapid convening of a Middle East peace conference to settle the Arab-Israeli conflict. He did not directly link the two issues, but, by referring to a set of "highly complex, interlocking problems" in the Middle East and by reviving the longstanding Soviet proposal for a peace conference, he appeared to support Saddam Hussein's earlier demand. In his last speech to the United Nations before his resignation, on November 29, Shevardnadze implicitly challenged the United States to accept movement toward an international conference on the Arab-Israeli problem and not to reject it out of "some occult fear of the word linkage."[84]

During the Primakov mediation efforts in February, considerable tension arose in U.S.-Soviet relations because of Moscow's willingness to compromise with Saddam. Whereas the United States insisted on Saddam's immediate and unconditional withdrawal from Kuwait, the Soviets were prepared to give him a period of time to withdraw, to consider lifting UN sanctions when he had withdrawn, and to provide him with assurances of protection in the aftermath of the war.[85]

Differing Visions. Even those Soviets who had supported the U.S. presence in the Gulf expressed concern about long-term U.S. intentions. Stanislav Kondrashov, for example, argued that Washington's

> gigantic military mechanism is working like clockwork, inevitably making Soviet generals and politicians bristle: after all, this is alongside our borders. After all, this is a show of U.S. power, which we have opposed for decades.

Are we now supposed to welcome it? . . . What if the Americans stay even after Saddam Hussein is gone?[86]

Soviet concern was heightened by Secretary of State Baker's suggestion in early September that the United States and Arab nations should establish a new "regional security structure" for the Persian Gulf to contain and roll back Saddam Hussein. He indicated that such an effort could require a sustained U.S. naval presence in the region.[87]

U.S. Concessions. Washington's efforts to forge an international coalition in support of its policy toward the Iraqi invasion led it to make unprecedented gestures toward Moscow. These included suggestions that the Soviet Union contribute forces to the multinational force, abandonment of opposition to a Soviet role in the Middle East peace process, modifications of proposed UN resolutions, and cautious movement toward linkage of Iraqi withdrawal from Kuwait with action to address the Arab-Israeli conflict.

U.S. suggestions that Moscow contribute forces to the multinational force were unprecedented. Washington had never before approved the dispatch of Soviet forces to a Third World area, much less encouraged it.[88] Administration officials argued, however, that, given the current policy of the Soviet Union, "a cooperative approach is warranted."[89]

In order to gain Soviet support for UN Resolution 665, the United States agreed to modifications in the language of the resolution, making references to the use of force less clear and referring to the UN's Military Staff Committee as the coordinating body for enforcing the resolution.[90]

The United States sought to allay Soviet concerns about its force build-up and long-term intentions. At the Helsinki summit in September 1990, President Bush assured Gorbachev that American troops in Saudi Arabia would leave when the crisis was over.[91] In talks after the summit, Baker and Shevardnadze discussed the prospect of a realignment of forces in the Persian Gulf. U.S. officials indicated that Baker and Shevardnadze had begun sketching out ideas for a long-term "regional security structure" for the Gulf. They indicated that Baker had modifed his original suggestion and was suggesting something more loosely organized.[92] Perhaps most important, the United States gradually moved toward acceptance of linkage between resolution of both the Gulf crisis and the Arab-Israeli conflict. At Helskini, President Bush had continued to assert that the issues of the Iraqi invasion and an international conference on the Middle East were not linked and that any effort to link them was "an effort to dilute the resolutions of the United Nations." Gorbachev, on the other hand, had stressed that the Gulf crisis and other disputes in the region were of "equal concern."[93]

Bush did drop remaining U.S. opposition to Soviet involvement in a Middle East peace conference, however, and, according to Administration officials, invited Moscow to play a greater diplomatic role. He also indicated that the United States was open to a peace conference provided the Iraq crisis was not on the agenda—in other words that there be no linkage.[94] In his speech to the United Nations on October 1, 1990, Bush held out more hope of possible movement on Arab-Israeli negotiations, indicating that Iraqi withdrawal from Kuwait could lead to "opportunities" to resolve other regional disputes, including the Arab-Israeli conflict. He subsequently asserted, however, that no linkage had been implied.[95]

The U.S.-Soviet joint statement of January 30, 1991, was the most dramatic concession made to Moscow by Washington. For the first time, by including language on both the Gulf crisis and the need to resolve other regional issues (particularly Arab-Israeli tensions), the United States implicitly acknowledged linkage between the two. The statement indicated that efforts to resolve other regional issues would be redoubled after the Gulf crisis ended. The statement also included language more flexible than that usually used by the United States, indicating that, if Iraq made a commitment to withdraw and took immediate steps to do so, hostilities could end.[96]

U.S. responsiveness to use of this language presumably reflected concern that Moscow's support for the coalition was weakening and that the Soviets might be tempted to join other nations calling for a ceasefire. Such a perception had been reinforced by Bessmertnykh, who, on the eve of his departure for Washington in January, had expressed reservations about the course of the war and U.S. intentions. Washington undoubtedly hoped that the joint statement would keep Moscow firmly within the alliance by providing assurances that Iraq's destruction was not sought and that the USSR would be part of any postwar diplomacy in the region. By seeking Soviet partnership in his Middle East initiative of mid-1991, Secretary Baker fulfilled the implicit commitment.

Prospects

The abrupt resignation of Foreign Minister Shevardnadze in late December 1990 raised questions in the West about Moscow's commitment to its policies in the Middle East and the Persian Gulf—as elsewhere. The Soviet Union's national crisis, the departure of other key backers of new thinking, and Gorbachev's move to the right in the period preceding the attempted coup further reinforced Western concerns.

The question of possible changes in Soviet policy also was raised by differences within the Soviet leadership and bureaucracy over policy in the Persian Gulf and Middle East. Criticism of Shevardnadze's policy toward the Gulf crisis was one reason cited for his resignation, and presidential adviser Yevgeniy Primakov made statements throughout the Gulf crisis suggesting that he gave greater priority to salvaging relations with Iraq than did Shevardnadze, who emphasized the need for harmony between Moscow and Washington.

Primakov also appeared more reluctant to modify Soviet positions with respect to Middle East issues than did Foreign Minister Bessmertnykh. In May 1991, as Bessmertnykh made his historic visit to Israel and sought partnership with the United States in a peace process based on compromise, Primakov reiterated the importance of direct Palestinian representation at any conference, portrayed Syria as the wronged party, and insisted that the United Nations play a central role in the negotiating process.[97]

Such differences appeared to reflect shades of emphasis rather than fundamentally different approaches, however. In spite of the dramatic domestic differences played out in Moscow in August, there were few strong challenges to the basic orientation of Soviet toward the Third World introduced by Gorbachev. Shevardnadze's successor, Bessmertnykh, was fired by Gorbachev because of his passive (some say, cooperative) performance during the August coup attempt. Bessmertnykh, however, had strongly endorsed and then pursued the policies of his predecessor, sending a reassuring message of continuity to the West. Soviet Foreign Minister Boris Pankin, appointed in late August 1991, was a strong proponent of new thinking, as is Russian Foreign Minister Andrei Kozyrev.

Moscow almost certainly will continue to give high priority to maintaining a relaxed international environment and expanding international economic relationships and will refrain from efforts to undermine U.S. positions by capitalizing on regional instability. A foreign ministry official wrote in 1990 that, if Soviet interests "clash with American interests, we must seek a resolution jointly. In other cases, American interests must not trouble us."[98] To the best of its ability, Moscow will continue to pursue political solutions to regional tensions and will encourage its clients to take moderate positions so as not to jeopardize broader interests.

The Middle East and Persian Gulf will retain their importance to Moscow because of their proximity, their wealth, and the dangers posed by chronic tensions. While progress in negotiations has reduced the danger of war, the Arab-Israeli conflict remains intractable and, in the absence of a settlement, the situation will remain volatile. The Arab states are no match for Israel, but the proliferation of nuclear and chemical weapons in the region increases the potential danger of any minor clash.

The Russian leadership will continue to support measures for UN participation in resolving regional conflicts in an effort to bolster its own weakened role in international processes. Moscow will urge the use of permanent members of the Security Council as guarantors of regional security as it has done with various regional conflicts in recent years. Thus far the Russians have found a broad consensus at the United Nations for a more active role by the secretary general in resolving conflicts and cooperating with regional organizations to create an environment for negotiations.

Reductions in arms sales to the Middle East probably will continue as Moscow pulls back from its commitments to client regimes and focuses on limiting competition. Gorbachev's reference in May 1990 to establishing limits on the basis of reciprocity indicated that Moscow would cooperate in controlling arms sales to the region. Moscow reacted slowly to proposals made by President Bush in May 1991 designed to control arms sales to the Middle East,[99] but did participate in the "unprecedented" meeting of the five permanent members of the Security Council, held in Paris in July 1991. The participants supported ridding the region of weapons of mass destruction and agreed in principle not to send arms to countries that threaten regional stability. They also agreed to draw up international rules for the export of weapons to "explosive regions" and to hold further meetings.[100]

Russian retrenchment does not mean that Third World states will lose all access to Russian weapons. While Moscow (or republic governments) will be increasingly unwilling to subsidize arms sales to Arab states, it may be willing to provide them with weapons from stockpiles that are being drawn down in Europe. And Moscow will continue to try to sell arms to those who can pay. While Soviet arms deliveries to the Middle East declined overall in 1989, for example, deliveries to Kuwait and Libya (both paying customers at the time) increased.

Russia also will continue to look for opportunities to sell arms in areas of strategic interest—even on generous terms. According to the Congressional Research Service, they had concluded more than $2.7 billion in arms agreements with Iran by the end of 1990,[101] and they have offered to increase sales to Egypt. They have lost two major arms clients—Iraq and Kuwait—and may hope to compensate by creating new markets in the conservative Gulf states.

In previous regional confrontations, both Washington and Moscow have been pressed to provide support and resupply. Any Russian leadership will be far less willing than before to provide rapid resupply to clients in conflict situations. The decision to halt arms shipments to Iraq after the invasion of Kuwait demonstrates that Russia will not support clients automatically but will weigh broader interests far more carefully than in the past.

In spite of the reduced danger of global confrontation, crisis management may become more difficult and time urgent as regional states that have acquired sophisticated and lethal weaponry may feel less constrained by the fear of superpower involvement; the Iraqi invasion, albeit a miscalculation, is a case in point. It is particularly ironic that key states in the

Middle East and Persian Gulf are acquiring intermediate-range ballistic
missiles just as the United States and the Soviet Union agreed to eliminate
such weapons from Europe. The advent of new thinking does not mean
that U.S. and Russian interests will coincide. As Stanislav Kondrashov has
warned, the interests of the two countries are not the same:

> America wants to dominate a region where there is so much oil, where Israeli
> interests . . . are still more important to it than Saudi interests, and which
> lies strategically close to the Soviet Union. What has changed in these
> principles of U.S. policy? It still relies on force and on assurances that force
> will be used in the interests of peace and stability. There are no grounds for
> doubting the sincerity of the assurances, but Washington reserves the right
> to determine what the interests of peace and stability are. Despite the level
> of cooperation reached between the United States and the USSR, the policies
> of the two powers are not and cannot be identical.[102]

New thinking does mean, however, that Moscow no longer believes the
expansion of its military presence in the Third World will give it greater
political security or that Moscow must counter every U.S. move. Unlike
Brezhnev, the new Russian leadership is not willing to pour arms into areas
of friction. Rather, Gorbachev advocated collective efforts to defuse conflicts "in all the planet's hot spots," and Yeltsin has continued these
efforts.[103] Their primary rationale for supporting regional settlements is to
ensure that local conflicts do not "engender confrontation" or increase
tensions between the superpowers.[104] This will remain a key Russian
objective for the foreseeable future as Moscow seeks to rebuild its shattered
political and economic structures.

Notes

1. Harry Gelman, *The Brezhnev Politburo and the Decline of Detente,* Ithaca,
Cornell University Press, 1984, pp. 26–27.
2. The Soviets used Syrian facilities for reconnaissance flights and conducted
joint naval exercises with the Syrians. They had access rights to facilities in both
Yemen and former South Yemen. Such access enhanced their logistics and reconnaissance capabilities in both the Mediterranean and Indian Ocean areas. The
Soviets also developed highly lucrative arms relationships with Libya, Iraq, and
Algeria. Their limited entree to such moderate Arab states as Jordan and Kuwait
came through arms sales.
3. The U.S.-Soviet joint communique of October 1, 1977, endorsed a comprehensive settlement to the Arab-Israeli conflict, incorporating all parties concerned
and all questions. Specific questions to be resolved included Israel's withdrawal
from territories occupied in the 1967 conflict; the resolution of the Palestinian
question, including insuring the legitimate rights of the Palestinian people; termi-

nation of the state of war and establishment of normal peaceful relations "on the basis of mutual recognition of the principles of sovereignty, territorial integrity, and political independence." It suggested the establishment of demilitarized zones and the stationing of UN troops or observers and international guarantees of agreed borders. It called for negotiations within the framework of the Geneva peace conference with the participation of all involved paraties including the Palestinians. ("U.S., U.S.S.R. Issue Statement on the Middle East," *Department of State Bulletin*, vol. 77 (November 7, 1977), pp. 639–40.

4. Galia Golan, "The Soviet Union in the Middle East After Thirty Years," in *The Soviet Union and the Third World: The Last Three Decades*, ed., Andrzej Korbonski and Francis Fukuyama, Ithaca and London, Cornell University Press, 1987, pp. 184–185, 192–193.

5. W. Raymond Duncan and Carolyn McGiffert Ekedahl, *Moscow and the Third World Under Gorbachev*, Westview Press, Boulder, San Francisco, and Oxford, 1990, pp. 71–75.

6. The normal presence of the Soviet Mediterranean Squadron consists of five to seven submarines, six to ten surface warships, and 14 auxiliary ships.

7. Richard Pipes' descriptions of Soviet efforts to build a major facility at Tartus in Syria to service vessels and submarines in the Mediterranean are specious. (*Commentary 89*), March 1990, p. 22) These facilities are no longer important for protecting Soviet sealanes.

8. *The Washington Post*, November 27, 1989, R. Jeffrey Smith, "U.S. Reluctant to Restrict Naval Arms," p. 1 and 4.

9. *The New York Times*, March 6, 1990, Youssef M. Ibrahim, "Arabs Fear End of Cold War," p. 1.

10. Richard F. Grimmett, Congressional Research Service report cited by *The New York Times*, August 11, 1991, Robert Pear, "U.S. Ranked No. 1 in Weapons Sales," p. 10.

11. Richard Grimmett, Congressional Research Service report, cited in *The New York Times*, August 11, 1991, p. 10.

12. Richard F. Grimmett, *Trends in Conventional Arms Transfers to the Third World by Major Supplier, 1982–1989*, Washington D.C., Congressional Research Service, 1990, p. 63.

13. The Soviet Union registered a substantial decrease in its share of Third World arms transfer agreements in 1988, falling from 50% in 1987 to 33% in 1988. The total value of its agreements also fell dramatically, from $19 billion in 1987 to $10 billion in 1988. See Richard F. Grimmett, *Trends in Conventional Arms Transfers to the Third World by Major Supplier, 1982–1989*, Washington, D.C., Congressional Research Service, 1990.

14. *Pravda*, June 26, 1990, p. 3.

15. *Reuters*, September 18, 1989.

16. *Pravda*, May 16, 1990, p. 5.

17. *Izvestia*, February 24, 1989, p. 3.

18. *The New York Times*, March 24, 1989, Thomas L. Friedman, "Spread of Missiles is Seen as Soviet Worry in Mideast," p. 2.

19. *Pravda*, September 12, 1987.

20. *The New York Times,* March 6, 1988, p. 3; *Wiener Zeitung,* February 4, 1990; *The New York Times,* September 30, 1990, p. 8, *The New York Times,* November 2 and 4, 1990.

21. *The New York Times,* September 30, 1990, p. 8.

22. *Pravda,* April 25, 1987, p. 5.

23. Aleksandr Bovin, *Izvestia,* August 26, 1989.

24. TASS, May 17, 1990.

25. *Komsomolskaya Pravda,* January 3, 1990, p. 3.

26. MENA, February 25, 1989.

27. TASS, May 27, 1986.

28. *Pravda,* April 25, 1987, p. 5.

29. *Izvestia,* January 7, 1989, Aleksandr Bovin.

30. *Baghdad Radio,* August 19, 1991; Jordanian daily *Sawt Al-Sha'b,* August 20, 1991; Libyan news agency *Jamahiriyah,* August 19, 1991.

31. *Pravda,* May 12, 1989, p. 5.

32. *Ha'aretz,* September 6, 1987.

33. William B. Quandt, ed., *The Middle East: Ten Years After Camp David,* William B. Quandt, "U.S. Policy Toward the Arab-Israeli Conflict," pp. 376–377.

34. *Pravda,* February 24, 1989, p.3. Foreign Minister Shevardnadze's speech at the headquarters of Egypt's National Democratic Party on February 23, 1989, contains the most extensive description of the Soviet leadership's views on the modalities of negotiations for an Arab-Israeli peace settlement.

35. *Izvestia,* June 30, 1990, p. 5.

36. Abu Dhabi *Al-Ittihad,* June 4, 1989; Kuwait *Al-Qabas,* August 23, 1989.

37. TASS, May 11, 1989.

38. *Pravda,* July 6, 1989.

39. TASS, September 24, 1989.

40. Relations with Oman and the United Arab Emirates were established in late 1985, with Qatar in 1988, and with Bahrain and Saudi Arabia in 1990.

41. *Vestnik Ministerstva Inostrannykh Sel SSSR,* August 1988, no. 15, pp. 27–46. Shevardnadze report to the Foreign Ministry.

42. *The New York Times,* August 28, 1990, Elaine Sciolino, "Peacekeeping in a New Era: The Superpowers Act in Harmony."

43. *Pravda,* July 4, 1987, and October 18, 1987.

44. Tehran Radio, January 8, 1989.

45. TASS, June 22, 1989.

46. Tehran TV, September 22, 1990.

47. *Al Iraq,* July 2 and 3, 1989.

48. TASS, August 2, 1990.

49. *Izvestia,* August 24, 1990, Aleksandr Bovin, "Political Observer's Opinion."

50. TASS, August 3, 1990.

51. *The Washington Post,* Michael Dobbs and Al Kamen, "U.S., Soviets Call For World Cutoff of Arms to Iraq," August 4, 1990.

52. *The New York Times,* September 9, 1990, Elaine Sciolino, "Soviet-Iraqi Tie: Marriage of Strained Convenience," *The Washington Post,* August 23, 1990, David Hoffman and David Remnick, "Soviets Resist Using Force."

53. *Izvestia,* September 4, 1990, Stanislav Kondrashov, "And This Time in Helsinki."

54. TASS, August 30, 1990.

55. *The New York Times,* September 4, 1990, Francis X. Clines, "Soviets Say Crisis Won't Mar U.S. Ties," p. A9.

56. *The New York Times,* September 4, 1990, Francis X. Clines, "Soviets Say Crisis Won't Mar U.S. Ties."

57. *The New York Times,* September 4, 1990, Francis X. Clines, "Soviets Say Crisis Won't Mar U.S. Ties;" *The Washington Post,* September 4, 1990, Michael Dobbs, "Soviet Spokesman Rebukes Military, Defends US Presence in Persian Gulf."

58. *Newsweek,* September 17, 1990, Margaret Garrard Warner, "The Moscow Connection," p. 24.

59. *The Washington Post,* August 18, 1990, David Remnick, "Gorbachev Cautious About Gulf."

60. *Izvestia,* August 15, 1990, Stanislav Kondrashov, "Together Against the Aggressor, What Then?"

61. TASS, August 3, 1990. Shevardnadze stated at a press conference on August 3 that he had responded to Baker's concern about Saddam Hussein's intentions by expressing confidence that Iraq would not resort to an overt invasion. He and Baker agreed at that time that they would meet again if the situation became aggravated. At this press conference, Shevardnadze emphasized that it was not easy for the Soviet Union to take the steps it was taking given its decades-long relationship with Iraq.

62. *The New York Times,* September 10, 1990, Bill Keller, "Bush and Gorbachev Say Iraqis Must Obey UN and Quit Kuwait."

63. *The Washington Post,* September 14, 1990, David Hoffman, "US May Seek Tougher Sanctions Against Iraq."

64. TASS, October 3, 1990.

65. *Newsweek,* September 17, 1990, Margaret Garrard Warner, "The Moscow Connection," p. 24.

66. *The New York Times,* August 8, 1990, Thomas L. Friedman, "U.S. Ready to Ask Soviets to Help Form Naval Force."

67. AFP, August 8, 1990.

68. *New York Times,* August 30, 1990, Elaine Sciolino with Eric Pace, "How U.S. Got U.N. Backing for Use of Force in the Gulf," p. A 1.

69. *The New York Times,* January 18, 1991; *The Washington Post,* January 20, 1990.

70. TASS, February 9, 1991.

71. *The New York Times,* February 19, 1991, Serge Schmemann, "Gorbachev Gives Iraqis a Peace Proposal," p. A1.

72. *The Washington Post,* August 18, 1990, David Remnick, "Gorbachev Cautious About Gulf."

73. *The Washington Post,* September 9, 1990, Michael Dobbs, "Soviet 'New Thinking' Faces Major Test in Persian Gulf Crisis."

74. *The New York Times,* August 10, 1990, Paul Lewis, "U.N. Council Declares Void Iraqi Annexation of Kuwait."

75. TASS, September 25, 1990.

76. *The New York Times,* October 3, 1990, Michael R. Gordon, "Top Soviet General Tells U.S. Not to Attack in Gulf," p. 1.

77. *Izvestia,* August 24, 1990, Aleksandr Bovin, "Political Observer's Opinion."

78. *The New York Times,* August 28, 1990, Elaine Sciolino, "Peacekeeping in a New Era: The Superpowers Act in Harmony."

79. *The New York Times,* February 14, 1991, Serge Schmemann, "Gorbachev's Envoy Sees 'Glimmer of Hope' After Talks With Iraqi Leader," p. A19.

80. TASS, September 6, 1990.

81. *The Washington Post,* September 7, 1990, Michael Dobbs, "Iraqi Envoy Asks Moscow to Seek Gulf Settlement."

82. *The Washington Post,* October 12, 1990.

83. TASS, August 20 and 21, 1990.

84. TASS, November 30, 1990.

85. *The Washington Post,* February 23, 1991, Michael Dobbs, "Soviets Press Plan for Iraqi Pullout Within Three Weeks."

86. *Izvestia,* September 4, 1990, Stanislav Kondrashov, "And This Time in Helsinki."

87. *The Washington Post,* September 5, 1990., David Hoffman, "Baker Proposes New Alliance to Contain Iraqi Aggression."

88. *Newsweek,* September 17, 1990, Margaret Garrard Warner, "The Moscow Connection," p. 25.

89. *The New York Times,* September 8, 1990, Andrew Rosenthal, "Bush Wants a Rise in Moscow's Force."

90. Text of UN Resolution 665, *The New York Times,* August 26, 1990.

91. *The New York Times,* September 10, 1990, Bill Keller, "Bush and Gorbachev Say Iraqis Must Obey UN and Quit Kuwait."

92. *The Washington Post,* September 12, 1990, David Hoffman, "Long-Term Gulf Security Arrangement Sought."

93. *The New York Times,* September 10, 1990, Bill Keller, "Bush and Gorbachev Say Iraqis Must Obey UN and Quit Kuwait."

94. *The New York Times,* September 11, 1990, Andrew Rosenthal, "Bush, Reversing US Policy, Won't Oppose a Soviet Role in Middle East Peace Talks."

95. *The Washington Post,* October 2, 1990, Ann Devroy, "Bush Offers U.N. Hope on Gulf," p. 1.

96. *The Washington Post,* January 30, 1991, Rick Atkinson and David Hoffman, "Commitment in Pullout From Kuwait Sought,", p. 1.

97. Primakov interview with *L'Unita,* May 15, 1991.

98. *Mezhdunarodnaya Zhizn,* April 1990, No. 4. "Reexamining Policy in the Third World", Andrey Kolosov, pp. 37–45.

99. *The Washington Post,* May 30, 1991, Ann Devroy, "President Bush Poses Mideast Arms Curb," p. A1.

100. TASS, July 11, 1991.

101. The Soviets supplied few arms to Iran between 1979 and 1983. Between 1983 and 1986, they reportedly signed $10 million worth of arms, a figure that increased rapidly in the last years of the decade. See Richard F. Grimmett, *Trends*

in *Conventional Arms Transfers to the Third World by Major Supplier, 1982–1989,* Washington D.C., Congressional Research Service, 1990; Richard F. Grimmett, Congressional Research Service report of 1991, cited in *The New York Times,* August 11, 1991, p. 10.

102. *Izvestia,* August 15, 1990, Stasilav Kondrashov, "Together Against the Aggressor. What Then?"

103. *Pravda,* September 17, 1987, p. 2.

104. Mikhail Gorbachev, *Perestroika: New Thinking for Our Country and the World,* New York, Harper and Row, 1987, p. 176.

3

Russian-American Cooperation in Latin America Since Gorbachev

W. Raymond Duncan

When Mikhail S. Gorbachev introduced "new thinking" in foreign policy after coming to power in 1985, few observers predicted the far-reaching effect it would have on Soviet-U.S. cooperation in managing regional conflicts in the Third World. While Gorbachev inherited his predecessors' reluctance to become directly engaged militarily on behalf of clients in Central and South America, it hardly seemed likely at the time that new thinking's emphasis on political settlement of conflicts would extend beyond rhetoric to direct diplomacy. This is especially true for the Caribbean Basin and Central America, where at the time Moscow was exploiting opportunities in Nicaragua to undermine U.S. influence in its strategic backyard. By 1989, however, Gorbachev's new thinking had produced dramatic revisions in Moscow's foreign policy that altered the nature of Soviet-U.S. relations in Third World conflicts.

In seeking to improve Soviet-American relations—so vital to Moscow's domestic economic rejuvenation program—the USSR announced a moratorium on arms shipments to Nicaragua in mid-1989, backed the UN-monitored February 1990 elections in that country, and promised to work closely with the newly elected post-Sandinista government of President Violetta Chamorro. Moscow, in addition, strongly endorsed regional peace efforts by the Central American presidents to end fighting in El Salvador and communicated its wish to cooperate formally with the United States in establishing a "permanent mechanism" to cut armed forces and weapons supplies in the region to the minimum required for self defense.

New initiatives have been pursued elsewhere in the Caribbean and Central American regions. In El Salvador, Yuri Pavlov, Chief of the Latin American Department of the Soviet Foreign Ministry, met with El Salvador's foreign minister in July 1990, and Pavlov's Deputy, Jan Burliay, met in San Salvador in August with Salvadoran President Alfredo Cristiani, the first visit of a Soviet official to El Salvador.[1] And the USSR recognized the government of Honduras, a staunch U.S. ally in the region, and has established a Moscow-Miami dialogue that recognizes the importance of the Cuban exile community in the U.S.—a shift away from strict attention to Havana. Indeed, following the failed August 1991 coup in Moscow, the Soviets announced in September that military troops soon would be withdrawn from Cuba—a surprise for Havana that generated mounting Soviet-Cuban frictions.[2]

In exploring how Soviet new thinking has played out in shaping Soviet-U.S. cooperation in Latin America, this chapter examines (1) Gorbachev's inheritance in Latin America regarding Soviet-U.S. cooperation and conflict, (2) new thinking for conflict management south of the Rio Grande, and (3) prospects for future Russian-U.S. cooperation.

Gorbachev's Inheritance

Gorbachev inherited a situation in Latin America, notably in the Caribbean Basin, that was not conducive to cooperative Soviet-American relations.[3] While Soviet-U.S. relations admittedly had gone up and down over the years, Soviet activities in Latin America, especially in the Caribbean and Central America, tended to foster adversarial political relations between Moscow and Washington. By the time Gorbachev came to power in 1985, Soviet competition with the United States—especially Moscow's military backing of Cuba, support for leftist regimes in Grenada and Nicaragua, and backing of guerrilla movements in El Salvador and Guatemala—had produced tensions. These dated back to 1960–61 when Fidel Castro turned toward the USSR for economic and military assistance and adopted Marxism-Leninism as Cuba's leading ideology. From that point on the Caribbean Basin and Central America remained focal points of Soviet-U.S. conflict, stimulating negative U.S. perceptions of the Soviet Union.

The period prior to Gorbachev's arrival on the scene especially fouled the waters of Soviet-U.S. relations. The emergence of Grenada's leftist New Jewel Movement and Sandinista Nicaragua in 1979 brought new anti-U.S. actors onto the stage, which Moscow quickly backed and Washington opposed. In the 1982 Falkland/Malvinas crisis, Moscow and Havana backed Argentina; Washington sided with Great Britain. The Kissinger Commission reported in 1984 that Soviet foreign policy makers were bent on expansionism, especially in the Moscow/Havana-managed support for violent revolution in Central America where they planned to establish Marxist-Leninist dictatorships aligned with the USSR.

By 1985, U.S. policy in combating communism in the western hemisphere assumed that a "domino theory" explained Soviet behavior—with Moscow supporting Cuba, which in turn sought to establish Marxist-Leninist states, beginning with Nicaragua, thence to El Salvador, and from there into the rest of Central America.[4] Once established, such states would then threaten Mexico to the north and Colombia and Venezuela to the South. The result would be an expanded Soviet presence with military bases threatening the Panama Canal, sea lanes of communication in the Caribbean, and other regional assets. Throughout the six-year period before Gorbachev's emergence, U.S. attention was focused on the Soviet and Cuban military build-up of Nicaragua, bolstering of Nicaragua's role in backing leftist guerrillas seeking overthrow of El Salvador's government, and aiding guerrillas elsewhere in the region. The huge Soviet military and intelligence presence in Cuba and Moscow's growing presence throughout Latin America[5] added to U.S. fears of communism spreading in the Americas.[6] Such perceptions helped generate President Ronald Reagan's policy of "rolling back" communism in leftist Third World states—as in Nicaragua where Washington's policies centered on bolstering the anti-Sandinista Contras and in El Salvador where aid was extended to a government fighting Cuban-backed leftist insurgents.[7]

Sources of Soviet-U.S. Conflict

In assessing Gorbachev's inheritance in terms of the legacy of Soviet-U.S. tensions in Latin America, three roots of regional tensions merit attention: (1) regional forces, including the Cuban factor (2) U.S. hegemony and (3) Soviet expansionism.

Regional Factors

Worth noting is the area's legendary reputation for political instability—a setting of civil wars pitting leftist guerrillas against formal governmental regimes. Such instability has not been caused by Soviet or Cuban activities, but arises from local and regional conditions. These include feudalistic land-holding structures, rising population growth and scarce resources, huge income disparities, and grinding poverty for the masses. But Moscow's and Havana's support for leftist insurgents and regimes—El Salvador's Farabundo Marti National Liberation Movement (FMLN), Grenada's New Jewel Movement (1979–1983) and Nicaragua's Sandinistas—exacerbated such local and regionally fed tensions and, therefore, contributed to the turmoil.

The Cuban Factor

Cuba has been a key regional element contributing to Soviet-U.S. conflict in the Third World. Until Fidel Castro's revolution and anti-Yanqui stance turned Moscow's head, the Soviets had for the most part written off Latin America—so far from Moscow's shores and so close to Washington—as generally within the U.S. sphere of interest. As Castro insinuated himself into the Soviet camp, his anti-imperialist policy objectives and support for leftist regimes and movements were viewed in Moscow as worthy of military and economic support. Cuba provided a strategic location for Soviet military and intelligence operations; Lourdes, outside Havana, is the largest Soviet intelligence installation outside the USSR. By following its own independent lines of action in the Third World, Cuba advanced Soviet interests by helping the Sandinistas seize and consolidate power, backing other leftist insurgents in the Caribbean and Central America, and by crafting a foreign policy paralleling Soviet interests in Angola, Ethiopia, and Mozambique.

U.S. Hegemony

U.S. perceptions have been another source of conflict with Soviet behavior in this part of the world. The United States is not unlike other great powers, whose security concerns typically are aroused by civil wars in adjacent, unstable border areas.[8] In 1954, well before Castro came to power in Cuba, the United States demonstrated its grave concern about communist inroads when it worked to unseat Guatemalan president Jacobo Arbenz Guzman, who had initiated radical economic and social reforms since coming to power in 1951—reforms the United States began to identify with communism. The United States backed a Guatemalan exile force, headed by Colonel Carlos Castillo Armas, that invaded Guatemala in June 1954 and took over the government despite Arbenz government appeals to the UN.

In April 1965 the United States intervened in the Dominican Republic, fearing that communists were involved in a rebellion that threatened U.S. interests. Well known, too, are the U.S.-backed Bay of Pigs invasion of Cuba in April 1961 as a result of the flowering Soviet-Cuban relationship and U.S. presidential, congressional, and popular fears of communism. The Cuban missile crisis in 1962 shocked the world, and the USSR and United States learned that nuclear war was possible—a lesson that forced both parties to look seriously at how, and in what ways, the threat of nuclear war might be reduced even while they maintained adversarial postures.

Soviet Expansionism

Soviet policy assumptions and behavior form another set of factors contributing to the adversarial character of Soviet-U.S. relations before Gorbachev. The combative character of Soviet-U.S. relations in Latin America evolved from the legacy of Soviet ambitions dating back to 1955, when Nikita S. Khrushchev began courting the Third World. In an effort to break Moscow's continental isolation, undercut United States containment strategy and compete more effectively with the United States, Khrushchev began to project Soviet power and influence into the Third World, seeking political legitimacy and political equality with the United States as a superpower actor on the world stage. These Third World goals led Moscow to expand its state-to-state relations with the developed countries of Latin America, notably in Mexico, Brazil, and Argentina, and to support anti-U.S. radical nationalist regimes and movements to project its influence and undermine U.S. interests.

Several key assumptions about policy-making in Latin America appear to have driven Moscow's activities before Gorbachev, assumptions that might be classified as "old thinking." These policy assumptions and guidelines can be identified as follows:

Political realism, defined as advancing state interests, competition with the United States for superpower status—through projected power and influence. Soviet ties with Cuba, Grenada and Nicaragua follow naturally; so, too, does working to undermine U.S. power in South America—as in supporting the Chilean Communist Party (PCCh) which sought the overthrow of Augusto Pinochet during the 1980s. In this assumption, loss of U.S. power is viewed as a gain for Soviet interests—a kind of zero-sum analysis of power politics.

Ideology, namely Marxism-Leninism, provides key formulas for defining friends and enemies; Marxism-Leninism makes Western capitalism and imperialism, led by the United States, a central adversary against which inevitable struggle must be waged. Marxist-Leninist Cuba and Nicaragua thus became important Soviet clients, and supporting leftist insurgents a strategic goal. Moscow frequently described trends in Latin America in terms of the "correlation of forces" between world capitalism/imperialism, on the one hand, and on the other, socialism/communism—two global forces locked into automatic opposition, with Moscow working to strengthen the former and weaken the latter through applied power. Ideology helped define where opportunities existed and where power must be applied, as in aiding Cuba and Nicaragua, courting leftist organizations like student groups, trade unions and local communist parties.

Military power offered the most certain form of power and one of the best ways to advance primary state interests and secondary ideological goals. In giving priority to military capabilities, Moscow provided massive amounts of free military assistance to Cuba and Nicaragua, conducted arms sales with Peru, and offered weapons sales to Argentina—actions that reenforced U.S. views of Soviet expansionism. Overall aid to Cuba ran at about $4–5 billion annually, and the Soviet navy deployed numerous task forces to Cuba and the Caribbean, as well as long-range naval reconnaissance aircraft; Nicaraguan received an estimated $2.3 billion in military aid between 1980 and 1988.

Exploiting regional tensions as a means of competing with the United States, by providing assistance to a participant in regional conflict, offered unique roads of influence to undermine United States power. So long as conflict could be managed in ways to avoid a direct Soviet-U.S. confrontation, various policies might be pursued, such as backing national liberation movements, aiding local communist parties, and taking active measures. The latter included disinformation—such as propaganda about an imminent U.S. "invasion" in Cuba or Panama—and support for front groups like the World Peace Movement, which have operated in the region.

Soviet activities in Latin America could be detached from the broader context of U.S. relations. In many respects Moscow's behavior in Latin America during the 1970s and early 1980s reflects its assumption that larger and more vital Soviet strategic and economic priorities in East-West relations would not be affected.[9] Although Brezhnev signed a 1972 memorandum of understanding regarding "codes of conduct" for superpower cooperation in the Third World, he continued to aggressively pursue Soviet interests to expand Moscow's presence and influence through Cuba, providing sophisticated fighter aircraft and deploying long-range Soviet warplanes, such as the TU-95 Bear D and the TU-142 Bear F reconnaissance aircraft that regularly patrolled the United States's east coast and the Caribbean Basin.

Cooperative Aspects of Soviet Policy Before Gorbachev

While Moscow's version of power politics led to assumptions and policies that put conflict management with the United States on the back burner, it would be inaccurate to depict Soviet policy in Latin America as totally devoid of cooperative elements. A systematic look at the record suggests various cooperative strands in Moscow's perceptions and policies that recognized a certain, if somewhat limited, degree of mutuality of interests in Soviet-U.S. relations as they played out in this region. Recognizing that perceived mutuality of interests is a necessary, if not sufficient, condition for regional security cooperation, a brief look at the cooperative elements of Soviet policy—elements that form the backdrop to Gorbachev's later policies in Latin America—is in order.

Cooperative aspects of Soviet behavior lay in the following policy traits. First, Moscow followed what might be termed "tacit cooperation;" that is, the Soviets made a number of unilateral decisions and initiatives that recognized Washington's interests. The Soviets, for example, restricted the transfer of certain types of military weapons to Managua, such as MiG fighters, knowing Washington's probable response. They did so at a time when they might have preferred to go ahead with MiG fighter deliveries, since the Sandinistas so badly wanted them and because Moscow at the time placed a premium on military solutions to conflict situations. The Soviets also paid lip service to regional peace efforts by Latin American presidents, as in the Contadora process, initiated in January 1983.[10]

Second, Moscow tended to avoid activities that might precipitate a strong U.S. reaction. Moscow's low-risk, cautious, approach to Third World conflicts has been noted frequently by scholars of Soviet foreign policy. Latin America was no exception to this rule. Moscow, for example, avoided direct aid to leftist insurgents *before* they attained power, as in Cuba, Grenada and Nicaragua; and Soviet theoretical writings on the peaceful versus the violent road to change generally stressed a parliamentary approach and state-to-state relations. Soviet writers, to be certain, endorsed violent change—an exception to their general line—during the early 1980s, using the Sandinistas as their model, but by the mid-1980s were again focusing on peaceful change. Caution and restraint in Soviet policy is reflected also in Moscow's restricting the number of personnel in Nicaragua before Gorbachev. The Soviets maintained around 250, whereas the Cubans sent in an estimated 7,500 military, technical, medical and educational personnel.[11]

Third, the USSR undoubtedly had learned lessons from previous Soviet-U.S. conflicts in Latin America. Because the October 1962 missile crisis brought the superpowers to the brink of war, the Soviets probably "learned" that the Caribbean Basin and Central American region ranked high in terms of U.S. sensitivities. The Soviets may have learned from that event that they could not follow their preferred option of greater military support in aiding the Sandinistas or El Salvador's rebels during the late 1970s and early 1980s. It seems likely that Moscow "learned" from the October 1962 missile crisis that its most judicious policy during a period of tension would be to adopt a low profile policy. Thus, when the United States intervened in Grenada in October 1983 and later mined Nicaragua's harbors in 1984, Moscow's response was cautious and restrained, much to the dismay of Castro, who called for a stronger Soviet reaction.

Successes and Failures in Latin America

Moscow could claim numerous successes in its Latin American policies by the time Gorbachev assumed power. The Soviets had developed a prominent presence throughout the region—well beyond what it had been during the 1950s—as evidenced by its broad diplomatic contacts, widened commercial relations, scholarship and exchange programs, and technical assistance projects. In bolstering Cuba and Nicaragua with economic and military aid, Moscow gained a direct physical presence in an important region next to its chief competitor and made possible the pursuit of foreign policies by these countries that challenged U.S. power and influence. Activities by Cuba and Nicaragua helped divert U.S. attention and re- sources away from other arenas more critical to the Soviets, strengthened Moscow's credentials as an "ally" of Third World states in the Nonaligned Movement and in the UN General Assembly, and caused major divisions within U.S. policy-making circles. In these respects it could be argued that Moscow's policies were successful.

A closer look at the record of Soviet policy in Latin America before Gorbachev—especially its approach to regional conflicts—suggests that Moscow's activities, by escalating tensions with the United States and the West, in effect were counter-productive to Moscow's more vital interests. Moscow's expanding military ties with Cuba and Nicaragua—coupled with Cuba's aid to leftist insurgents in Central America, Nicaragua's ties with Central American leftists, and Soviet/Cuban activities elsewhere in the Third World—were undermining broader Soviet strategic and eco- nomic imperatives by:

1. Stimulating international tensions, while at the same time bogging down a beleaguered Moscow in costly and protracted civil wars on behalf of economic basket cases, as in Nicaragua.
2. Fostering an expensive Soviet-U.S. arms race and legitimizing Wash- ington's Strategic Defense Initiative (SDI), which would cost even more to defend against, thus adding to Moscow's economic burdens.
3. Hindering mutually advantageous commercial and trade ties with the United States, which were becoming more crucial to Soviet economic recovery by the mid-1980s.
4. Creating the impression that Moscow was a threatening power that must be opposed forcefully.[12]
5. Anchoring Moscow with costly economic burdens, notably in Cuba, at a time when overall military expenses were undermining a sagging Soviet economy.[13]

Gorbachev's Approach to Conflict Management in Latin America

Gorbachev's approach to conflict management in Latin America mir- rored the basic elements of Moscow's new thinking in Soviet foreign policy.

Recognizing that previous Cold War tensions and expansionism in places like Central America have produced more costs than benefits, new thinking drew upon older cooperative elements in Soviet foreign affairs, while formulating new themes and objectives designed to improve the overall Soviet-U.S. political relationship. This effort in effect linked Third World strategies and tactics with broader Soviet strategic and economic priorities, such as reducing arms spending and gaining access to U.S. aid, trade, and technology.

The New Thinking Backdrop to Cooperation in Conflict Management

Gorbachev's new thinking—with its Latin American variants—stressed the following policy guidelines:[14]

Mutual security. This key goal in Russian-U.S. cooperation in managing Third World conflicts means that all must feel secure if anyone is to feel secure. Moscow thus ceased military shipments to Managua in 1989, recognizing that United States security interests must be recognized in Soviet-Nicaraguan ties if the overall Soviet-U.S. political relationship was going to improve. Mutual security has greatly modified Moscow's previous zero-sum analysis of Soviet-U.S. competition in Third World conflict arenas; Moscow now emphasizes cooperation with the United States to reduce Third World tensions as opposed to exploiting conflict to undermine U.S. influence and expand Russian power.

Soviet-U.S. formal cooperation in managing regional conflict. Gorbachev emphasized joint cooperation between Moscow and Washington; conflicts must be resolved through negotiation among Soviet-U.S. and Third World actors.

Political settlement of Third World conflicts. The Russians now seek peaceful negotiation of regional conflicts, as in Central America, notably Nicaragua, through a process of national reconciliation (or power sharing) that can be advanced by unilateral, bilateral Russian-U.S. diplomacy, and multilateral negotiations utilizing United Nations (UN) auspices, and respect for international law.

Deideologizing foreign policy. Ideology has been sharply downgraded in the sharpened focus on designing a foreign policy more strictly in terms of Russian national interests.

De-emphasizing military force. In contrast to past reliance on expanding military power as the main instrument of influence in foreign relations, the Gorbachev years underscored unilateral, bilateral, and multilateral diplomacy.

Focusing on global interdependence. Unlike the old days of a zero-sum games of power politics—where a United States loss tended to be viewed as a Soviet gain, Gorbachev's diplomacy highlighted how all states are mutually vulnerable and therefore must work together in resolving global problems.

One of the biggest problems during the pre-Gorbachev period of Soviet power projection in the Third World was the formulation of foreign policy on the basis of Marxist-Leninist ideological principles. During the 1970s, for example, Soviet policy makers and academicians instructing Moscow's upcoming generation of foreign policy leaders, stressed that detente was simply "another form of class struggle."[15] Many of Gorbachev's think-tank supporters—as in Moscow's Institute for the Study of the USA and Canada—stressed that prior to new thinking, "ideology often ran against Soviet national interests, with many things done in the Third World that were not in Soviet interests," such as projecting military power, weapons and technology into Third World conflict arenas on the side of leftist-leaning insurgents and filling power vacuums with Soviet/Cuban forces.[16] Soviet and Cuban intervention in Angola in 1975, Ethiopia in 1978–1979, and Grenada and Nicaragua in 1979 are cases in point.

Some Soviet observers believed that this approach led to "imperial overreach" and a heavy economic burden. At the same time, Moscow's ideologized perceptions of power politics fostered "conflicting interests"— a mutual denying of goals in Soviet-U.S. relations largely created by extensive weapons transfers to pro-Soviet supporters, as opposed to developing "parallel" or "common" interests through carefully crafted diplomacy.[17] Gorbachev's new thinking was designed to foster the latter. In contrast to old ideological policy guidelines, members of the Institute for the Study of the USA and Canada now urge that:

> Soviet foreign policy must advance Soviet economic positions . . . so they need to adopt policies of tension-reduction with the U.S. and the West . . . they must create a web of relationships with the U.S. that advance each side's interests.[18]

Cooperative Policy Techniques Since Gorbachev

Unilateral, bilateral, and multilateral forms of cooperation have been pronounced in Russian-Latin American relations since Gorbachev. In terms of unilateral cooperative activities, Moscow has stressed the cooperative elements of new thinking in its stepped-up diplomatic contacts throughout the region. In meeting after meeting with Latin American presidents, Soviet and now Russian diplomats have underscored the need to reduce the threat of nuclear war, build zones of peace and cooperation, reduce military spending, strive for universal and total disarmament backed by international verification, and seek more international control over the environment.[19] In his April 1989 meetings with Castro in Cuba, Gorbachev again underscored the importance of new thinking—such as the avoidance of armed force in the settlement of conflict—as the basis of Moscow's Latin American policy. Gorbachev's Treaty of Friendship and Cooperation with Castro contained numerous articles bearing the imprint of such new thinking. Other unilateral measures have included Moscow's cut-off of weapons transfers to Nicaragua in 1989, pressure on Nicaragua's Sandinistas to hold free and fair elections in February 1990, making clear it was not directly aiding El Salvador's FMLN, and leaning on Cuba to agree to withdraw its 50,000 troops from Angola as part of the Angola/Namibia settlement of December 1988.[20]

Moscow, in addition, increasingly backed the Central American peace process, launched by the five Central American presidents in Esquipulas, Guatemala, in June 1986. In August 1987, the five presidents met again in Esquipulas, this time signing what became known as the "Esquipulas II Accords." These accords—entitled "Procedure for the Establishment of a Firm and Lasting Peace in Central America"—called for political reconciliation within each of the Central American countries, democratizing their political processes, and the cessation of civil and international hostilities. In promoting "national reconciliation"—language taken directly from Soviet new thinking, Esquipulas II called for a cease-fire in countries where insurgents were active, amnesty policies to encourage the cease-fire, dialogue between governments and insurgents, and promotion of pluralism and democracy—including free and honest elections at an early date—a clear pressure on Soviet-backed Nicaragua.[21] That Moscow has strongly endorsed these principles is illustrated by continuing Russian diplomatic pressure on Nicaragua's Sandinistas since the February 1990 elections to ensure the transition to the new government of President Chamorro.

Bilateral forms of cooperation have been pursued through various policy techniques, including periodic discussions with high-level U.S. decision-makers during and between summit meetings, and communications through letters, memoranda, and public statements on issues of mutual concern. Such activities have been especially pronounced regarding Central America, notably Nicaragua and El Salvador, since the Bush Administration came to power in January 1989. In the dramatic case of Soviet arms cut-off to and pressure on Nicaragua's Sandinistas to hold elections in February 1990, the remarkable close collaboration between U.S. Secretary of State James Baker and Soviet Foreign Minister Shevardnadze—and between Assistant Secretary of State for Inter-American Affairs, Bernard Aronson, and his Soviet counterpart, Yuri Pavlov, has been well documented.[22] Among the elements facilitating cooperation between the two superpowers must be included:

1. The Bipartisan Accord with Congress on March 24, 1989, which enlisted Democratic support for a new U.S. policy on Central America and bolstered U.S. pressure on the Soviets to promote a political settlement in Nicaragua through deeds and not simply slogans.[23]
2. Pressure by Bush on Gorbachev, through a letter of March 27, 1989, to initiate a shut-off of the arms pipeline fueling violence in the region—which would provide a signal of Moscow's serious intention to cooperate on the political management of Central American conflict.[24] Shortly before Baker's first formal meeting with Gorbachev and Shevardnadze in Moscow on May 10, Gorbachev responded to Bush's letter by indicating that Moscow had ceased weapons shipments to Nicaragua.[25]
3. A genuine desire on Moscow's part to reduce its position in Central America and Cold War tensions with Washington, and as the Soviets have acknowledged, a growing recognition of the linkage between cooperation on regional conflicts such as Nicaragua and improvement in Soviet-U.S. relations.
4. Agreement by Aronson and Pavlov on the mechanism for halting Sandinista arms shipments to El Salvadoran insurgents—the UN Observer Group in Central America (ONUCA), the group in place to monitor compliance with Article VI of the Central American Agreement, known as the Esquipulas II Accords, which prohibits the use of territory to aid guerrilla operations in neighboring states.
5. Agreement by both Pavlov and Aronson that elections in Nicaragua would be in the interests of the Soviets and the United States.[26]

Multilateral cooperation has transpired largely through Moscow's significant steps in backing UN peacekeeping and international law as key mechanisms of "disengaging the troops of warring sides and observing cease fires and armistice agreements."[27] In pressing for an expanded UN role in conflict resolution and mediation among belligerents, Moscow has supported the establishment of new UN peacekeeping operations, including UN military observers to oversee its withdrawal from Afghanistan and Cuban combat troops from Angola, UN truce monitors at the Iran-Iraq border, and the military forces and civilians in both the UN Transition Assistance group in Namibia and the UN Observer Group in Central America (ONUCA).[28]

On the Central American scene, the USSR joined the United States and other members of the Security Council in November 1989 in supporting unarmed military observers to monitor the commitment by Central American governments to stop aiding insurgents. Civilians from the UN and the Organization of American States (OAS) monitored the February 1990 Nicaraguan elections and have taken active roles in the contra demobilization and repatriation processes since then.[29] Following Chamorro's election victory over the Sandinistas, the UN Security Council voted in March 1990 to endorse the second stage of the Central American operation by sending in some 800 lightly armed UN soldiers to collect the weapons of the contras in Honduras or in enclaves inside Nicaragua. Another UN and OAS civilian group supervised the eventual repatriation and relocation of the rebels. These Soviet-U.S. supported actions have resulted in the first use of UN peacekeepers in the Western Hemisphere. The Soviets, in addition, leaned on Cuba and Angola not to walk away from quadripartite (Angola, Cuba, United States, and South Africa) negotiations during 1988, in which the Soviets sat as observers, leading to the Angola/Namibia settlement and beginning of Cuba's withdrawal of 50,000 troops.[30] Finally, Moscow has supported continuing UN efforts to mediate a political agreement on military reform and cease-fire in El Salvador.

Such efforts to deal with conflict resolution through political and diplomatic techniques illustrate Moscow's new perceptions and practices regarding Soviet-U.S. security cooperation.[31] Where Moscow's "old thinking" undermined the mutuality of Soviet-U.S. interests in places like Central America, new thinking has tried to minimize a conflict of interests between the USSR and United States by changing U.S. perceptions of Soviet behavior.[32] Where Moscow's "Old thinking" discouraged Washington from cooperating—because it did not envision a "positive pay-off structure" nor hopeful "shadow of the future" through cooperation[33]— new thinking has stimulated cooperation by signalling a positive pay-off.[34]

Factors Facilitating New Thinking in Latin America

Gorbachev's efforts were necessary ingredients for stimulating Soviet-U.S. cooperation in managing regional conflict. New Russian perceptions prepared the ground for progress in cooperative conflict management— looking for ways to work jointly with the United States and UN, down-grading the role of force in resolving disputes, upgrading diplomacy and political processes and dismissing ideological formulas. Without these changes, Nicaragua's Sandinistas might still be in power, UN-backed talks between the FMLN and El Salvador's government might never have occurred, and Moscow, Cuba, and Nicaragua might still be full steam ahead in support of leftist insurgents throughout the region. Moscow's aversion to the use of force in the settlement of regional conflicts—be they in the Middle East or Central America—has become a feature of late twentieth century world politics.

Still, a balanced assessment of Soviet-U.S. cooperative progress must examine the role of other key elements in the complex equation of forces promoting cooperation in Third World regions such as Central America. These include:

The Changing International Setting. New thinking in the USSR contributed to the collapse of communism in Eastern Europe, which in turn has undermined external support for leftist Third World regimes, like Cuba and Nicaragua. As for Cuba, the demise of East European communism—combined with slipping Soviet aid and the USSR's internal turmoil—has weakened Havana's external economic and political support, sharply undermining Castro's capability as an actor bolstering leftist insurgents in Third World settings. While the shifting international setting has not ended Castro's penchant for supporting leftist regimes, a decline in Cuban interventionist power serves Soviet-U.S. cooperation. Soviet, East European, and Cuban shifts in world politics undoubtedly were not lost on the Sandinistas in the late 1980s. Sensing a retreat of external support for their revolution, they cooperated with Nicaragua's internal opposition to set up processes in 1989 that facilitated Soviet-U.S. cooperation and the February 1990 elections.[35] Since then, the Cubans have departed, and Soviet aid virtually ended.[36]

U.S. Pressure on the Soviets. Soviet cooperation has in part responded to U.S. pressure. Cooperation is a two-way street, with each side working on the other not to defect. The Bush administration on more than one occasion has exerted diplomatic pressure on the USSR to promote a more "cooperative" relationship. Washington objected to continuing high levels of Cuban and Nicaraguan assistance to Nicaragua in violation of Esquipulas II, pressured for proof of Moscow's good faith in real cooperation when its actions seemed to the contrary, cited Soviet and Cuban complicity in arming Salvadoran guerrillas, and generally faulted the Soviets on regional conflicts as means to urge fuller cooperation.[37] Five days following his confirmation on June 14, 1989, Bernard Aronson took his first flight as the State Department's top Latin American expert. Rather than heading for Latin America, he flew directly to Moscow to meet with Yuri Pavlov to convince Moscow that the Bush team, unlike the previous administration, was seriously prepared to work with Moscow on managing Central American conflict.[38]

Regional Factors. The role of Central American presidents, led by Oscar Arias, then president of Costa Rica, in pushing for a political settlement to Central American conflict has facilitated Soviet-U.S. cooperation. Their agreement of August 1987, Esquipulas II, in calling for joint UN/OAS monitoring of the peace process, provided an international legalistic mechanism for Moscow-Washington cooperation.[39]

Dividing Complex Issues into Negotiable Parts. Central America's presidents, the Soviets, and the United States have been able to divide the complex security problem into smaller components more easily negotiated. Esquipulas II, for example, was important in this respect, providing a common text and legalistic mechanism justifying all sides pursuing the same goal. Article VI of Esquipulas II prohibited the use of territory to aid guerrilla operations in neighboring states, and the UN Observer Group in Central America (ONUCA) was designed to monitor compliance with Article VI. Nicaragua wanted U.S. support in the UN for deployment of this peacekeeping force, so that ONUCA might ensure that the contras in Honduras did not infiltrate Nicaragua, while the United States insisted that ONUCA also monitor the clandestine flow of arms from Nicaragua to the FMLN. Aronson and Pavlov agreed that the United States would support ONUCA's deployment and Moscow would accept U.S. evidence of arms-flow violations, even if the UN force was incapable of confirming the allegations.[40]

Time Urgency and Fiscal Constraints. For the Soviets, time urgency and fiscal constraints were generated by deteriorating economic and political conditions, rising domestic complaints about Third World expenses, and Nicaragua's own beleaguered economy—coupled with Cuba's sagging economic conditions, which cost Moscow about $4–5 billion annually. The Bush administration, meanwhile, needed to end its political war with Congress over support for Nicaragua's contras and realized that Congress wanted to come down on the side of democratic processes in Latin America. Cooperating with the Soviets to produce "free and fair" elections in Nicaragua followed, given Soviet incentives and Washington's positive experience in working with Soviets to reach the 1988 quadripartite accords on Angola/Namibia.[41]

Prospects for Future Russian-American Cooperation

Prospects for future Russian-American cooperation in managing conflict in Latin America are promising in several respects. The improved Russian-U.S. relationship in the post Cold War Era has widened each side's perceptions of the mutuality of their interests and opened the way for collective action. More and more the interests of Russia and the United States have converged in ways facilitating cooperation to resolve regional conflict. Certainly this has been true in Central America, where Soviet new thinking has helped spawn a multilateral (UN/OAS) arrangement for dealing with conflict in Nicaragua and El Salvador—identifying key issues on which both sides continue to try to reach agreement (e.g., restricting arms transfers to competing power contenders) and generating a positive atmosphere in their relations.[42]

Soviet-U.S. cooperation in the Gulf crisis of 1990–1991 and announcement at the July 1991 Soviet-United States summit meeting that the two superpowers would sponsor a Middle East Peace Conference in October vividly illustrate how far the positive dimensions of Soviet-U.S. relations have come since the early 1980s. In effect, Moscow's new thinking has ended the Cold War era, paving the way for a post Cold War period in which the kind of collective security originally intended by the framers of the UN has a chance. Russia now sees cooperation—with the United States and UN—as a legitimate and less expensive way to influence events and resolve regional conflicts from the Persian Gulf to Central America. The United States-Soviet strategic arms treaty signed in Moscow in July 1991 at the summit meeting underscores the new cooperative spirit. Soviet participation in U.N. collective security operations—as in the 1990–91 Persian Gulf crisis—and in backing efforts to resolve conflicts, as in Nicaragua and El Salvador, should have "carry-over" effects into future Latin American crises and disputes. Indeed, Russian commentators, in observing how far Moscow-Washington relations have progressed in managing conflict in Central America, now regularly refer to new thinking in Russian-American relations.[43]

Russian-U.S. cooperation, in addition, has improved in terms of creating institutionalized procedures for managing conflict and more clearly defined norms and "rules" of behavior for regulating superpower behavior—notably in Central America—through continuous communication at the state-to-state level and joint participation in a newly revived and strengthened UN peace-keeping operations. When added to regional pressures for peacefully managing Central America's tensions—especially through the efforts of the Central American presidents—the 1990s are shaping up as an era truly distinct from the 1980s. Electoral defeat of leftist Sandinistas in Nicaragua, positive relations between Moscow and Nicaragua's new government, and the demise of General Manuel Noriega's regime in Panama add significantly to this positive view of the future. This trend gains added value in view of Soviet cooperative activities during 1990, such as the talks held by Pavlov and his deputy with El Salvador's foreign minister and president, the Miami-Moscow dialogue—in which Russian foreign policy advisers are now in contact with Castro's foes in the Cuban exile community—and Russian diplomatic relations with Honduras.

The Cuban Factor

Russian-U.S. cooperation on Cuba has taken new dimensions since the failed August 1991 coup in Moscow. Speaking at a press conference held jointly with U.S. Secretary of State James Baker, Gorbachev announced in September that Moscow had decided to withdraw Soviet military troops from Cuba—yielding to a goal long pressed by the U.S. Moscow had been openly decreasing its military presence in Cuba for some time—cutting Soviet "technicians" from 3,200 in January 1990 to 1,500 by October 1991, with another 500 scheduled to leave in late 1991.[44] Before Gorbachev's announced military withdrawal in September, the U.S. State Department had estimated the entire remaining Soviet presence in Cuba at about 5,400—a figure that included some 1,200 military advisers, 2,200 troops, and about 2,000 civilian technicians; most of the latter worked at Moscow's sophisticated intelligence-gathering installation at Lourdes outside Havana.[45] As the talks on withdrawal proceeded, Moscow identified some 2,800 "servicemen" and a total of about 4,000 people including family members, who would be pulled-out on a stage-by-stage basis.[46]

Indicative of Moscow's reduced use of Cuban facilities are Soviet naval and air deployments to Havana, which have declined in recent years. A Soviet task force visited Havana in 1988 after a two year gap in a series of such visits (27 deployments since 1970).[47] While the number and type of Soviet vessels (four ships: an Udaloy, a Krivak, a Boris Chilikin, and a Tango) were consistent with those of the previous deployments, this visit lasted only 30 days compared to the average 45 days. The Soviet ships spent about half the time in Cuban ports; the remainder circumnavigated the island and conducted ASW/aid defense exercises with the Cuban navy. The force did not enter the Gulf of Mexico as in previous visits. Bear D and Bear F deployments to Cuba continued the 1988 trend of fewer than normal—three of each compared with usual totals of seven-to-nine Bear Ds and five Bear Fs. This trend is consistent with the lower naval operational tempo noted elsewhere.[48]

In the post Cold War and post August 1991 coup era, when the USSR unravelled politically and was in grave economic distress—and where the Soviet-East European Council for Mutual Economic Assistance (CEMA) no longer exists—Cuba simply has become less important, indeed less relevant, in Russian foreign policy priorities. Such a trend had already become distinct by the late 1980s, as Moscow's backed away from support of leftist Third World regimes and movements. During the Cold War days of Soviet-U.S. competition in the Third World (1955–1985), Cuba cooperated with the Soviets in regional interventions to advance Cuban-Soviet interests—a factor enhancing Havana's value and influence in Moscow. Those days had disappeared by 1990, as communist political systems disappeared in East Europe, economic turmoil mounted in the USSR and Gorbachev's power came under siege. By 1991, Havana's challenge had become more one of working out economic deals with ex-Soviet republics to survive as Russian aid dwindled, supply-lines from Moscow failed and Cuba's economic conditions dramatically worsened.[49]

Such pressures had clearly begun to squeeze the Soviet-dependent Cuban economy by 1990. A former high level Cuban official involved in negotiations with the USSR, who defected to the U.S. in July 1990, reported that Moscow's transition to a market economy and scheduled cuts in aid to Cuba probably would cripple Havana's economy unless Castro introduced radical economic change—which Castro did not do during the October

1991 Fourth Party Congress.[50] The official, Ramon Gonzalez Vergara, Vice Secretary of the former Soviet Council for Mutual Economic Assistance in Moscow until his defection, detailed the tense discussions in Moscow in early 1990, when the USSR informed Cuba of its intention to reduce its support drastically in practically all areas of economic aid from barter trade to subsidized prices for Cuban products.[51] And former Soviet Deputy Prime Minister Leonid Abalkin, during a visit to Havana in April 1990, warned that Cuba's debt to the USSR (estimated at $24 billion, according to published Soviet figures) would be payable in dollars beginning in 1995.[52]

The economic future for Cuba looks grim in light of Russian and East European political confusion and striving for some form of market economies. Russian and East European moves toward a hard currency and free enterprise trading system will exert increasing pressure on the Cuban public in light of trends at work by 1990. During 1990, prices of Cuba's staple foods rose, the bread ration has been cut, and fuel consumption was slashed drastically in the wake of a shortfall in Russian oil shipments of nearly 14 million tons and the surge in world oil prices due to the Persian Gulf crisis.[53] In response, Castro has continued to exhort Cubans to work harder, declared a new slogan of "socialism or death," and tried to prepare the country for even harder times ahead—a "special period in a time of peace," in effect an era of draconian austerity as Russian aid flows dwindled. By 1991, as food and fuel rationing mounted, he increasingly spoke of the "O option," pointing toward a bleak future of broken trade ties with the USSR.

These and other pressures have already forced trends in Cuban foreign policy favorable to Russian-U.S. management of conflict in places like Central America. Cuba has increasingly supported the Central American peace process, strengthened ties with South American governments (Brazil and Venezuela), and cooperated to some extent in the 1990–91 Gulf crisis.[54] Cuba is working toward winning friends and trade partners among Latin America's established governments, rather than creating enemies by backing subversive leftist movements. Such foreign policy initiatives have been underlined by Castro's publicized appearance at the first Ibero-American Summit Conference in Guadalajara, Mexico, in mid-July 1991,[55] Havana's hosting of the Pan American Games in late July 1991—perhaps its most ambitious international event in recent years—and its pressing toward increased foreign investment from Latin America, as announced at the Fourth Party Congress in October 1991.[56]

Limits on Russian-American Cooperation

Russian cooperation with the United States in managing conflict in Latin America, however, is by no means unlimited. Restrictions on Moscow's capability to cooperate with Washington include the following:

Difficulties in Enforcing Regional Settlements. While Moscow and Washington may agree with the U.S. on how to manage a crisis or conflict through cooperation and diplomatic accords to contain it, ending such conflict and enforcing the spirit of agreed-upon terms between contending parties may prove more difficult. Nicaragua is a case in point. Despite their loss of government power in the February 1990 elections, the Sandinistas retain power in Nicaragua's political setting—through control of the military intelligence service—which has produced Sandinista-led violent protests against President Chamorro's administration since February 1990.[57] Rural Sandinista supporters reportedly also have harassed government sympathizers since the 1990 elections.[58] Government property requisitioned by the Sandinistas when they left power in 1990 became source of bitter struggle for the Chamorro government in 1991.[59]

Difficulty in Breaking Deadlocks Between Governments and Guerrillas. Conflict in Central America, long before the Soviets and Cubans entered the scene, has been generated by local and regional forces—groups with independent agendas, perceptions, and power capabilities. The ups and downs of the UN-mediated peace talks between negotiators for the FMLN and Salvadoran government during 1989–1991 illustrate the point.[60] FMLN guerrillas follow their own dictates, if and when they agree among themselves, and the extreme right-wing Salvadoran military strongly opposes doing business with the leftist guerrillas—UN mediated or not. In Guatemala, right-wing military and other political groups oppose national reconciliation and power-sharing with leftists.

Cuban Foreign Policy. Despite Cuba's foreign policy patterns that parallel Soviet new thinking in Latin America, Cuba has demonstrated its own independent line of action time and again—in ways that undercut closer Soviet-U.S cooperation. An unmarked twin-engine airplane carrying North Korean anti-aircraft missiles and other weapons bound for leftist Salvadoran guerrillas, for example, crashed in eastern El Salvador in November 1989.[61] That Cuba may have been behind shipments of this type—transshipped through Nicaragua is suggested by the reported upbraiding Cuba (and Nicaragua) received from the Soviet Union shortly thereafter.[62]

The United States Assistant Secretary of State for Inter-American Affairs, Bernard Aronson, accused Cuba in June 1991 of continued logistical and arms support to violent revolutionary groups, such as El Salvador's FMLN—made possible by Cuba's high level of military spending backed by Soviet assistance to Cuba.[63] Aronson went on to state that Moscow "could do more to prevent Cuban support for violent groups like the FMLN and encourage internal reform."[64] The Cuban Foreign Ministry quickly issued a denial of United States allegations, saying that Havana provided only political support to the rebels.[65] That the Russians do not wish to lose their strategic ties with Cuba—where, for example, the Lourdes intelligence-gathering installation is the largest outside the USSR—remains a stumbling block in United States-Soviet cooperation.

Continued Anti-U.S. Rhetoric Pursued by Moscow. Moscow continued—at least through mid-1990—to lace its verbal support of the Central American peace process and cooperation with the United States with hostile rhetoric not helpful for the cooperative process. In commenting on the seventh summit conference of Central American presidents in April 1990, for example, *Pravda* charged the U.S. with "brazen exploitation of the economic backwardness, social inequality, and instability of governments." in Central America and "frequent incitement of the region to violence and war."[66]

Difficulty in Diagnosing Issues in Ways That Facilitate Soviet Cooperation with the U.S. One of the more interesting questions about future Russian cooperation with the United States in Latin America is the nature of future conflicts and how they will be diagnosed. Some issues may prove difficult regarding cooperative diplomacy at the unilateral, joint, or multilateral level. Cases that come to mind in this category are the militant Islamic coup attempt in Trinidad during July-August 1990, ethnic conflict (Indian groups versus non-Indian power groups), drug trafficking, environmental deterioration and refugees.[67] Future cases may involve the activities of Latin American military groups, such as in Brazil's discovery in October 1990 of a 15-year-old secret military program to make an atomic bomb—an event affecting the interests of both Moscow and Washington.[68] Brazil has not signed the nonproliferation treaty intended to limit the spread of nuclear weapons.

The Future

Given events in Russia since the failed August 1991 coup—such as the demise of the Communist Party, purges of the KGB, Interior Ministry, and military forces; rise in power of Russia's Boris Yeltsin; ex-Soviet republic's transition to independence; and a Russian economy in turmoil—predicting the future is hazardous at best. If we assume, however, that some form of centralized "Soviet" decision-making remains in Moscow, several trends seem likely. The record since 1988–1989 points toward future progress in arms control, demilitarization proposals, and political settlement of regional conflicts. As a new Russian "security regime" evolves in Latin America, it likely will take shape through collaborative U.S. and Soviet groups working within international legal mechanisms that have operated in ending Nicaragua's civil war and international subversion. Such legal mechanisms—which offer an international legalistic regime justifying a common strategy of cooperation—include UN peacekeeping efforts, OAS

Observer Groups, and Central America's state-to-state peace efforts. Esquipulas II, among other goals, calls for an end to regional subversion, while the UN's ONUCA was created to monitor compliance with Esquipulas II. Future cooperation within these emerging channels appears highly likely, given Moscow's and Washington's disposition toward international verification of the resolution of interstate/intrastate conflicts in Central America.[69] Such Russian cooperation in a new security regime is consistent with Moscow's goal of lowering the costs and risks of their involvement in the Third World.

What will happen to Russian relations with Cuba? The Moscow-Miami dialogue is especially significant, for it represents the first time Moscow has recognized Castro's Miami-based enemies as a political factor in Russian-U.S. cooperation. It also may signal Moscow's belief that Miami's Cubans may be destined to play a more significant role in a potential post-Castro Cuba, should deteriorating economic conditions on the island undermine Castro's political power. Russian leaders likely will pursue down-graded ties with Havana—a point Boris Yeltsin has made clear. Whether such conditions will lead to Castro's demise remains to be seen.

At the same time, Moscow will continue joint backing of International Atomic Energy Agency (IAEA) standards to prevent proliferation of nuclear weapons into Third World countries (e.g., close monitoring of nuclear suppliers to developing countries such as Argentina and Brazil); support for UN pressure on members to enforce sanctions that prohibit trade or arms shipments into regional crises, e.g., Brazil's trade in arms and food with Iraq in the 1990 Gulf crisis; and using multilateral diplomacy, collective security, and UN measures in territorial conflicts—as in a future war over the Falklands/Malvinas. All in all, it has been a remarkable period of Russian-U.S. cooperation in Latin America.

Notes

1. *The Washington Post,* October 18, 1990, p. 1.

2. The troop withdrawal announcement of September 11, 1991, by TASS was a bitter pill for the Cubans to swallow. The Cuban Communist Party newspaper, *Granma,* wrote a scathing editorial on this September surprise in Havana, and Soviet Deputy Foreign Minister Valeriy Nikolayenko described the Soviet-Cuban consultations on this matter as "difficult." *Granma*'s editorial was printed on September 14, 1991. On the Nikolayenko discussions with the Cubans, see Federal Broadcast Information Service (FBIS)-Latin America, September 23–24.

3. Students of Soviet-U.S. relations have emphasized in recent studies that cooperation in security matters—such as arms control—may be hindered or facilitated by the nature of the overall political relationship that exists between the USSR and the United States at any given time. Because Soviet activities in Latin America were undermining the overall relationship–thus impeding international

conditions favorable to Gorbachev's goal of reduced military spending and a revitalized economy—it became increasingly clear to his team that Caribbean and Central American policies needed a change designed to improve U.S. perceptions of Soviet behavior if progress were to be made on the larger issues. See Alexander L. George, "Factors Influencing Security Cooperation," in Alexander L. George and Philip J. Farly and Alexander Dallin, eds. *U.S.-Soviet Security Cooperation: Achievements, Failures and Lessons.* New York: Oxford University Press, 1988, p. 607.

4. See U.S. Departments of State and Defense background paper, "Nicaragua's Military Build-Up and Support for Central American Subversion" (Washington, D.C.: July 18, 1984); and *ibid.,* "The Soviet-Cuban Connection in Central America and the Caribbean" Washington, D.C.: March 1985).

5. See Departments of State and Defense background paper, "Nicaragua's Military Build-Up and Support for Central American Subversion" (Washington, D.C.: July 1984); *ibid.,* "The Soviet-Cuban Connection in Central America" (Washington, D.C.: March 1985); *ibid.,* "Challenge to Democracy in Central America" (Washington, D.C.: June 1986); and *Ibid.,* "Democracy in Latin America and the Caribbean: The Promise and the Challenge" (Washington, D.C.: June 1987).

6. See *The Washington Post,* January 1, 1987, p. 1.

7. On the Reagan Doctrine, see Walter Lefever, *The American Age: American Foreign Policy at Home and Abroad Since 1750.* New York: W. W. Norton, 1988, pp. 677 ff; also James A. Nathan and James K. Oliver, *United States Foreign Policy and World Order.* Glenview, Illinois: Scott, Foresman and Company, 1989, 4th edition, pp. 425 ff.

8. See Evan Luard, *Conflict and Peace in the Modern International System.* Albany: State University of New York Press, 1988, chapter four; also p. 288 and Appendix I.

9. For a discussion of East-West and Third World linkage before Gorbachev, See W. Raymond Duncan and Carolyn McGiffert Ekedahl, *Moscow and the Third World Under Gorbachev.* Boulder, Colorado: Westview Press, 1990, Chapter four.

10. The Contadora group—Mexico, Venezuela, Colombia, and Panama—met on the Panamanian island of Contadora in January 1983 to offer formulas for the negotiated settlement of Central American conflict. They proposed to serve as a mediator by searching for peaceful negotiated outcomes in Central America, and they crafted a set of principles designed to promote discussions between the United States and Nicaragua, and, in El Salvador, between the government and leftist insurgents. Such principles included limiting arms flows, prohibiting all foreign bases, withdrawing external advisers (including Cuban, East European, and U.S) and ending support for insurgents. This group was joined by four other South American countries—the Contadora Support Group. For background reading, see G. Pope Atkins, *Latin America in the International Political System.* Boulder, Colorado: Westview Press, 1990, pp. 322–326.

11. U.S. Department of State, "The Soviet-Cuban Connection in Central America and the Caribbean" (Washington, D.C.: March 1985).

12. Vyacheslav Dashishev, of the Institute of the Economics of the World Socialist System, wrote that Brezhnev had squandered opportunities created by the

attainment of strategic parity and detente with the United States—exploiting detente to build up Soviet military forces, which in turn generated an arms race with the United States that undercut the weaker Soviet economy. Dashishev also argued that Brezhnev had no clear idea how Moscow's expansionism into Third World countries, like Nicaragua, would serve state interests. Vyacheslav Dashishev, *Literaturnaya Gazeta*, May 18, 1988.

13. Soviet analysts today argue that the Third World "economic burden" comprises much of the legacy of pre-Gorbachev Third World strategies. "In this respect," said one Soviet analyst, "the Third World has not helped the Soviet Union . . . this is the cost of imperial overreach." Author's interviews with members of the Institute for the Study of the U.S.A. and Canada, Moscow, January and May 1990,

14. See Duncan and Ekedahl, *The Soviet Union and The Third World Under Gorbachev*, chapter four.

15. Conversation with Dr. Peter Gladkov, Head of Section, Institute for the Study of the U.S.A. and Canada, D.C., May 1990.

16. *Ibid.*

17. *Ibid.*

18. Author's private conversations with staff members of the Institute for the Study of the U.S.A. and Canada, January 1990.

19. See the *Federal Broadcast Information Reports* (FBIS) - Latin America, covering Foreign Minister Shevardnadze's trip to Mexico in October 1986, the first visit by a Soviet foreign minister to a Latin American country other than Cuba; Deputy Foreign Minister Viktor Komplektov's visits to Brazil, Uruguay, and Mexico shortly thereafter; Boris Yeltsin's travels to Nicaragua in March 1987; Shevardnadze's return trip to Latin America in the fall of 1987, when he met with top officials in Brazil, Argentina, Uruguay, and Cuba; and, of course, Gorbachev's historic visit to Cuba in April 1989 and Shevardnadze's return trip to Nicaragua in October 1989. Various Latin American presidents, meanwhile, were visiting Gorbachev and Shevardnadze in the USSR during this period. Soviet trips to Latin America averaged around 13 per year during 1976–1984; they jumped to around 20 per year after 1985.

20. On the story of Soviet pressure on the Sandinistas to hold elections in February, 1990, see Michael Kramer, "Anger, Bluff—and Cooperation," *Time Magazine*, June 4, 1990, pp. 38–45; and *The Washington Post*, May 30, 1990, p. 1.

21. See Robert Pear, "Central America Negotiates on Its Own," *The New York Times*, March 19, 1989. President Oscar Arias of Costa Rica played a key role in Esquipulas II, for which he won the Nobel Peace Prize.

22. Kramer, "Anger, Bluff—and Cooperation," *Time Magazine, op. cit.* Baker and Shevardnadze provided *Time Magazine* with key information, and made Aronson and Pavlov available for extended interviews, because, as Kramer notes, they took ". . . pride in what they have accomplished." See p. 38.

23. Kramer, "Anger, Bluff—and Cooperation," *op. cit.*, p. 39.

24. *Ibid.*

25. Gorbachev's letter arrived on May 6, 1989, late in the evening of the day before Baker left for Moscow. *Ibid.*, p. 39.

26. *Ibid.*, pp. 40–41.

27. See *Pravda*, September 1987, p. 1.

28. See Thomas G. Weiss and Meryl A. Kessler, "Moscow's U.N. Policy," *Foreign Policy*, No. 79 (Summer 1990), pp. 94–112.

29. *Ibid.*, p. 108.

30. For a discussion of Soviet activities during these sessions, see Duncan and Ekedahl, *Moscow and the Third World Under Gorbachev*, pp. 171–175.

31. On the successes and failures of Soviet-U.S. security cooperation, see George, Farley and Dallin, *U.S.-Soviet Security Cooperation: Achievements, Failures and Lessons*; Kenneth A. Oye, "Explaining Cooperation Under Anarchy: Hypotheses and Strategies," *World Politics*, 37, No. 1 (October 1985), pp. 1–24; and Robert Axelrod and Robert O. Keohane, "Achieving Cooperation Under Anarchy: Strategies and Institutions," *World Politics*, 37, No. 1 (October 1985), pp. 226–254.

32. The significance of perceptions has been strongly emphasized in the study of conflict management, because decision-making in ambiguous settings is heavily conditioned by the ways in which the actors think about their problem. See Axelrod and Keohane, "Achieving Cooperation Under Anarchy: Strategies and Institutions," pp. 245–46.

33. Studies on security cooperation argue that a positive pay-off structure and hopeful shadow of the future are requisites to prevent one party from defecting from joint management of conflict in an ambiguous setting. See Axelrod and Keohane, "Achieving Cooperation Under Anarchy," and Oye, "Explaining Cooperation Under Anarchy."

34. Gorbachev's letter to President Bush, indicating that Moscow had ceased sending weapons to Nicaragua, is discussed in *The Washington Post*, May 16, 1989, p.22.

35. See *The Washington Post*, August 5, 1989, p.24.

36. See *The Washington Post*, April 7, 1991, p. 23.

37. In his speech to the annual meeting of the Organization of American States, November 14, 1989, Secretary of State James A. Baker III cited the downing of two planes in El Salvador, reportedly carrying Soviet-made anti-aircraft missiles into El Salvador, to support his charge that Moscow's support of liberalization in Eastern Europe had not been echoed in Central America, where Moscow still worked with Cuba and Nicaragua to aid Marxist insurrection forces such as the FMLN. He said, "Soviet behavior toward Cuba and Central America remains the biggest obstacle to full, across-the-board improvement in relations between the United States and the Soviet Union." *The Washington Post*, November 14, 1989, p.32.

38. The story of how Aronson and Pavlov cooperated in reaching agreements on the Nicaraguan issue is well covered in Kramer, *op. cit.*

39. By then, Nicaragua had already accepted U.N. monitoring of its February 1990 elections, and congressional rejection of more military aid for the contras had put President Bush on notice that the majority of lawmakers were ready for a full-blown diplomatic approach to the conflict in Nicaragua. See *The Christian Science Monitor*, August 15, 1989, p.4

40. On the importance of breaking up issues into negotiable pieces, see Alexander L. George, "Factors Influencing Security Cooperation," in George, Farley and Dallin, *op. cit.,* p. 671.

41. See *The Washington Post,* February 28, 1990, p. 1.

42. For background reading on these important elements of Soviet-U.S. cooperation, see George, "Strategies for Facilitating Cooperation," p. 697.

43. *Pravda* (in Russian), April 10, 1990, p. 1.

44. *Caribbean Report,* October 3, 1991, RC-91–08, p. 1.

45. *Ibid.*

46. Moscow TASS in English, 30 September 1991, FBIS-Latin America, October 1, 1991, p. 19.

47. See *Proceedings,* U.S. Naval Institute, May 1989, p. 230.

48. *Ibid.,* pp. 230–31.

49. See Castro speeches to the Fourth Party Congress of the Cuban Communist Party, held in early October 1991. By mid 1991, only 38 percent of goods expected from the USSR had arrived. FBIS-Latin America, October 14, 1991.

50. *The New York Times,* September 13, 1990, p. 1

51. *Ibid.*

52. *Ibid.*

53. *The Washington Post,* August 30, 1990, p. 1.

54. As a member of the UN Security Council, Cuba backed resolutions to (1) condemn Iraq's invasion of Kuwait and (2) to declare Iraq's annexation of Kuwait null and void. Cuba abstained on the vote to order a trade and financial boycott of Iraq and on the vote to give the United States and other nations the right to enforce the economic embargo against Iraq by halting shipping to and from that country. *The New York Times,* August 27, 1990, p. 7.

55. See *The New York Times,* July 18, 1991, p. 5.

56. See *The Washington Post,* July 29, 1991, p. 1; also FBIS-Latin America, October 14, 1991 [full report on the Fourth Party Congress of the Cuban Communist Party].

57. The Sandinistas-backed labor unions, for example, won a broad package of concessions on wages and economic policy in July 1990—after building barricades and burning vehicles at major intersections throughout the capital, bringing it to a standstill. See *The New York Times,* July 10, 1990, p. 1; July 11, p. 3, and July 12, p. 5.

58. *The Washington Post,* March 5, 1990, p.1.

59. See *The New York Times,* June 25, 1991, p. 1.

60. See *The Washington Post,* May 10, 1991, p. 22.

61. *The Washington Post,* November 26, 1989, p. 1.

62. *Le Monde,* November 30, 1989, p. 48.

63. Statement of Bernard Aronson, Assistant Secretary of State for Inter-American Affairs Before he Subcommittee on Western Hemisphere Affairs, House of Representatives, June 20, 1991, issued by Secretary Aronson's office.

64. *Ibid.*

65. George Gedda, Associated Press report made available by CBS news, June 20, 1991.

66. *Pravda* (in Russian), April 10, 1990, second edition, p. 1.

67. On the militant islamic coup attempt in Trinidad, see *The New York Times,* July 31, 1990, p. 1, and *The New York Times,* August 31, 1990, p. 1. On lack of cooperation on such issues as the environment and refugees, author's interview with V. Zaemsky, Soviet Embassy, June 8, 1990.

68. *The New York Times,* October 9, 1990, p. 1.

69. This prognosis is based on the proposition that the USSR remains intact as opposed to dissolving into independent republics.

4

U.S.-Russian Cooperation in Africa

Peter Clement

Talking during the tour with Foreign Ministry staffers who deal with Africa, I invariably asked them why our Africa policy has become deadlocked to a certain extent, what was the main mistake in it? Almost all the people with whom I talked agreed that the main mistake was the universal ideologization of our relations. Soviet diplomats strove at all costs to turn Africa into a "socialist-oriented continent." The socialist choice was imposed on everyone—without consideration for historical, economic, or national features. And generous aid flowed as a mark of gratitude.

The economic model espoused by socialist-oriented African countries has turned out to be bankrupt almost everywhere. And if states were still managing to keep their heads above water somehow, it was largely thanks to Soviet injections into their collapsing economies. The dozen "friendly states which made the socialist choice" turned into a heavy burden on our declining budget. Perestroyka has placed a revision of relations in the agenda. We could no longer allow ourselves to base those relations on free aid. The public was asking more and more persistently: Can we act as a charity, given our poverty?

—M. Yusin in *Izvestiia*

Upon assuming the post of CPSU General Secretary in March 1985, Mikhail Gorbachev inherited a foreign policy best described as a gloomy series of policy cul-de-sacs: relations with the United States and Western Europe were in deep freeze after the Soviets had walked out of the INF negotiations. Both sides now hurled rhetorical barbs reminiscent of the early Cold War years. The East-West competition, moreover, continued to color regional conflicts in the Third World, where Moscow found itself mired in a growing number of costly counterinsurgency wars with no end in sight; indeed, the USSR was extending increasingly large amounts of military and economic aid to fledgling Marxist regimes in Afghanistan, Angola, Ethiopia, Mozambique, Nicaragua, and Cambodia. The viability of these regimes was shaky at best. In addition, well-developed client relationships with Cuba and Vietnam continued to tax Soviet resources.[1]

Gorbachev could only look at the Third World with a great sense of irony. After all, hadn't comrade Brezhnev boasted just four years earlier that these Third World achievements were tangible evidence of the growing shift in the world correlation of forces in favor of socialism? These words seemed all the more absurd in 1990, with the collapse of socialism not only in Eastern Europe, but the very citadel itself—the USSR. And how bitterly ironic was the fact that Moscow—once the patron and ideological beacon for those national liberation groups seeking to destroy the status quo established by Western "imperialism"—was now itself in the uncomfortable position of propping up dictatorial Marxist regimes against a series of would-be "liberators" backed by the West?

Resolving these nettlesome Third World conflicts has frequently proved to be a more difficult task than the more dramatic policy shifts enunciated by Gorbachev since 1985. Granted, Gorbachev had to skillfully maneuver his way through party politics to build support for the shift on INF, improved ties the West, and the unilateral reduction of Soviet military forces—not to mention Moscow's acquiesence to a unified Germany in NATO. Still, in effecting changes in Third World policy, he not only had to deal with party and military critics, but with external forces beyond his control: the local Marxist regimes—many of which exhibited a great degree of autonomy, despite their dependence on Soviet aid; anti-Marxist insurgencies who were seriously undermining the viability of the USSR's client regimes; and foreign rivals—the U.S., Western Europe, and South Africa—who nurtured these insurgent groups.

Gorbachev's Inheritance in Africa

These dilemmas of Moscow's Third World policies were exemplified by the USSR's position in Africa at the time Gorbachev took the reins of power in the Soviet Union:

Angola

In Angola, the Soviet-backed MPLA regime was beleaguered by an ever-expanding civil war with UNITA guerrillas led by Jonas Savimbi. UNITA had solidified its hold on the southeastern quadrant of the country while continuing its guerrilla tactics throughout the country—even in Luanda. Moreover, UNITA seemed more than likely to hold its own, as South Africa and, to a much smaller degree, the United States continued to provide financial and material support for the struggle against the Soviet-backed MPLA regime in Luanda. The Cuban troop presence had escalated to some 40,000–45,000 following major campaigns in the summer of

1983 and the subsequent incursion into southern Angola by some 10,000 South African regulars in pursuit of SWAPO guerrillas.[2]

Beyond the troubles on the battlefield, Moscow had growing concerns about the actions and motives of its ostensible client regime in Luanda. Indeed, the MPLA embarked on important diplomatic forays apparently without informing its Soviet benefactors, and then offered little detail about the state-of-play once it started negotiating with other players. In early 1984, for example, the MPLA entered into serious talks with the South Africans—and U.S. intermediaries—without including the Soviets. These talks culminated in the Lusaka Accord of February 16, which called for the withdrawal of South African forces from southern Angola in exchange for Luanda's commitment to restrain SWAPO guerrillas from entering the areas after the departure of the South Africans. Moreover, the MPLA government continued to talk with U.S. officials throughout 1984, this time about a broader Namibia settlement. By late 1984, it became clear that Angolan President dos Santos implicitly accepted a linkage between the presence of Cuban forces in Angola and Namibian independence—a position that Moscow and Havana continued to oppose. In short then, Gorbachev faced the possibility that the USSR would be cut out of a major regional deal—as in the case of Rhodesia in 1979–1980—despite its long-term relationship with the MPLA.[3]

Mozambique

In Mozambique, the situation paralleled that of Angola, with a few important exceptions. Moscow and Havana were not as invested in Mozambique, as there were no Cuban combat forces there; and moreover, Moscow had far less "prestige" at stake, since it was much less directly involved in the Machel regime's rise to power following Portugal's divestiture of its African colonies in the mid-1970s. Two other critical differences included Mozambique's geographical situation—touching directly on South Africa's northeastern border—making a direct Soviet or Cuban combat role extremely problematic; and Maputo's dearth of fungible natural resources, which also made any serious role an expensive proposition, unlike oil-rich Angola. Still, Moscow and Havana had provided a good deal of advisory support, and Soviet arms deliveries had played an important role in sustaining the Marxist regime of Samora Machel against South African-backed RENAMO insurgents. Consequently, the Soviets were clearly unhappy when Machel exluded them from ongoing talks with South Africa that culminated in the Nkomati accords with South Africa in March 1984; the accords stipulated that neither side would permit its territory to be used by indigenous groups to prepare attacks against each other.

Thus, as Gorbachev came to power in 1985, he found that Moscow's sizable investment and involvement in southern Africa did not insure the

USSR's inclusion as a main party to regional settlements. On the contrary, Moscow was being denied its "rightful role" as a global superpower as its own clients pursued separate regional deals with the dominant regional player, South Africa—brokered in part by Moscow's main adversary, the United States.[4]

Horn of Africa

The situation in the Horn of Africa was not much brighter. While there was little chance of a U.S.-brokered deal between Ethiopian strongman Mengistu and the Eritrean and Tigrean insurgent groups, Moscow nonetheless saw little chance of any breakthroughs in the increasingly costly and devastating civil war. Still, Moscow felt Ethiopia was an important investment to maintain. Of Moscow's numerous African clients, only Ethiopia could claim some broader relevance to Soviet geostrategic and security interests by virtue of its location astride the Red Sea and across from the Arabian peninsula. Moreover, the loss of Soviet influence in Egypt and Sudan during the 1970s made Ethiopia all the more important. This was amply demonstrated by the significant amount of Soviet economic assistance—grants and economic credits totaling some $980 million—to Ethiopia between 1980 and 1984.[5] Miltary aid levels were even higher between 1980 and 1985, when Ethiopia imported over $2.5 billion in arms from its Warsaw Pact benefactors—primarily the USSR.[6]

Despite this massive investment, Moscow could hardly feel secure since so much rested on the fortunes of the ruthless and somewhat mercurial Colonel Mengistu. To offset this dependency, Moscow had spent nearly a decade trying to persuade Mengistu to ceeate a vanguard party in Ethiopia—one through which Moscow hoped to cultivate future leaders and establish a certain ideological tradition. Mengistu finally did create a Workers' Party of Ethiopia (WPE), but it was largely the same cast of characters who had run the military dictatorship since the mid-1970s.[7] Mengistu also adopted a Soviet-style constitution and proclaimed Ethiopia a "Peoples' Republic" in the fall of 1986, but most observers recognized this for the cosmetic change that it was.

Soviet Policy Under Gorbachev: The Unfolding of New Thinking in Africa

At first glance, Gorbachev's policies in Africa seemed riddled with contradictions. At the February 1986 Party Congress, Gorbachev clearly signaled Moscow's fading interest in the Third World. Third World clients were not mentioned by name—except the tantalizing reference to Afghanistan as a "running sore from which Moscow desired to withdraw its forces." More ominously for Moscow's clients, Gorbachev did note that the Soviet Union could only render foreign aid according "to the extent of its abilities" and that it was mainly "through their own effort, every people create the material and technical base needed for building the new society."[8] In short, Gorbachev already was signaling that young Marxist states would have to assume greater responsibility for building socialism—without massive Soviet support.

While these and subsequent comments by Soviet leaders strongly suggested an imminent Soviet retrenchment in the Third World, events on the ground suggested a different story. From 1986 to 1989, arms deliveries and related military assistance to such key clients as Afghanistan, Angola, Ethiopia, and Nicaragua often reached record levels.[9] Not surprisingly, these deliveries coincided with major new and unprecedented government offensives in several of these regional conflicts.

Meanwhile, Gorbachev was effecting dramatic shifts in Soviet policy that gave greater credibility to his claims of "new thinking" about Soviet concepts of security and global interdependence: the INF breakthrough at Reykjavik, renewed START talks, the February 1988 announcement of a two-year timetable for withdrawl from Afghanistan, and the unilateral 500,000 man cut in the Soviet military revealed in Gorbachev's 7 December 1988 address to the UN.

The sheer momentum of these moves strongly suggested there would soon be a "spillover" into the arena of other Third World regional conflicts. Indeed, as Gorbachev noted shortly after the Afghan withdrawal announcement, "we hope the Geneva accords on Afghanistan will lend an impulse to the process of settling regional conflicts."[10]

Angola

Throughout the latter half of 1988 a growing U.S.-Soviet dialogue on southern Africa facilitated the conclusion of an Angolan-Cuban-South African accord on Namibian independence in December 1988. During June 1988 talks in Cairo, for example, U.S. and Soviet officials consulted on the sidelines as U.S. Assistant Secretary of State Chester Crocker mediated talks between representatives from Cuba, Angola, and South Africa.[11] During a New York meeting the next month, Crocker acknowledged that U.S. and Soviet officials continued to be in close contact as the pieces of a Namibian settlement began to fall into place.[12] When the terms of the accord were finalized in Brazzaville, Congo, in mid-December, Crocker described the ongoing US-Soviet cooperation a "case study" of superpower efforts to resolve regional conflicts. In turn, Crocker's Soviet counterpart, Deputy Foreign Minister Adamishin highlighted "the brilliant role" played by Crocker, as well as the "reasonable position finally adopted by South Africa."[13] The final terms included the phased with-drawal of 50,000 Cuban troops by July 1991, and the application of UN resolution 476 on Namibian independence, by which South Africa would reelinquish control of Namibia and abide by the results of a UN-sponsored election. The United States and the Soviet Union continued to play a key role in the implementation of the Brazzaville accord, serving as observers on a commission of appeals to resolve any disputes that might arise.[14]

Given the combustible nexus of actors in the Angolan-Namibian situa-tion—SWAPO, UNITA, Angolans, South Africans, Soviet advisers, and Cuban troops—the successful application of this accord was far from assured. Indeed, when attacks in Namibia by Angolan-based SWAPO guerrillas in March 1989 threatened to upset the accords, both superpowers consulted in their role as commission members, and strongly reiterated their support for the accord. South African troops, together with UN forces, monitored the withdrawal of some 1000–2000 SWAPO guerrillas north of the 16th parallel in Angola.[15]

Potentially the most destabilizing element in the equation was the UNITA issue. The notable absence of any reference to the UNITA-MPLA civil war in the Namibia Accords underscored their fragility. U.S. negotia-tors had long sought MPLA-UNITA reconciliation as one of the key elements of a "package settlement" on Namibian independence. It became increasingly evident however, that the key players—including the United States and the USSR—had "agreed to disagree" on this one, as most public statements during the Brazzaville signing ceremony noted that the issue of Angolan "national reconciliation" was an "internal matter." The differ-ences, presumably, were not about whether to hold MPLA-UNITA talks, but rather the terms of such a dialogue. Indeed, there is evidence that Moscow had told the MPLA to talk with UNITA well before the Namibia accord was finalized. For example, as early as March 1988, senior Soviet diplomats reportedly told MPLA leaders to negotiate with UNITA. In July 1988, Soviet Deputy Deputy Foreign Minister Petrovskiy told press cor-respondents in Harare that the USSR backed U.S. efforts to mediate between the MPLA and UNITA. Then, in July 1988, Deputy Foreign Minister Adamishin publicly called on the two sides to enter into direct negotiations.[16]

While both superpowers continued to publicly call for a resolution of the Angolan civil war, they also continued to provide arms and assistance to the Angolan combatants. Faced with Congressional concerns that Wash-ington was "selling out UNITA in the aftermath of the Namibia settle-ment," Bush administration officials were quick to announce that the United States would not establish ties to Luanda or give away any "carrots" until national reconciliation is under way; they also noted that support of UNITA "will continue undiminished."[17] U.S. aid levels to UNITA were in part symbolic, as that aid was minuscule when compared with the continued massive infusions of Soviet military aid to the MPLA regime.

Despite the seeming superpower deadlock on Angola, there were indications of Soviet weariness with the 14-year-old war—and a corresponding shift in strategy. In early 1989, for example, Soviet diplomats in Luanda were surprisingly vocal about Moscow's misgivings, telling foreign journalists that only a political accord could end the war, and that the USSR was no longer willing to sponsor major new summer offensives like those of previous years. (The USSR reportedly sent arms to Angola in 1988 valued at $1 to 1.5 billion.)[18] The absence of a major offensive in the summer of 1989 did suggest a change in Soviet thinking. In retrospect, the major full-scale offensives in 1987 and 1988 may have been similar to those in Afghanistan—a last chance effort for the military to turn the tide on the battlefield before turning to a diplomatic solution. Even if the military failed to prevail, the Soviets may have calculated that these offensives would likely improve the MPLA's overall bargaining position before sitting down to formal negotiations. The absence of a new big offensive in the summer of 1989 thus assumed greater importance as a possible indicator of Moscow's changing strategy.

Soviet officials were also more blunt about other aspects of the Soviet-Angolan relationship, further fueling speculation that the USSR was in the process of altering its policies there. One Luanda-based Soviet diplomat candidly told a foreign reporter that Moscow was making no profit in Angola—economic or political—and that Angola was saying it could no longer pay for Soviet arms because it was a "poor country."[19] Such public recriminations probably reflected the private dialogue between Moscow and Luanda. Indeed, it probably was no coincidence that such comments appeared just as Angolan President dos Santos called for a cease-fire, and other Angolan military leaders acknowledged that back-channel contacts with UNITA had been initiated.[20]

Despite continued sporadic fighting and small offensives on the ground throughout 1990, the prospects for a breakthrough on the Angolan civil war seemed to pick up as the United States and USSR began to focus greater energies on this issue. During the March 1990 Namibian independence ceremonies in Windhoek, Soviet Foreign Minister Shevardnadze stated that "Angola might provide a good opportunity to repeat the collaboration that produced the Namibian independence."[21] He also held private talks on Angola with U.S. Secretary of State Baker—who in turn met with Angola President dos Santos; following that meeting, U.S. officials said that the MPLA leader was showing more flexibility about talking with UNITA.[22]

In late September, UNITA chief Savimbi expressed hope that a cease-fire could be in place by the end of 1990, largely because of "the growing involvement of the superpowers—especially the Soviet Union—in peace negotiations.[23] Savimbi's optimism was based on meetings between his representatives and Soviet officials in Lisbon in late September—the first direct contacts betwen the USSR and UNITA. According to UNITA officials, the Soviets said they were "looking for a solution" to the civil war. This meeting was confirmed by the Soviets. At the Soviet Foreign Ministry's daily press conference, a spokesman said the Soviet role was designed to "promote an early achievement of national reconciliation in Angola in a more efficient way." He added that Soviet and U.S. experts were assisting the protagonists in the ongoing talks.[24]

Meanwhile, at the September session of the UN General Assembly, Secretary Baker and Foreign Minister Shevardnadze raised the Angolan issue during their bilateral talks in New York. The MPLA-UNITA talks dragged on through the fall, stymied on the issue of legalizing UNITA as a political party, as the Luanda government insisted that UNITA could not be recognized until after an amendment to the constitution permitting a multi-party system. Issues surrounding the timetable for a full election in late 1991 also were a source of contention.[25]

The major breakthrough in the Angolan negotiations occurred in December 1990, as U.S. and Soviet leaders renewed their efforts to reach a settlement. During a major bilateral ministerial in Washington that month, Shevardnadze and Baker met with MPLA and UNITA officials to push for progress. Baker met with Angolan Foreign Minister Van Dunem, while Shevardnadze held a private session with Savimbi—the first meeting between any high-level Soviet official and the UNITA leader. Interestingly, *Izvestiia* characterized Savimbi as a "young and witty man who knows a lot about events in the Soviet Union . . . and who puts forward a program in . . . the spirit of our perestroyka."[26] The lengthy *Izvestiia* account of the Baker-Shevardnadze talks also reflected Moscow's growing impatience with the stalled MPLA-UNITA talks, and seemed to lean on the MPLA to be forthcoming. Noting that "it has become increasingly obvious that the conflict in Angola has no military solution," the authors went on to urge the two sides "to consider that it is not their patrons . . . but they themselves who will have to pay for their obstinacy in drawing out the war."[27] Moreover, the article also explicitly acknowledged Soviet-Angolan disagreements, by stating that the difference in emphases in both sides' statements indicated the talks were "complicated."[28] Presumably, Shevardnadze's meeting with Savimbi was not well received by the MPLA side. U.S.-Soviet efforts evidently helped resolve the MPLA-UNITA deadlock, as both sides agreed in January 1991 to a general timetable and sequence of change as the prelude to a general election.

By May 1, 1991, the MPLA and UNITA finally reached a settlement on a cease-fire. According to Soviet diplomats, the difficult negotiations were kept on track largely through the intervention of U.S. and Soviet officials, as well the good offices of Portuguese mediators; they also noted that Cuba contributed to the peace process—not as participants in the negotiations, but by their "balanced and sensible policy, and the withdrawl of Cuban troops from Angola."[29] On the occasion of the 31 May signing ceremonies between dos Santos and Savimbi, TASS issued a government statement applauding the Angola settlement—and the U.S.-Soviet cooperation that helped facilitate it. Toward that end, it reiterated that the USSR intends to "rigorously fulfill" the agreements, including stopping the deliveries of weapons to this country.[30]

Ethiopia

For a number of reasons, Ethiopia did not figure prominently in the growing U.S.-Soviet cooperation in regional conflicts. For one, Ethiopia was not a serious impediment to U.S.-Soviet relations, as were Afghanistan and, to a lesser degree, Angola. Moreover, the insurgency war in Ethiopia was more "self-contained" than that in Angola, where there was an intricate overlapping of diverse and competing interests among the Angolans, Namibians, Cubans, and South Africans. Because the Ethiopian combatants were almost exclusively indigenous ethnic groups—and because Castro refused to permit Cuban forces to be used against the Eritreans—the war had less of an impact on neighboring states, let alone the United States and the USSR.[31]

In the 1985–1987 period, Gorbachev seemed to be trying to maintain Soviet influence in Addis Ababa—i.e., salvaging a respectable payoff from an expensive 13-year "investment" in the regime of Mengistu Haile Mariam—while trying to persuade the ruthless Ethiopian dictator to employ some new thinking in the seemingly endless successionist war with Eritrean and Tigrean guerrillas. As early as 1987, Soviet officials signaled their growing unhappiness with Mengistu's policies, as they stepped up pressure for him to conclude a political settlement with the insurgent groups.[32] Consequently, the Soviets reduced arms deliveries, tightened up credit terms, and pushed Mengistu to undertake economic reforms.[33] An abortive coup against Mengistu in May 1989 resulted in the execution of nine generals and mass arrests in the officer corps; this episode further underscored the magnitude of Moscow's difficulties in trying to continue its collaboration with the Ethiopian dictator. Mengistu made some major changes in opening up the economy and permitting some private ownership of property; more important, he also agreed to open a dialogue with the Eritrean Peoples' Liberation Front in June 1989. In September, former U.S. President Jimmy Carter entered these talks as a mediator in a round of talks held in Atlanta. Still, progress was slow in coming. Moscow signaled its continuing unhappiness with Mengistu in March 1990, when Soviet Foreign Minister Shevardnadze pointedly omitted Ethiopia from his 11-country African tour.

Despite the formidable progress in U.S.-Soviet cooperation elsewhere in Africa, Ethiopia posed seemingly insurmountable obstacles to U.S. and Soviet negotiators. Thus, while the U.S.and Soviets enjoyed some success in providing food assistance to remote areas of Ethiopia, there was little progress on the thornier issue of the civil war, for a number of reasons: the long history of the Eritrean movements; the diverse policies and goals of other groups, such as the Tigrean Peoples' Liberation Front; and above all, the mercurial Mengistu, who seemed totally uncompromising and bent on preserving his personal power at all costs. Despite cutbacks in Soviet military assistance, Mengistu proved wily in eliciting aid from other donors—most recently Israel. By 1990, it was clear that Gorbachev was looking beyond Mengistu, as he successfully moved to put some distance between the USSR and Mengistu. Increasingly, public criticism, drawdowns in military aid, and calls for a negotiated settlement with the insurgents were designed to bolster Moscow's chances of landing on its feet in a post-Mengistu era. The demise of the Mengistu regime came surprisingly quickly in the spring of 1991. Following a series of military victories by Eritrean and Tigrean insurgent forces in February and March, observers predicted that Addis itself would fall within weeks.[34]

Mengistu himself was desperately seeking to rally support, traveling to military camps around the country and imposing mandatory conscription of students at Addis Ababa University.[35] Moscow's shifting policies contributed to Mengistu's downfall. Its failure to renew a major arms accord in 1990, the drawdown of Soviet advisory personnel, and hard-nosed bargaining on trade issues came to haunt Mengistu in the critical early months of 1991.[36] Moscow's insistence on hard currency payments for oil, for example, led to critical fuel shortages, which led to gas rationing in Addis; similarly, Ethiopian troop morale reportedly was influenced by the cutoff of Spviet deliveries in late 1990.[37]

These Soviet moves, however, failed to persuade Mengistu to engage in serious negotiations until it was too late. Still, as late as May 6—2 weeks prior to Mengistu's hasty flight from Addis to Zimbabwe—senior Soviet Foreign Ministry officials were urging Mengistu publicly to talk with his adversaries. The Deputy Chief of the Foreign Ministry's Africa Department, for example, asserted that military victories by either side only served to escalate the conflict, and that all the parties should seek "national reconciliation" through "compromise."[38]

Mengistu's departure on 22 May coincided with the onset of talks between the remaining "rump government," the various insurgent groups, and a U.S. mediator. Soviet participation was specifically excluded by the various guerrilla leaders; a Soviet spokesman sheepishly acknowledged that while no Soviet official could be an observer at the negotiations, "one would be at hand"—presumably a gesture extended by the U.S. side in light of growing U.S.-Soviet cooperation on most regional issues; indeed, just 10 days later U.S. and Soviet officials issued their joint statement on the internal Angolan settlement between the MPLA and UITA.[39]

Prospects for Future U.S.-Russian Cooperation in Africa

A number of factors suggest solid possibilities for U.S.-Russian cooperation in resolving local African conflicts and problems in the next few years: radically altered Russian priorities in the post-August 1991 coup era, the improved Russian relationship with the West, Moscow's efforts to integrate Russia into the world economy, and the Kremlin's commitment to new thinking about international security and proposals for institutionalizing these new concepts on a global basis.

Radically Altered Russian Priorities

The ongoing domestic revolution in Russia promises to be a long-term process that ensures a Russian preoccupation with needs and priorities at home. This domestic preoccupation is quite apparent in comments by numerous officials, not least of all former Foreign Minister Shevardnadze— as well as his successors. Since 1988, he had become more outspoken about the limits of Russian assistance and the futility of pursuing military solutions instead of political solutions. In this regard, his March 1990 tour of nine African states was most revealing. At various points of his itinerary, Shevardnadze emphasized the primacy of economic reconstruction and the need for political compromise solutions. He also stated that the United States and the Soviet Union were "moving away from competition to cooperation" in Africa—a clear signal that Moscow would not let past commitments or ideology obstruct its efforts to promote settlements in the region.[40]

Deepening Relations with the West and Integration into the World Economy

Moscow's shifting priorities are highlighted by the radical turnabout in Soviet thinking about its economic linkages to the world economy and its consequent efforts to join the Western community. As long as domestic economic reconstruction remains the primary driving issue in Russian politics—and remains linked to growing ties to the West and increased integration into the international economy—Moscow will have strong incentive to sustain a constructive engagement of the West in pursuit of solutions to regional problems. In short, Russia's dire need for Western economic aid and credits,technology and know-how, as well as its need to redirect its resources toward its own needs should sufficiently curb the desires of any Russian leadership—including a more hardline or xenophobic one—from looking toward the Third World for new imperial conquests. With the end of the Cold War in Europe, it becomes increasingly difficult for Moscow to justify almost any Third World commitments on the basis of common ideology or anti-U.S./Western motives; this was most recently evidenced by Gorbachev's unilateral decision to remove Soviet troops from Cuba in September 1991. Even if the current revolution and dissolution of the old USSR were somehow reversed, a more traditionalist-minded leadership dominated by "old thinkers" would still have difficulty trying to compete with the United States in the Third World again. In any case, Russia's domestic problems suggest that the Third World is less likely to be the backdrop for such a competition.

New Soviet Thinking on "Security" and Global Interdependence

Part and parcel of Gorbachev's radical policy shifts has been the emergence of a "weltaunschaung"—new thinking—to replace the worn and discredited ideology of his predecessors. One can cite numerous examples of this new thinking, but perhaps the most remarkable one was Shevardnadze's defense in the Supreme Soviet of Moscow's policy in the Persian Gulf crisis during the late fall of 1990:

> It was politically and psychologically difficult for us to take such a position, by virtue of our advanced and multilateral ties with Iraq and the existence of a Friendship and Cooperation Treaty in 1972.
>   But we could not act otherwise, for there are principles, norms of international law, such concepts as respect for the inviolability of established borders and observance of world law and order. *If we had acted otherwise, we have rendered null and void everything done in recent years by our state in the international arena.*[41]

That was a remarkable admission of the degree to which Gorbachev and his new thinkers had become "prisoners of their own logic," in that Moscow was continually on the line to demonstrate that new thinking was not merely words and rhetoric, but real deeds, performed consistently over time. In keeping with this approach toward multilateral solutions to regional tensions, Shevardnadze's address to the Fall 1990 session of the UN General Assembly augured well for continuing U.S.-Soviet collaboration in resolving conflicts in Africa. That said, there actually are few remaining conflicts where Moscow would have a direct stake. The United States and USSR facilitated an internal settlement in Angola in June 1991, and the warring parties in Mozambique are in a similar "endgame" there. And, the rapid denouement of situation in Ethiopia obviated the need for a U.S.-Soviet role in resolving the civil war—though the longer term prospects there remain cloudy. Still, on a broader level, the Soviets could play a cooperative role in reducing tensions in Africa. Thus, some of Shevardnadze's ideas could apply to Africa—his professed desire to counter the "arithmetical" approach to military parity and security utilized by so many states, for example. To remedy this problem, he reiterated an earlier call for an international registry for certain kinds of armaments to insure a certain level of "transparency" that should lead to a more stable balance of power in various regions. He also called on the UN to play a greater role in resolving conflicts, even to the point of using force under the aegis of the UN's Military Staff Committee. Moscow's deft use of the UN during the Persian Gulf situation underscores its apparent commitment to the UN as a forum to resolve new Third World crises.[42]

Emerging Political Constituencies

Another domestic factor that could positively effect the prospects for U.S.-Russian cooperation is the rise of new political constituencies within Russia—the Supreme Soviet and its international affairs subcommittees, the Republics, the media, and public opinion. Indeed, the newly independent republics—not only the free Baltic states, but Ukraine and others—are already asserting their roles on certain foreign policy issues. Other actors, such as the media, have actively exploited glasnost and the August 1991 revolution to offer some bitter and critical observations about the political and economic costs of Moscow's Third World involvement. In this regard, both Angola and Ethiopia had come under close press scrutiny in the Russia. A 6 June 1990 article in *Literaturnaya Gazeta* entiled "The Angolan Knot—the Balance Sheet of the African Items in Our Budget" offered a devastating critique of Moscow's continuing involvement in Angola. The author, for example, asserted that the USSR has become "hostage" to its policy in Angola and questions the MPLA's desire for peace. He argued there was a caste of Angolan officials who see the war as a means of insuring their personal prosperity—and said he had personally seen their "luxurious villas and imported cars," despite Angola's poverty-stricken economy. More biting, perhaps, was the comment that "one need not think that they (Soviet advisers) are experiencing deprivations only for the sake of internationalist ideas," but also economic benefit, as their salaries—$700 a month in hard currency—"from the Soviet budget" is better than "400 rubles a month in Kostroma."[43] A less cynical, but equally critical, review of Soviet policy in Angola appeared in the 20 July *Izvestiia*; the author pointed up the contradictions in Soviet tactics, noting that "top leaders" advocate negotiations, while Soviet military advisers recommend and plan "inadvisable" military offensives that set back the talks. The article left no doubt that a negotiated settlement with UNITA was the only way out of this conflict.[44]

Ethiopia too had come under attack in the Soviet press during the pre-coup period of the Gorbachev era. One *Izvestiia* reporter wrote in a March 1990 article that Soviet military aid is based on a bilateral accord that specifically states that Moscow is to "rebuild the Ethiopian military *with a view to repulsing foreign aggression.*" In a detailed discussion, he stated the aid was designed to defend against Somalia in the late 1970s but not "for an internal conflict that has dragged on for years." The author also indicated that Addis Ababa owed the USSR 2.86 billion rubles—primarily for military aid, and that it would be "very hard" for the Ethiopian military to put up a fight against the Eritrean and Tigrean insurgents without such aid. The author then expanded his critique into a broadside against indiscriminate arms sales, noting that 100,000 Soviet AK-47 kalashnikovs—captured by Israel in the 1967 six-day war with Egypt—had recently been sold to Ethiopia by Israel. The messages here were quite clear—it was time to re-think the panoply of all Soviet dealings in the Third World.[45]

While such media pieces reflect a liberal, reformist perspective, they nonetheless do reflect the views of the general public—which predictably is preoccupied with the great economic hardships within Russia itself. In this environment, Moscow would be hard-pressed to justify any major new foreign commitments abroad, and probably will face growing pressure to reduce existing relationships—including those with Cuba and North Korea, who also have come under heavy media attacks in 1990.

Barriers to Cooperation

Despite these positive indicators, there nonetheless remain other factors that could impede U.S.-Russian cooperation. While most of the liberal and reform-minded media savaged many of Moscow's past Third World policies, there were other actors who were a bit more reluctant to completely disengage from the Third World. For example, the ongoing Iraq crisis has revealed the continued reservations of some Arabists within the MFA—as well as some military officials—about new thinking and the primacy of Russian-Western relations. Thus, Deputy Foreign Minister Belonogov implicitly challenged Shevardnadze's joint statement with the U.S. when he expressed to the Supreme Soviet his disquiet over the U.S. military buildup in the Gulf. Concerns about this US threat also were expressed by the former chief of Warsaw Pact forces, General Lobov, later that month.

Similar "old thinking" was evident in the media debate on policy toward Cuba, where a "Cuba lobby" of Soviet diplomats and academics pointed out the benefits of ties to Cuba. In this context, it is worth noting that even Shevardnadze—as late as November 1989—felt sufficiently pressured to assert that Moscow had certain responsibilities to its longtime allies and clients, that they could not just be "dropped" because of the changing circumstances in the USSR. Implicitly, he was conceding to the "prestige and reliability" arguments used by old thinkers to justify a continuing Soviet role abroad. By the time of his Africa tour in March 1990, it was clear he felt more comfortable in forcefully arguing his own position:

> Yes, the achievements of the revolution must be defended, but the situation sometimes arises whereby a continuation of armed domestic conflicts and clashes becomes a factor that threatens it. Particularly when there is no military solution to domestic problems, as we were told in Angola in Mozambique.[46]

Although there can be little doubt as to who was prevailing in these policy debates, the events of late 1990 suggested a greater degree of uncertainty in Russian policy calculations on foreign policy questions. Gorbachev's rejection of the Shatalin economic reform program, Shevardnadze's resignation in December 1990, Gorbachev's turn to the right, and the growing prominence of the KGB and the military in dealing with managing domestic problems—"crime and economic sabotage" as well as "nationalist provocations" in the Baltics—raised questions about the possibility of new shifts in foreign policy. By naming Aleksandr Bessmertnykh as Shevardnadze's successor in December 1990, Gorbachev clearly signaled his desire to keep U.S.-Soviet relations on track. Bessmertnykh, a "new thinker," former Ambassador to the United States and career diplomat, faced difficult challenges in his brief eight month tenure—notably, trying to convince Western audiences that the increased prominence of the KGB and military in the first half of 1991 did not portend a major shift from Gorbachev's goal of economic and political reform.[47] The postponement of the scheduled U.S.-Soviet February 1991 summit underscored that challenge. In that regard, the growing attacks on Shevardnadze's handling of arms control—he was portrayed as a prisoner of U.S. interests—did not auger well for U.S.-Soviet cooperation when the traditionalist critics of new thinking appeared to be in the ascendancy.[48]

The failed traditionalist coup of August 1991 radically altered the internal political landscape in the USSR, subsequently complicating any mid-term predictions about foreign policy. The treaty talks between the center and the republics—most of all Yeltsin's RSFSR and the Baltic states—altered the conduct of Soviet foreign policy. Besides these factors,

new conflicts or crises in the Third World could emerge, ones not as neat
and clear cut as Saddam Hussein's blatant seizure of Kuwait. In any event,
Hussein's unpredictable behavior did complicate and test U.S.-Soviet cooperation; U.S. and Russian interests could possibly collide in a situation less
obvious—for example, internal turmoil in Iran.

On balance, trends in Soviet Africa policy under Gorbachev do augur
well for U.S.-Russian collaboration in resolving any future African conflicts.
Since his February 1986 Party Congress speech, Gorbachev has consistently
preached the need for economic belt-tightening in the Third World, the
need for new economic policies, and the importance of political solutions
to regional problems. Former Foreign Minister Shevardnadze was increasingly candid in pointing up the need for these clients to fashion compromises and focus on economic development tasks rather than political power.
Even without Gorbachev on the scene, it is difficult to imagine Moscow—
even one led by a repressive, xenophobic leadership—plunging back into
the Third World as it did in the 1970s.

The application of new thinking in Russian foreign policy, as well as the
turn of events within Russia itself, clearly indicate that the heyday of
Russian military and economic largesse is over—as are Russian military
adventures in the Third World.[49] With the dramatic shift in U.S.-Russian
relations and the collapse of the East-West divide in Europe, Third World
leaders can no longer play their "ideology" card to elicit U.S. and Russian
aid for their cause. Increasingly, they will have to turn to both parties, or
the UN or regional groups, to resolve their local conflicts.

Notes

1. For broader studies of Soviet Third World policy in the 1980s, see Alvin Z.
Rubinstein, *Moscow's Third World Strategy,*(Princeton: Princeton University Press,
1988.; Francis Fukuyama, *Moscow's Post-Brezhnev Reassessment of the Third World,*
(Rand Corporation R-3337-USDP, February 1986; Elizabeth K. Valkenier, *The
Soviet Union and the Third World: An Economic Bind* (New York: Praeger Studies,
1983.); Carol Saivetz and Sylvia Woodby, *Soviet-Third World Relations* (Boulder:
Westview Press, 1985), and more recently, W. Raymond Duncan and Carolyn
McGiffert Ekedahl, *Moscow and the Third World Under Gorbachev,* (Boulder:
Westview Press, 1990).

2. For a detailed account of Moscow's position at the time of Gorbachev's rise
to power, see Peter Clement, "Moscow and Southern Africa," in *Problems of
Communism*, Vol. XXXIV, No. 2, March-April 1985, pp. 29–50.

3. Ibid., pp. 35–39.

4. Ibid., pp. 39–43.

5. See the State Department May 1986 publication *Warsaw Pact Economic Aid
to Non-Communist LDCs 1984* p. 12. for year-by-year breakdowns of extensions of
economic aid.

6. For arms import figures, see *World Military Expenditures and Arms Transfers 1986,* US Arms Control and Disarmament Agency, publication #127, April 1987, p. 116.

7. See Peter Clement, "The USSR and Sub-Saharan Africa: A Balance Sheet" in Carol Saivetz, ed., The Soviet Union In The Third World, (Boulder: Westview Press, 1989), pp. 150–171.

8. For the complete text of the Gorbachev speech, see Foreign Broadcast Information Service, Daily Report–Soviet Union (cited hereafter as *FBIS-USSR,* 26 February 1986.

9. See, for example, the regional sections of *Soviet Military Power,* 1985–1989 editions for detailed on the size and types of stepped-up arms deliveries to key Soviet clients in the Third World.

10. Gorbachev interview with *The Washington Post,* May 22, 1988.

11. Victor Mallet, "Namibia and Angola Talks End on Note of Optimism," in *The Financial Times,* June 27, 1988 p. 32.

12. Michael Berlin, "Angola Talks Yield Progress," in *The* Washington Post, July 14, 1988, p. 1.

13. William Claiborne, "Cuba, Angola, South Africa Sign Accord," in *The Washington Post,* December 14, 1988, p. 1.

14. Ibid.

15. E.A. Wayne, "Namibia Peace On Track," in *The Christian Science Monitor,* April 20, 1989, p. 8.

16. Neil MacFarlane and Helen Kitchen provided the details of these Soviet entreaties to the MPLA. See Neil MacFarlane, "The Soviet Union and Southern African Security," in *Problems of Communism,* March-June 1989, p. 83. MarFarlane provides an excellent discussion of broader Soviet thinking on southern Africa as well.

17. E.A. Wayne, "Angola-Namibia Accords, Part II," in *The Christian Science Monitor,* February 23, 1989, p. 8.

18. James Brooke, "Angola Gives Hints of Willingness to Seek Political Solution to War," in *The New York Times,* January 28, 1989, p. 4.

19. Ibid.

20. Ibid.

21. John Goshko, "US,Soviets Cooperate on Angola Conflict," in *The Washington Post,* April 16, 1990, p. 22.

22. Ibid.

23. Frank Swoboda, "Angola Rebel Calls Cease-Fire Likely by Year'send," in *The Washington Post,* October 1, 1990, p. 23.

24. TASS, 2 October 1990, as reported in *FBIS-USSR,* October 3, 1990, p. 11.

25. Swoboda, op. cit.

26. A. Blinov and V. Nadein, "Date For Summit Announced," *Izvestiia,* 14 December 1990, p. 4.

27. Ibid.

28. Ibid.

29. Moscow Radio in Afrikaans, 29 May 1991, citing Soviet MFA Africa Division Chief Kazimirov.

30. TASS International Service, 31 May 1991.

31. Raymond W. Duncan, *The Soviet Union and Cuba: Interests and Influence,* (New York: Praeger, 1985), p. 135.

32. Ekedahl and Duncan, op. cit., pp. 180–181.

33. Ibid.

34. Jane Perlez, "As Rebels Surge in Ethiopia," in *The New York Times,* March 23, 1991, p. 1.

35. Ibid.

36. Clifford Krauss, "Ethiopia's Dictator Flees; Officials Seeking US Help," in *The New York Times,* May 22, 1991, p. 1.

37. Perlez, op. cit.

38. TASS, 6 May 1991, as reported in British Broadcasting Corporation, *Summary of World Broadcasts,* May 8,1991, p. 1.

39. Xan Smiley, "Death Knell Sounds for Soviet Power in Africa," in the *Daily Telegraph,* May 26, 1991, p. 13.

40. See the detailed and revealing assessment of Shevardnadze's trip and the comments of his staffers in M. Yusin, "New View of Africa," in *Izvestiia,* March 31, 1990, p. 5.

41. TASS, September 11, 1990.

42. TASS, September 25, 1990.

43. Vladislav Yanelis, "The Angolan Knot: The Balance Sheet of the African Items in Our Budget," in *Literaturnaya Gazeta,* June 6, 1990, p. 15.

44. M. Pavlov, "We, the Americans, and the War in Angola," in *Izvestiia,* July 20, 1990, p. 4.

45. G. Ustinov, "Ethiopian Version: How Our Cooperation is Developing in the Military Sphere," in *Izvestiia,* March 30, 1990, p. 5.

46. TASS, March 26, 1990.

47. Melvin A. Goodman, "Who Is Bessmertnykh?", in *The Christian Science Monitor,* 31 January 1991, p. 7.

48. See, for example, the debate on whether to ratify the Treaty on Conventional Forces (CFE) published in *Sovetskaya Rossiya,* 9 January 1991, p. 5.

49. For a recent overview of Moscow's retrenchment in the Third World, see Melvin A. Goodman, "Gorbachev's Retreat," in *The Christian Science Monitor,* October 4, 1990, p. 6.

5

Soviet and American Peacemaking Efforts in Regional Conflicts in Asia: Afghanistan and Cambodia

Daniel S. Papp

Of the many issues that divided the United States and the Soviet Union during the Cold War, few had greater impact on East-West relations than "regional conflicts." Frequently, the U.S. and the U.S.S.R. found themselves supporting opposite sides in military confrontations in Asia, Latin America, the Middle East, and Sub-Saharan Africa. Fortunately, despite their frequent juxtaposition, U.S.-Soviet conflict never eventuated.

Nevertheless, the impact that regional conflicts had on East-West relations was extensive. During the 1950s and 1960s, the growth of Soviet involvement with Third World states led many Americans to conclude that the U.S.S.R. had embarked on a policy of global expansion that had to be contained. U.S. involvement in the Vietnam War was one result of this conclusion. Later, during the 1970s and early 1980s, Soviet military diplomacy in Afghanistan, Angola, Ethiopia, Mozambique, Nicaragua, and elsewhere led directly to the collapse of detente and the rearming of the United States.

However, during the middle and late 1980s, several forces emerged that provided new opportunities to manage, deescalate, and resolve regional conflicts. These forces included but were not limited to changing political, economic, and military outlooks within the United States and Russia; new perspectives on the part of some of the combatants in regional conflicts about acceptable solutions to the conflicts; more effective involvement on the part of non-combatant regional actors in efforts to manage, deescalate, and resolve regional conflicts; and more effective involvement by extra-regional actors additional to the superpowers in efforts to manage, deescalate, and resolve conflicts.

In this study, we will examine U.S. and Soviet efforts to manage, deescalate, and resolve the conflicts in Afghanistan and Cambodia. These two Asian conflicts had extensive impact on the U.S.-Soviet relationship, and that relationship had extensive impact on events in Afghanistan and Cambodia as well. But before we explore the U.S. and Soviet role in peacemaking in Afghanistan and Cambodia, we will first examine the broader U.S. and Soviet contexts within which those Afghan and Cambodian peacemaking efforts of the 1980s and early 1990s proceeded.

Establishing the Context for Peacemaking: The Reagan Doctrine and Gorbachev's "New Thinking"

As the 1980s opened, many Soviet client governments and pro-Soviet governments in the Third World were under siege. The governments of Angola, Ethiopia, Mozambique, and Nicaragua fought against indigenous movements supported by external forces. In Cambodia, the government survived primarily because of the presence of over 100 thousand Soviet-armed and equipped Vietnamese troops. In Afghanistan, the presence of over 100 thousand Soviet combat troops played a major role in keeping that government in power in its struggle against the Mujahadeen.[1]

Meanwhile, momentous events and processes that had significant impacts on the Third World conflicts listed above were underway in both the United States and the Soviet Union. In the United States, the Reagan administration had come to power, avowed to strengthen American military might and end the free hand it believed the Soviet Union had in its Third World policies.[2] In the U.S.S.R., the old Brezhnev regime was winding down, soon to be replaced by the short-lived regimes of Yuri Andropov and Konstantin Chernenko. These regimes in turn were replaced by Mikhail Gorbachev's, which brought with it new perspectives on how Soviet domestic and foreign policies should be run.

The interplay between U.S. and Soviet outlooks on and policies in the Third World during the early and middle 1980s played a key role in establishing the conditions that led to international peacemaking efforts in Third World conflicts in subsequent years. We here provide only an outline of that interplay before we turn to our primary tasks, the analysis of U.S. and Soviet peacemaking efforts in Afghanistan and Cambodia.

The Reagan Doctrine and American Views of Soviet Third World Policies Before the Gorbachev Revolution

Ronald Reagan became president in January 1981, carrying the views that during the 1970s, the Soviet Union had undertaken "the most brazen imperial drive in history," and that the United States, because of a combination of the "Vietnam syndrome," weak leadership, and insufficient attention to its military, had not responded adequately to that drive. To Reagan, it was time for the U.S. to act. As Reagan's Secretary of Defense Caspar Weinberger said in 1981:

> This Soviet [expansion], unchallenged in recent years by the United States, has led to Soviet gains and the growing perception that the Soviets and their proxies can act with impunity. This trend must be halted and then reversed.[3]

Reagan's Third World containment strategy included the U.S. military build-up; U.S. efforts to establish a "strategic consensus" in the Middle East;[4] active use of U.S. military forces; and as the 1980s wore on, increasing U.S. support for anti-Soviet insurgencies around the world. The latter policy became known as the "Reagan Doctrine."

Under the auspices of the Reagan Doctrine, the U.S. expanded military assistance to the Mujahadeen in Afghanistan,[5] and began providing assistance to UNITA in Angola, anti-communist forces in Cambodia, and the Contras in Nicaragua. In some cases, U.S. assistance was sizeable. For example, in 1986, the U.S. sent at least 100 million dollars of military assistance to the Mujahadeen. In other cases, the U.S. sent limited amounts of military aid. Thus, also in 1986, anti-communist forces in Cambodia received only 3.5 million dollars of military assistance. Nevertheless, by the middle 1980s, it was evident that the United States had adopted a world-wide policy of providing military assistance to those fighting in the Third World against Soviet clients and the Soviet Union itself.

This policy encountered some domestic American opposition. However, this opposition little deterred Reagan, whose commitment to opposing pro-Soviet and Soviet forces in the Third World may best be gauged by his willingness to permit a climate to prevail in the White House that contributed directly to the Iran-Contra affair.

Meanwhile, even during the early 1980s, some analysts in the U.S.S.R. began to doubt the wisdom of Soviet military diplomacy in the Third World, and questioned the U.S.S.R.'s role in Third World affairs.[6] Some Soviet analysts acknowledged that Soviet clients in the Third World might be defeated despite Soviet support,[7] and others suggested to pro-Soviet Third World states that they rely on their own resources for development and security.[8]

In a policy sense, the activist, expansion-oriented, Soviet military diplomacy of the late 1970s in the Third World also changed, giving way to less expansionist Soviet behavior in the Third World in the early 1980s. While the Kremlin did not abandon any of its Third World positions, by the early 1980s it had adopted a policy of consolidating, not expanding, its Third World presence and influence.[9] The reasons for this policy change were numerous, but a significant question remained: would the U.S.S.R. opt to "consolidate in place," or would it choose to "retrench and consolidate?"[10]

It was not entirely surprising, then, that as early as 1983, U.S. and Soviet officials began to talk with each other about their differences over regional issues. By 1986, U.S. and Soviet officials had held discussions covering Afghanistan, Cambodia, Central America, the Middle East, and southern Africa. At first, these meetings were purely informational, but over time, they led to improved U.S.-Soviet understanding of each others' positions on regional conflicts. As we shall see, they also contributed to peacemaking efforts in the middle and late 1980s in Afghanistan, Cambodia, and elsewhere as well.

Gorbachev's New Thinking, Soviet Third World Policy, and U.S.-Soviet Third World Peacemaking Efforts

Despite U.S.-Soviet discussions on regional issues, not much had changed in the U.S.-Soviet relationship in the Third World by 1985. In Third World conflicts around the world, the U.S. supported one side, and the Soviets the other. The few efforts that did exist to manage, deescalate, or resolve regional conflicts had no real hope of success.

Gradually, however, following Mikhail Gorbachev's accession to power in the Kremlin in March 1985, the new Soviet leader began to alter the U.S.S.R.'s perspective on international affairs. Gorbachev's "New Thinking" (novoe myshlenie) on international affairs affected all areas of Soviet foreign policy. Importantly, several aspects related directly to Soviet Third World policy and the Soviet role in Third World conflicts. These aspects included: 1) a desire to end U.S.-Soviet Cold War competition; 2) an acceptance of the view that conflicts in the Third World could undermine the U.S.-Soviet relationship; 3) an awareness that many Soviet Third World activities cost much and gained little; 4) an emphasis on political rather than military dimensions of security; 5) an acceptance that many "wars of national liberation" were "regional conflicts;" and 6) a stated desire to resolve regional conflicts via "national reconciliation" rather than military victory.[11] Each deserves separate comment.

To Gorbachev, one of the highest priorities for Soviet foreign policy was to curtail U.S.-Soviet Cold War competition. From Gorbachev's perspective, that competition sapped Soviet economic strength, weakened the U.S.S.R.'s international position, and because of the arms race, mortgaged the Soviet Union's future. As far as Gorbachev was concerned, unless Soviet foreign policy changed, the U.S.S.R. would continue to lose international prestige, the threat of war would continue, and chances for success in his domestic programs would be reduced.

Closely related to this outlook was Gorbachev's acceptance of the view that conflicts in the Third World could undermine U.S.-Soviet relations. Historically, this was an easily demonstrable fact that had been evident during the 1970s, but Brezhnev and his colleagues chose to ignore it. However, given the centrality of improved U.S.-Soviet relations to Gorbachev's entire program, Gorbachev's acceptance of this view was a critical conceptual breakthrough.

At the same time, proponents of New Thinking argued that many of the U.S.S.R.'s Third World activities cost much and gained little for the U.S.S.R. While this perspective had begun to develop during the early 1980s, it became increasingly evident during the middle and late 1980s that the Kremlin poured billions of rubles into the Third World without getting much in return. Afghanistan and Vietnam were but two cases in point.

Aware that his country's military expenditures were undermining its economic strength; concerned that those expenditures elicited military responses from others that jeopardized Soviet security; and convinced that the U.S.S.R. was involved directly or indirectly in several apparently unwinnable conflicts in the Third World, Gorbachev also asserted that the countries of the world—the U.S.S.R. included—had to increase their emphasis on political dimensions of security and decrease their attention to its military dimensions. This emphasis on political dimensions of security applied not only to East-West and Sino-Soviet relations, but also to conflicts in the Third World. Political dimensions of security implied a need to talk and negotiate, not fight.

Equally important, Gorbachev and his supporters moved away from the concepts of "progressive forces" and "wars of national liberation," and toward the concepts of "conflicts of interest" and "regional conflicts." As minor as these changes in terminology may appear, they were critical in an ideological sense since they provided the U.S.S.R. with tremendous policy flexibility. Whereas the U.S.S.R. was duty bound to support "progressive forces" in "wars of national liberation," the U.S.S.R. could proceed with practically any policy it chose when "conflicts of interests" led to "regional conflicts."

Finally, in keeping with the need for negotiations implied by "political dimensions of security" and the flexibility implied by "regional conflicts," Gorbachev urged that regional conflicts be settled via "national reconciliation." At one time or another, New Thinkers in the Soviet hierarchy urged that national reconciliation be pursued to end regional conflicts in Afghanistan, Angola, Cambodia, Ethiopia, Mozambique, Nicaragua, and elsewhere as well.

These six aspects of Gorbachev's New Thinking evolved over time, and they provided a significant part of the context in which U.S. and Soviet peacemaking efforts proceeded. But they were not the entire context. Not all Soviet leaders accepted New Thinking and its implications, and on the policy level, the U.S.S.R. during late 1985–1987 provided large quantities of weapons to its clients in Angola and Nicaragua; helped support large Vietnamese offensives in Cambodia; and stepped-up and brutalized its own military operations in Afghanistan. Contextually, New Thinking played a critical role in U.S.-Soviet Third World peacemaking, but neither it nor the Reagan Doctrine provided the entire context.

U.S. and Soviet Peacemaking in Afghanistan

On April 14, 1988, representatives of the governments of Afghanistan and Pakistan signed three separate agreements concluded under United Nations auspices that in many people's eyes removed the Afghanistan conflict from the international agenda. These three agreements included one on "Non-Interference and Non-Intervention," a second on "Voluntary Return of Refugees," and a third on the "Settlement of the Situation Relating to Afghanistan." Additionally, the United States and the Soviet Union signed a "Declaration of International Guarantees" on the Afghan settlement. Together, the four accords entered into force on May 15, 1988.[12]

The path toward the four accords was a long and tortuous one, beginning in November 1980 when the United Nations General Assembly authorized Secretary General Kurt Waldheim to explore possibilities for a political solution to the Afghan conflict. Negotiations eventually began under U.N. auspices in June 1982 between the government of Pakistan and the Soviet-installed Afghan regime. These so-called "proximity talks" led to the May 1988 accords.

For our purposes here, that is, the analysis of U.S. and Soviet peacemaking efforts in Afghanistan, the path toward the Afghan accords, and American and Soviet involvement in their realization, can best be divided into four distinct periods. Each will be discussed separately.

Warfare and Pre-Negotiations: April 1978–June 1982

From April 27, 1978, when units of the Afghan air force and armored forces seized power in Kabul, through the December 1979 Soviet invasion of Afghanistan and the November 1980 U.N. authorization of U.N. Secretary General Kurt Waldheim to explore a political settlement to the Afghan conflict, up until the actual beginning of Afghan-Pakistani proximity talks in June 1982, no meaningful negotiations on the Afghan conflict took place. On the Kabul regime/Soviet side, unsuccessful efforts were undertaken to win the war militarily. Conversely, a constellation of forces centered on the internally-divided Afghan Mujahadeen countered the

Kabul/Soviet effort. Countries as diverse as China, Egypt, Iran, Saudi Arabia, and the United States provided military support to the Mujahadeen.

With the Soviet Union maintaining that the government of Afghanistan had invited it into that country, and with most of the rest of the world rejecting that assertion, there was little about which to negotiate. In January 1980, a U.N. Security Council resolution calling for an unconditional withdrawal of foreign troops from Afghanistan was vetoed by the U.S.S.R., but on January 14, the U.N. General Assembly passed it, 104 to 18, with 18 abstentions. Later in January, the Islamic Conference also condemned the invasion, and on February 19, the European Community's Foreign Ministers Meeting called for the neutralization of Afghanistan under international guarantees following a Soviet withdrawal. Shortly thereafter, India announced its opposition to "technical" neutrality for Afghanistan, but proposed that a "regional solution" to the crisis be found, with India acting as mediator. Not surprisingly, Pakistan rejected India's proposal, concerned about the dominant role India might play because of its role as mediator. And in late March, Fidel Castro offered to help find a regional settlement. Nothing came of these proposals, and the United States and the Soviet Union played no discernible role in any of them.[13]

On April 17, 1980, however, Babrak Karmal, installed as the Afghan leader by the Soviets during their December 1979 invasion, proposed separate bilateral discussions be undertaken between Afghanistan and Iran, and between Afghanistant and Pakistan. Given the relationship between the Karmal government and the Kremlin, there was no doubt that the U.S.S.R. supported Karmal's proposal, and may have initiated it. Less than a month later, the Kabul government offered another set of proposals for a negotiated political settlement to the conflict, proffering that the United States and the Soviet Union should serve as international guarantors against external interference. Shortly thereafter, on May 15, U.S. Secretary of State Edmund Muskie rejected Karmal's proposals as "cosmetic and ambiguous." U.S. goals remained the withdrawal of Soviet troops, the restoration of Afghan neutrality and non-alignment, and noninterference by external forces in Afghanistan's internal affairs.[14]

Meanwhile, even with Karmal's negotiations proposal, the Soviet goal remained the maintenance of the Babrak Karmal regime in Kabul. Given the near certainty in 1980 that the withdrawal of Soviet troops would lead to the collapse of the Kabul government, from the Soviet perspective, there was truly little about which to negotiate. Thus, in all likelihood, Karmal put his negotiations proposal forward in the hope of improving his government's (and the Soviet's) image, and of splitting the anti-Soviet/anti-Kabul front.

Throughout the rest of 1980 and most of 1981, the U.S.S.R. continued to assert that it was in Afghanistan by invitation because of external

Chinese, Pakistani, and American involvement there. In October 1980, Karmal visited the Soviet Union, and both he and Soviet President Leonid Brezhnev called Afghan-Soviet ties "irreversible."[15] Neither the Kremlin nor the Kabul regime changed their positions significantly during the first seven months of 1981 despite efforts to arrange negotiations by the European Community and the United Nations. Indeed, on August 5, an official Soviet Foreign Ministry statement rejected these efforts to arrange negotiations as "unacceptable interference" in Afghanistan's internal affairs.[16]

But in August 1981, the Afghan government, supported by the Soviets, began to change its position. It now expressed willingness to meet jointly with Pakistan and Iran in the presence of the U.N. Secretary General, and stated that it would also accept wider international discussions. But on the core issue, the presence of Soviet troops in Afghanistan, the Karmal regime insisted that Soviet forces could remain in Afghanistan as long as Kabul and the Kremlin desired. Thus, the war dragged on into 1982 with no hope of negotiations in sight.

Negotiations and Stalemate: June 1982–Early 1986

The first movement toward a negotiated settlement in Afghanistan came in June 1982 when the Afghan government and Pakistan began their first round of "proximity talks" in Geneva. Diego Cordovez, the U.N.'s Under Secretary General for Special Political Affairs and Special Envoy to the proximity talks, was the key to the negotiations as he shuttled between the Afghan and Pakistani delegations. This arrangement was necessary because Pakistan did not recognize the Afghan regime, and sitting with it to negotiate would imply recognition.

Neither the United States nor the Soviet Union were party to the proximity talks. The United States continued to insist on Soviet withdrawal from Afghanistan, restoration of Afghan neutrality and nonalignment, and noninterference by outside force in Afghanistan's internal afairs. At the same time, the U.S. continued to provide weapons to the Mujahadeen. While the U.S. took no part in negotiations, it did remain in close contact with Pakistan about the negotiations.. Meanwhile, the Kremlin, although not a party to the proximity talks, sent high-level observers to the Geneva talks. According to some reports, Soviet observers not only observed, but also crafted the Afghan government's positions.[17]

In many respects, the proximity talks were modeled on the proposal for Afghan-Pakistani negotiations put forward by Karmal in August 1981, with the significant exceptions that Iran was not included and Afghanistan and Pakistan did not meet face-to-face. Thus, the Soviet position on international negotiations had clearly changed; the Kremlin no longer rejected participation in negotiations by parties beyond Southwest Asis as meddling in Afghanistan's internal affairs. There were at least two explanations for the changed Soviet outlook. First, the Kremlin may have become aware that its refusal to support extra-regional involvement in negotiations was eroding its international reputation. Second, the Soviet Union may have hoped to drive a wedge between the United States and Pakistan via negotiations.

In any event, despite agreement on the agenda for discussion,[18] the first round of Afghan-Pakistani proximity talks accomplished little. The Afghan government continued to insist on direct negotiations between itself and Pakistan, international recognition, an end to foreign intervention that it did not request, and international guarantees before Soviet troops were withdrawn. Pakistan insisted on the withdrawal of Soviet troops, a free choice of government by the Afghan people, and a return of refugees. In short, although the Afghan government and Pakistan met in Geneva, neither had changed its previous positions. Negotiations had begun, but stalemate continued.

Despite extensive optimism expressed by U.N. Special Envoy Diego Cordovez, the second round of proximity talks, held again in Geneva from April 11–22, 1983, and June 12–24, 1983, also accomplished little. Cordovez announced on April 23 that "substantial progress" had been made in negotiations that were "95 percent complete;"[19] but it gradually became apparent that three stumbling blocks remained: 1) the timetable for a Soviet troop withdrawal; 2) the timetable to end external support for the Mujahadeen; and 3) the type of government that would exist in Kabul after the Soviet military withdrew. Without settlement of these issues, no agreement on Afghanistan was possible.

Each of these three stumbling blocks was substantive. On the first, Pakistan insisted on a rapid timetable of three to six months for a Soviet withdrawal. The Kabul regime intimated that the Kremlin wanted at least 18 months. Pakistan—and the United States—were concerned that the Soviet Union would use this time to shore up the Kabul regime and attack the Mujahadeen. On the second issue, the Afghan and Soviet governments wanted a guarantee that all outside aid to the Mujahadeen would stop immediately. Neither Pakistan nor the United States could guarantee that, even had they wanted to, since Iran and China, neither of whom were parties to the proximity talks also provided aid to the Mujahadeen. Directly related to this was disagreement over when aid should stop. The Kabul government—and the Kremlin—wanted immediate termination of aid to the Mujahadeen upon signing of an accord, with no limits on Soviet aid to the Kabul regime,with the Soviet Union withdrawing its forces after aid to the Mujahadeen had ended. Pakistan—and the United States—opposed the sequential nature of this proposal, and wanted military aid to both sides in Afghanistan drawn down simultaneously in proportion to the rate of Soviet troop withdrawal. On the third issue, without the Mujahadeen being party to the negotiations, their acquiescence to a settlement could not be assured. This virtually guaranteed that at least one, if not all, of the seven major factions that made up the Mujahadeen would challenge and seek to topple the Kabul regime after an agreement was reached. In essence, then, even though the proximity talks raised hopes for a settlement, too many obstacles remained at the end of 1983 for any political solution to be seriously contemplated.

Little progress was achieved in 1984 and 1985, either. A January 1984 call by the Islamic Conference for an international conference to assure Afghanistan's nonalignment was heatedly rejected by the Kabul government, and a third round of proximity talks in August 1984 yielded nothing. Even Mikhail Gorbachev's March 1985 accession to power failed to energize negotiations despite Gorbachev's April 1985 order to the Politburo to undertake "a hard and impartial analysis of the Soviet position [in Afghanistan] and see a way out of the situation."[20]

The fourth and fifth rounds of Afghan-Pakistani proximity talks, held in Geneva in June and August 1985, also produced little discernible progress. Nevertheless, U.N. Special Envoy Diego Cordovez now argued that three of the four elements of an overall agreement had been "all but finalized."[21] However, Soviet troops remained in Afghanistan; the two sides at the proximity talks still differed substantially on both the timing of a Soviet withdrawal and the timing of the termination of external aid to the Mujahadeen; and no meaningful discussions had taken place on the composition of the future Afghan government. By mid-summer 1985, then, despite Cordovez's optimism, all the major disagreements of previous years persisted. To make matters worse, some observers even believed that Soviet military activities in Afghanistan intensified in the months following Gorbachev's accession to power.[22]

Late in 1985, this diplomatic logjam appeared to begin to break up. In his November 1985 Geneva summit meeting with Ronald Reagan, Gorbachev omitted two long-standing Soviet positions on the conflict, the first that Soviet troop withdrawals from Afghanistan were exclusively a Soviet-Afghan affair, and the second that any country that opposed the Soviet military presence in Afghanistan had to talk directly to the Kabul government, not Moscow.[23] Shortly after the Geneva summit, in an apparent effort to test Soviet sincerity, the U.S. government on December 10, 1985 sent a letter to U.N. Special Envoy Diego Cordovez declaring that it would be a guarantor of accords on Afghanistan as expressed in a draft guarantee document drawn up in the proximity talks, provided the talks could resolve the "central issue of Soviet troop withdrawal and its interrelationship to the other instruments."[24] This letter was in keeping with Ronald Reagan's proposal put to the United Nations in his 1985 address to that body's General Assembly that the U.S. and U.S.S.R. encourage warring parties in regional conflicts to seek political settlements and that the U.S. and Soviet Union then enter into bilateral talks to end their own military involvement in regional wars.

This letter marked a significant change in the U.S. position. Before this, the U.S. had been extremely noncommittal about its willingness to serve as a guarantor of an eventual agreement. Admittedly, the U.S. provided extensive support to the Mujahadeen, and discussed the Afghan situation and the proximity talks extensively with Pakistan, but the U.S. had not had a direct role in negotiations. The December letter changed this. At the same time, there was extensive disagreement within the U.S. government about whether the new U.S. position was authorized, and about who had authorized it.[25] Nevertheless, the U.S. was on public record as a guarantor of a not-yet-concluded agreement.

Meanwhile, during the December 1985 sixth round of Afghan-Pakistani proximity talks, Afghan Foreign Minister Mohammed Dost showed Diego Cordovez the text of an Afghan-Soviet agreement on Soviet troop withdrawals. Pleased with the text, Cordovez submitted to the Afghans and the Pakistanis a draft memorandum of understanding based on the Afghan-Soviet text.[26] For the first time, with both the stated U.S. intent to serve as a guarantor and a specifically-stated (but not public) Afghan-Soviet withdrawal timetable, concrete progress at the proximity talks appeared possible.

Despite this movement, problems remained. The United States expressed concern that the Cordovez initiative would cut off all external aid to the Mujahadeen as soon as it went into effect, and that the Soviets would then under the Cordovez initiative have six months to withdraw and to undertake offensives against the weakening Mujahadeen.[27] An equally significant problem was that the Mujahadeen themselves had never been part of the negotiating process. Whether they would accept any agreement remained to be seen.

Indeed, a strong case could be made that the movement on the Soviet side of the ledger was designed to have an impact on international public opinion and to buy time for additional military action, not to reach a political settlement. Even Gorbachev's statement at the Twenty-Seventh Congress of the Communist Party of the Soviet Union on the U.S.S.R's position on negotiations could be interpreted in this light. To Gorbachev, Soviet troops could be withdrawn from Afghanistan:

as soon as a political settlement is reached that will ensure a real cessation of armed intervention from outside in the internal affairs of the Democratic Republic of Afghanistan and will reliably guarantee its nonresumption.[28]

In most respects, this was the same position that the Soviet Union had taken for years—Soviet forces would be withdrawn only after external aid had ended and only after a political settlement had been reached, thereby assuring the Kabul regime's survival. After almost a year of Gorbachev's rule, the Soviet position on the Afghanistan situation had changed little.

Endgame: Early 1986–April 1988

However, as 1986 continued, it became increasingly clear that the Soviet Union had in fact changed its strategy. Changes were evident in Afghan politics, in the field, and at the negotiating table. In Afghan politics, the former head of Afghanistan's secret police, Najibullah, replaced Babrak Karmal as leader of Afghanistan's ruling People's Democratic Party of Afghanistan (PDPA) in May 1986. In the field, Soviet and Afghan military activities escalated noticeably, with frequent offensives, increased firepower, and greater brutality. And in diplomatic and negotiating circles, Gorbachev and other Soviet leaders stressed their desire to withdraw forces from Afghanistan.

In May 1986, the seventh round of Afghan-Pakistani proximity talks witnessed several significant moves by Moscow through its Afghan ally.[29] For the first time, the Soviet-Afghan coalition submitted a concrete proposal for a withdrawal timetable. Although Pakistan (and the United States) rejected the proposed four year timetable as too long, at least the Soviet-Afghan coalition had made a concrete proposal. For their part, the Soviets and Afghans rejected Pakistan's three month withdrawal timetable as too short.

There were other indications of new momentum as well. At the seventh round, Afghan Foreign Minister Dost ended his insistence that he meet directly with his Pakistani counterpart, Yaqub Khan. The two sides also agreed that agreements would be legally binding. Most importantly, the Afghan government accepted simultaneous implementation of all four parts of the impending agreement. This was a critical change since it meant that Kabul—and Moscow—had abandoned their insistence on sequential implementation.

An eighth round of proximity talks began in July 1986, but achieved no major successes. Most attention for the last half of the year centered on activities away from the proximity talks. Gorbachev's July 28 Vladivostok speech was one of the major events. In this speech, the Soviet leader expressed once again the Kremlin's desire to withdraw from Afghanistan, although he did not change the formula for withdrawal. He also promised to withdraw six regiments of Soviet troops from Afghanistan.[30]

As a second major set of activities, the Soviets also accelerated the pace of combat in Afghanistan as Soviet forces increasingly employed indiscriminate bombing and ground firepower. Meanwhile, the Mujahadeen began to receive U.S.-supplied "Stinger" anti-aircraft missiles. At the same time, the promised Soviet withdrawal of six regiments proved long on show and short on substance. Three of the six regiments were anti-aircraft units with no utility in Afghanistan.

A third series of events in December 1986 and January 1987 gave grounds for renewed optimism. In his July Vladivostok speech, Gorbachev had broached the concept of "national reconciliation" for opposed groups in Afghanistan, but little else was said about it in following months. Then, in December 1986, Afghan leader Najibullah during a trip to the U.S.S.R. announced that his government had adopted "national reconciliation" as its own policy. This was a marked departure from previous Afghan government—and Soviet—denunciations of the Mujahadeen, but in keeping with Gorbachev's developing "New Thinking" on Soviet foreign policy. The question was whether this policy change—as well as Najibullah's New Year's Day 1987 speech announcing a temporary cease-fire starting on January 15, calling for open contacts with the Mujahadeen, and mentioning the possibility of a coalition government including guerilla leaders[31]—was a strategic change signifying a desire to end the conflict, or a tactical change designed to improve the Najibullah government's international image and divide further the Mujahadeen and their allies.

The Soviet and Afghan governments sent more signals in January 1987 that the change in policy was strategic. The Afghan government set up a Commission for National Reconciliation, which held its first meeting in January, in Kabul.[32] More importantly, Soviet Foreign Minister Edward Shevardnadze and CPSU Party Secretary and Head of the International Department Anatoli Dobrynin journeyed to Kabul in January as well. During their visit, they praised effusively the Afghan decision to adopt national reconciliation. Shevardnadze observed that "a political settlement is not a distant perspective, but a reality of today," and both Shevardnadze and Dobrynin emphasized that the success of national reconciliation would lead to the withdrawal of Soviet troops from Afghanistan.[33] Although no agreement was in sight, opportunities to overcome some of the stumbling blocks preventing an agreement were being established.

Meanwhile, from the American perspective, the Soviets were attempting the "Vietnamization" of the war by creating a situation that would allow them to withdraw their forces, have Afghan forces take over the fighting, and reach a political settlement to the conflict, all with the pro-Soviet Afghan government still in place. Moscow's insistence on a three to four year timetable for withdrawal also concerned U.S. officials. "The Soviet timetable of three to four years," said one U.S. State Department representative, "is a timetable for consolidation and not of withdrawal."[34]

To this point, other than promising under certain conditions to serve as a guarantor of an agreement, the U.S. still had not played a direct role in negotiations. But goaded by intimations of movements in the Soviet position, the U.S. sent Under Secretary of State for Political Affairs Michael Armacost and Presidential Special Assistant on Near East and South Asian Affairs Robert Oakley to Pakistan on January 18, 1987, to discuss Afghanistan with Pakistani officials. Soviet Deputy Foreign Minister Anatoly Kovalyev visited Islamabad on January 17, and met the same Pakistani officials the U.S. representatives did. The U.S. saw the Soviet move as an effort to influence Pakistan before Washington could.[35]

But once again, the optimism raised in December and January dissipated in February and March. In February, Soviet commandos and paratroopers launched a major offensive against Mujahadeen bases, breaking the three week old cease-fire,[36] At the end of the month, large-scale Afghan bombing raids on Mujahadeen bases in Pakistan nearly led to a Pakistani walk-out from the ninth round of the proximity talks.[37] Tension between Pakistan and Afghanistan escalated further in late March when Afghan planes attacked Afghan refugee and Mujahadeen targets in Pakistan once again, killing over 180 people, and when Pakistan a week later shot down an Afghan plane that ventured into Pakistan. In the first three months of 1987, Afghan planes violated Pakistan's airspace 323 times, compared to 251 times in all of 1985 and 757 times in 1986.[38]

Meanwhile, the Mujahadeen also escalated the war, firing 288 rockets at Kandahar Airport in early March. Additionally, the United States provided the Mujahadeen with more and more "Stinger" surface-to-air missiles, which the Afghan insurgents used to devastating effect. In March, they destroyed at least 15 Soviet and Afghan aircraft.[39]

Quietly, though, the search for a political solution to the conflict moved forward. After the Pakistanis decided to stay at February's ninth round of proximity talks, they increased the time they found acceptable for a Soviet withdrawal from four months to seven months. Importantly, the Soviets reduced the time they insisted upon from four years to 18 months. The question of the composition of the regime that would rule Afghanistan after the Soviet withdrawal was also discussed, although nothing was resolved.[40]

Another channel of possible settlement also opened in early 1987 as Soviet, American, and Pakistani diplomats, all apparently individually, established contacts with Zahir Shah, the former king of Afghanistan, in Rome. Zahir Shah still enjoyed extensive support in Afghanistan, and had potential to be a bridge between Najibullah's People's Democratic Party of Afghanistan (PDPA) and the Mujahadeen.[41] However, neither the PDPA nor the Mujahadeen had been in contact with Zahir Shah. With neither of the two in-country antagonists pursuing contacts with the former king, the contacts that others had with him were clearly merely exploratory.

Throughout the rest of 1987, the U.S.S.R. provided several more indications that it was prepared to withdraw militarily from Afghanistan. But at the same time, it gave no indication that it intended to abandon Najibullah and the PDPA. In May, Gorbachev expressed a willingness to accept Zahir Shah as a member of a post-Soviet withdrawal coalition government.[42] Other Soviet sources implied that the Kremlin was prepared to talk directly with the Mujahadeen in an international conference that would include the U.S.S.R., the U.S., Pakistan, the Kabul regime, and the Mujahadeen.[43] And in December, the Kremlin declared it was ready to withdraw its forces from Afghanistan within twelve months of a political settlement, down from the 18 months it had argued for in March.[44] At the same time, the Soviets stepped up their military activity throughout Afghanistan, but the cost frequently was high.

The last few months of 1987 and the first few months of 1988 offered a dizzying panorama of public and private maneuvering by almost all the actors involved in the Afghanistan drama. In November, just before the Washington Summit at which the Intermediate Nuclear Forces (INF) Treaty was signed, Soviet sources aired rumors that a Soviet military withdrawal was imminent.[45] During late 1987, the U.S.S.R. also began indirect contacts with the Mujahadeen through Pakistan's orthodox Jamaat-e-Islami party. These contacts were aimed at exploring possible directions for a political settlement in Afghanistan, including a post-withdrawal government. Meanwhile, senior Soviet and U.S. officials travelled respectively to Afghanistan and Pakistan to conduct talks.[46] During his January 1988 trip to Pakistan, U.S. Under Secretary of State for Political Affairs Michael Armacost met with Mujahadeen leaders, and one of them informed the American that Afghan insurgents were ready "to undertake arrangements that would facilitate the orderly withdrawal" of Soviet troops.[47] During his January 4–6 trip to Afghanistan, Soviet Foreign Minister Shevardnadze declared that the Kremlin would like 1988 to be "the last year of the presence of Soviet troops" in Afghanistan. Implicitly, Shevardnadze made it clear that the U.S.S.R. had become more concerned about its own withdrawal than about the future of Najibullah or the PDPA.[48]

But it was left to Mikhail Gorbachev in a February 8, 1988 statement to establish the conditions that brought the endgame to a close. In his statement, Gorbachev declared that Moscow and Kabul had agreed that if agreements were signed by March 15, the Soviet withdrawal could begin on May 15 and be completed within 10 months. This was two months faster than the best previous Soviet withdrawal offer, but two months longer than Pakistan and the Mujahadeen wanted. Gorbachev also agreed to the U.S. "front-loading" formula, that is, the U.S. insistence that a larger portion of Soviet troops be withdrawn at the beginning of the withdrawal process than at the end. Another major Soviet concession was Gorbachev's observation that it was "none of our business" about what form of government ruled in Kabul following the U.S.S.R.'s withdrawal.[49] This could not have been too pleasing to Najibullah, but it underscored how far the Kremlin's position had evolved over time.

Immediately after Gorbachev's statement, Soviet Deputy Foreign Minister Yuli Vorontsov, on February 10–11, journeyed to Pakistan to meet with senior government officials there. In his meetings, Vorontsov stressed that Gorbachev's statement opened the opportunity for a rapid settlement of the Afghan problem, that Pakistan should not delay a settlement, and that the internal settlement in Afghanistan was a matter for the Afghans themselves.[50] Pakistan's Minister of State for Foreign Affairs Zain Noorani travelled to Washington on February 17 for discussions on Afghanistan with the U.S. According to Noorani, the U.S. supported Pakistan's insistence on creating a coalition government before an agreement was signed.

On February 23, discussions between U.S. Secretary of State George Shultz and Mikhail Gorbachev in Moscow moved the American and Soviet positions on Afghan negotiations closer together. Going into the Moscow talks, Shultz had expressed support for the creation of a coalition government in Kabul before an agreement was signed. At the end of the talks, Shultz stated only that such a government would be "desirable," but that the issue was "fundamentally up to the Afghans."[51] The U.S. was now closer to the Soviet position than to the Pakistani position.

On March 2, another round of the Geneva proximity talks opened. After two weeks, despite pledges by all involved parties to reach a quick solution, the talks were deadlocked. Pakistan continued to insist on a coalition government before an agreement could be reached, and the Soviets and Kabul insisted that the form of a future Afghan government was an internal Afghan affair. A second sticking point was U.S. insistence that the Kremlin end military aid to the Afghan government when the U.S. cut off its aid to the Mujahadeen. Soviet spokesmen argued this was not a part of the Geneva negotiations.[52] By mid-March, then, the optimism of early 1988 was beginning to fade once again.

On March 17, the Soviets stated that even if no agreement was reached in Geneva, they would remove their troops anyway. At a series of Shevardnadze-Shultz talks in Washington on March 22–23, the Kremlin even promised to withdraw its forces by the end of 1988, but would not agree to end aid to the Kabul regime. When the U.S. would not change its position on insisting for a simultaneous end to U.S. and Soviet aid, Shevardnadze simply warned that "the Afghan question can be resolved without U.S. guarantees."[53]

After his Washington visit, Shevardnadze returned to Moscow and then went on to Kabul on April 3. Four days later, Afghan leader Najibullah and Mikhail Gorbachev himself both flew to Tashkent, and issued a declaration that committed the Soviets and the Kabul regime to act in accord with Gorbachev's February 8 statement, including beginning the Soviet withdrawal on May 15. Notably, in its discussion of the formation of a coalition government, the statement did not mention Najibullah's PDPA.[54]

From that point, events moved rapidly. On April 8, U.N. Special Envoy Cordovez declared the accords on Afghanistan would be ready to sign on April 14. The same day, Gorbachev told CPSU party leaders in Tashkent that the Politburo had "found approaches" to obtain a settlement. On April 10, Gorbachev affirmed that Soviet troops would begin their withdrawal on May 15. On April 13, George Shultz flew to Geneva, and on April 14, the accords were signed.

What had happened to the two major outstanding points of disagreement? Pakistan's desire for a coalition government had been ignored, with Islamabad acceding to a U.N. statement issued through Diego Cordovez and supported by all four involved governments that "all concerned will therefore promote the endeavors of the Afghan people to work out arrangements for a broad-based government and will support and facilitate that process."[55] As for the American insistence that Soviet aid stop when U.S. aid stopped, the Soviets essentially gave in to the U.S. position by insisting through Shevardnadze that Soviet aid to the Kabul government was justified, and that the Geneva accords called for the end of external "interference but not aid" to the Mujahadeen."[56] Hence the way was cleared for the April 14 signing.

Afterward: Afghanistan Since the Accords

The Soviet withdrawal started on schedule on May 15, and nine months later on February 15, 1989, the last Soviet combat forces withdrew from Afghanistan. There were occasional allegations of too-slow Soviet withdrawal during the nine month interregnum, and after the withdrawal, some reports indicated that small contingents of Soviet forces remained or had been reintroduced to Afghanistan. Other reports indicates that Soviet aircraft carried out bombing attacks against targets in Afghanistan from bases within the U.S.S.R. But nevertheless, the key point remained, on February 15, 1989, Soviet combat forces left Afghanistan.

But fighting continued. The Geneva accords did not end the Afghan war, but reduced the level of overt superpower involvement in the war. The Mujahadeen, who from the first had never been parties to the proximity talks, fought on, still receiving aid (although at more limited levels) from the U.S. and other sources. The Soviets, for their part, continued to provide military and economic assistance and advice to the Najibullah government, which despite everyone's expectations to the contrary, continued to survive, if not prosper.

Throughout the withdrawal process, the Soviet government gave indications that it was distancing itself from but not abandoning the PDPA. At one time, Gorbachev indicated that the PDPA's role in a new government in Afghanistan would depend on its "capacity for constructiveness,"[57] and after Soviet Deputy Foreign Minister Yuli Vorontsov was named Ambassador to Kabul in October 1988, he made it clear throughout his 11 month ambassadorial tenure that his country sought a political solution to the continuing conflict that might or might not include the PDPA. Eduard Shevardnadze made the same point when he visited Najibullah in Kabul in January 1989.[58]

Moscow also conducted direct negotiations with several Mujahadeen commanders following the 1988 Geneva accords.[59] Vorontsov himself engaged in some of the dialogue, and also travelled to Rome to meet with former Afghan King Zahir Shah in December 1988.[60] Earlier, in November, the Soviet government proposed a U.N.-sponsored conference to arrange for a nonaligned, neutral, and demilitarized Afghanistan. Gorbachev repeated this call in his December 7, 1988 U.N. speech, during which he also called for an Afghan ceasefire, an end to outside arms deliveries by all forces, and the deployment of a U.N. peacekeeping force to Kabul.[61] All indications were the Soviets were serious about their desire to end the conflict, and they were not confident about the future of Najibullah.

Nevertheless, Najibullah survived on into 1989 and 1990. One reason for this was that the cooperation that had occasionally been displayed between Mujahadeen forces during the Soviet occupation of Afghanistan dissipated rapidly during and after the Soviet withdrawal. But a second reason for Najibullah's survival was the Kremlin's provision of large quantities of military aid. Direct Soviet military assistance to the Afghan regime was higher in 1988 than in 1987, and higher again in 1989 than 1988. Indeed, between March 1989 and July 1989, the Kremlin provided Najibullah's government with 550 SCUD missiles, 160 T-55 and T-62 tanks, 615 armed personnel carriers, and 1,600 five-ton trucks.[62] Soviet troops had withdrawn, but Soviet support for Najibullah, the PDPA, and the Afghan government had not ended.

The United States continued to provide military assistance to the Mujahadeen as well, primarily because the United States by 1990 had achieved only one of its policy objectives in Afghanistan, the removal of Soviet forces. Others still remained, as restated by a senior U.S. official in April 1990, including the establishment of a representative Afghan government through self-determination, the return of refugees to Afghanistan, and the establishment of an independent and nonaligned Afghanistan.[63]

Nevertheless, because of the changing international situation and the seeming irrelevance of Afghan affairs to most Americans in the light of those changes, pressures built for an American policy alteration. More and more Americans including several prominent Congressional leaders openly questioned where U.S. policy was headed. Therefore, when in February 1990 Soviet General Secretary Gorbachev proposed on the first anniversary of the Soviet withdrawal from Afghanistan a ten-point peace plan that included a ceasefire, an end to U.S. and Soviet arms shipments to the respective sides, and a proposal for an externally supervised election, the American response, although negative, showed distinct signs of change. The U.S. dropped its insistence that Najibullah renounce power immediately; accepted the possibility of an interim role for him as a new government was formed; and saw some wisdom in the termination of Soviet and American arms shipments.

By May 1990, more movement had occurred. During discussions between Baker and Shevardnadze in Moscow in May, the U.S. and the U.S.S.R. agreed that elections should be held, supervised by the United Nations and the Conference of Islamic Countries; that Najibullah could run for the presidency if he first surrendered power to an international authority; and the PDPA could participate in the elections as a political party. The Americans and the Soviets had compromised. The Soviets now accepted elections (they previously had opposed elections, fearing the PDPA would be badly defeated), and the Americans were now willing to permit Najibullah and the PDPA to possibly participate in a future government. Problems still existed over arranging a transitional authority and over convincing Najibullah to step aside during the transition, but the Americans and Soviets had come a long way.

The two foreign secretaries made further progress during their August 1990 Irkutsk meeting and their December 1990 Houston meeting. Thus, by the end of 1990, the two sides agreed on the need for a ceasefire, a transitional period leading up to a general election, the establishment of a representative coordinating body to govern Afghanistan during the transition period, and an end to weapons deliveries to the combatants. However, they disagreed over how to achieve many of these agreed-upon needs. The Kremlin also evidenced concern that, even in the event of a U.S.-Soviet agreement to curtail arms shipments to Afghanistan, the Mujahadeen could continue to receive arms from Iran, Pakistan, Saudi Arabia, and elsewhere as well. Importantly, however, the U.S. and the U.S.S.R. agreed to work with each other and with the combatants in Afghanistan to narrow the disagreements.

Further U.S.-Soviet discussions during the first half of 1991 produced no major breakthroughs on these disagreements. Nevertheless, in May, the Bush administration significantly altered American policy by omitting from the U.S. federal budget for the first time since 1980 a request for funding for the Mujahadeen. But Afghanistan was not—and never had been—exclusively an American-Soviet issue. The Mujahadeen, Pakistan, and Najibullah himself opposed all or part of the proposed American-Soviet concept. Most Mujahadeen continued to view Najibullah and the PDPA as anti-Islamic, and refused to accept a ceasefire as long as Najibullah ruled the DRA. Even Najibullah's continued offers for national reconciliation, negotiations, and a coalition government failed to dissuade many Mujahadeen from continuing their efforts to overthrow the PDPA government.

The negotiating process, then, had been a partial success for the United States. One primary U.S. objective had been achieved, but other major goals had not been. U. S. officials admitted that they had miscalculated the strength and staying power of Najibullah's government, but would not state for the record if they would have negotiated differently or reached different conclusions if they had realized Najibullah would survive. As for the Soviets, negotiations must be regarded as a nearly complete success. Soviet forces were withdrawn, and despite the Kremlin's apparent willingness to accept the collapse of the regime it had installed, that did not happen until April 1992. From the U.S. and Soviet perspectives, then, both sides were better off with the conditions that prevailed in Afghanistan at the start of the new decade than during most of the old, but for the Afghans themselves, the killings continued.

U.S. and Soviet Peacemaking in Cambodia

Until very late in the 1980s, neither the U.S. nor the Soviet Union had an extensive role in efforts to manage, deescalate, and resolve the Cambodian conflict. In many respects, American unwillingness to become involved in Cambodian affairs may best be explained as a continuation of the U.S. Vietnam War "hangover." Additionally, U.S. policy was complicated by the continuing issue of 2,500 U.S. servicemen listed as missing in action. For most of the 1980s, the United States therefore remained satisfied to follow the lead of the Association of Southeast Asian Nations (ASEAN) in policies towards Cambodia. For the U.S., the primary concern relating to Cambodia until 1989 was the Soviet-Vietnamese relationship. Following the Vietnamese withdrawal from Cambodia in 1989, the U.S. chief concern became preventing the return to power of the Khmer Rouge.

Meanwhile, the Soviet Union had been relatively satisfied with the situation in Cambodia throughout the early and middle 1980s. Throughout this period, the Soviets gave constant and unquestioning military and diplomatic support to Vietnam in the Cambodian conflict. At the same time, the Kremlin acquired for itself military bases in Vietnam at Camranh Bay and Danang, provided itself with a strategic foothold on China's southern flank, and established itself as a political player in Southeast Asia. The U.S.S.R. funnelled as much as five to six billion dollars per year in military and economic assistance to Vietnam,[64] but to the Kremlin, the benefits were well worth the costs.

Throughout the 1980s, the primary tasks of Soviet diplomacy in Southeast Asia were to expand its own role in the region, to minimize Chinese and U.S. influence there, and to prevent the establishment of an effective anti-Vietnamese front.[65] After Gorbachev acquired power, Soviet spokesmen began to call for the resolution of the Cambodian conflict as well as national reconciliation in Cambodia. Nevertheless, the Kremlin continually asserted that the Cambodian conflict was caused by Chinese, ASEAN, and U.S. meddling, and that the end result of any political settlement must be the continuation of the Vietnamese-installed regime in Cambodia, although perhaps Cambodian resistance forces other than the Khmer Rouge could be included. Additionally, the Soviet role in Cambodia was complicated by Sino-Soviet and Sino-Vietnamese bilateral relations.

For our purposes here, that is, the analysis of U.S. and Soviet roles in peacemaking in Cambodia, international efforts to find a solution to the Cambodian conflict can best be divided into five periods. Each period will again be discussed separately.

Conflict Without Negotiations: January 1979–June 1982

The roots of the Vietnamese invasion of Cambodia extend far back into history, but the proximate causes of the invasion were attacks by Pol Pot's Khmer Rouge regime against Vietnam throughout its rule from 1975 to 1978; the carnage caused in Cambodia by the Khmer Rouge during their rule; Vietnam's long-standing desire to create a federation of Indochinese states with itself at the head; and Vietnam's assurance of Soviet support, codified in the November 1978 Soviet-Vietnamese Treaty of Friendship and Cooperation.

Vietnam's December 1978 invasion quickly overthrew Pol Pot and established a client government, the People's Republic of Kampuchea (PRK), under Heng Samrin. But in February 1979, China launched a "punishment operation" against Vietnam. This "punishment operation" did not go well for the Chinese, but it elevated the Vietnamese occupation of Cambodia to a new level of international concern.

Unfortunately for the Vietnamese, they had also failed to "mop up" all Khmer Rouge elements during their invasion. These elements returned to the jungle and launched a guerrilla war against the Vietnamese occupiers.[66]

Many operated from base camps near and in Thailand. This opened yet another channel in the Cambodian drama as Thailand and increasingly other ASEAN states became involved in the conflict as well. Indeed, by fall 1979, ASEAN managed to gather together 91 countries to vote for its U.N. resolution condemning Vietnam for its invasion of Cambodia.

During 1980, Vietnamese forces launched several attacks against Cambodian refugees and Khmer Rouge guerrillas in Thailand. Vietnam's actions not only drove the ASEAN alliance closer together, but also led the United States to undertake a four day airlift of munitions to Thailand. As for negotiations, Vietnam continued to argue that the Cambodian situation was irreversible. Given this Vietnamese attitude, and given the insistence of the Cambodian resistance, China, and ASEAN states that the Vietnamese-installed PRK government was illegitimate, it was not surprising that the diplomatic contacts between a number of regional states concerning the Cambodian conflict during 1979 and 1980 did not lead to any negotiations on Cambodia.

The major event regarding negotiations in 1981 occurred in July when the United Nations sponsored a major international conference on Cambodia in New York. Vietnam, the Soviet Union, and most Eastern European countries did not participate, but 93 other countries did, including the United States. However, ASEAN's resolution calling for the disarmament of all U.N. factions, the withdrawal of Vietnamese forces, and the holding of free elections did not pass, primarily because China opposed disarming the Khmer Rouge. The U.S. supported China's position, hoping that it might influence China on future Indochina-related issues.[67]

Meanwhile, Vietnam was willing to accept a political solution to the Cambodian situation only if it was completely on her own terms: Hanoi asserted that it would withdraw some of its troops from Cambodia only if all supplies reaching Cambodian insurgents were blocked, and if Cambodian insurgent forces in Thailand were completely disarmed. Of course, this would have left Vietnamese troops in Cambodia fighting against insurgents whose capabilities would be steadily dwindling. Inevitably, Vietnam's "solution" would have left the PRK government in power. The Soviets supported Vietnam's positions unquestioningly. There were no discernible differences between Vietnamese and Soviet positions.

Deadend Diplomacy: June 1982–Early 1985

After considerable pressure from China and ASEAN, the three leading anti-PRK insurgent groups banded together in June 1982 to form the Coalition Government of Democratic Kampuchea (CGDK). Consisting of the Khmer Rouge, Prince Norodom Sihanouk's Sinanoukist Liberation Army (ANS), and Son Sann's Kampuchean People's National Liberation

Front (KPNLF), the CGDK did little inside Cambodia to strengthen the anti-Vietnamese/PRK opposition. However, it did increase the international credibility of the anti-PRK forces, and it provided the Khmer Rouge with a veneer of respectability that they previously did not have. The coalition also provided the ANS and the KPNLF with additional fighting capability in the field. Importantly, the alliance also solidified for China an avenue via Thailand through which it had been providing support to the Khmer Rouge. At the same time, the leaders of the CGDK disliked one another intensely, and disagreed continually over policy. The CGDK was purely a marriage of convenience.

Throughout this period, several states outside Southeast Asia including India, Japan, and Australia sought to mediate the conflict, but none made any headway.[68] At the same time, ASEAN and the CGDK occasionally put forward proposals of their own. They too achieved little. Vietnam proposed political solutions as well, even as it launched major military operations against insurgent forces every dry season. Meanwhile, as before, the Soviet Union completely supported Vietnam's positions, while the United States followed ASEAN's lead on the Cambodian conflict. Neither superpower expended any diplomatic effort to arrange or participate in negotiations.

By early 1985, then, there appeared to be no solution to the Cambodian conflict. Vietnam's occupation of the country appeared ordained to continue, and perhaps over time even be accepted by the international community. The Soviet Union supported Vietnam's occupation of Cambodia and the PRK government in every respect, and provided the wherewithal for Vietnam's military adventures. Meanwhile, despite the Reagan Doctrine, the United States provided no material support to the CGDK. The U.S. condemned the Vietnamese occupation of Cambodia and supported the CGDK diplomatically, but it did nothing to try to arrange a political solution to the conflict. U.S. and Soviet diplomats met on occasion to discuss the Cambodian situation, but in every sense of the word, a stalemate was in place in Cambodia.

Soviet Pressures, Economic Problems, and Diplomatic Pre-Negotiations: Early 1985–July 1988

All this was about to change,but slowly. Changes were closely related to three factors, Vietnamese military successes in Cambodia, the accession to power of Mikhail Gorbachev in Moscow in March 1985, and Vietnam's worsening economic situation.[69]

The impact that Vietnam's military successes in 1984–85 had on Vietnam's attitudes toward the Cambodian situationout is easy to detail. In December 1984, Vietnam launched a major dry season offensive that by March 1985 gave it control of 15 CGDK base camps and allowed it to seal much of the Cambodian-Thai border. Given these results, Vietnam's Foreign Minister Nguyen Co Thach declared in April 1985 that Vietnam would withdraw its forces from Cambodia by 1995. In August, he moved the date up to 1990.

On the second point, at first, little appeared to change following Gorbachev's assumption of the General Secretary's position. Indeed, when Konstantin Chernenko died and Mikhail Gorbachev replaced him as CPSU general secretary, Vietnam sent a 16-man delegation headed by Vietnamese Prime Minister Pham Van Dong and Politburo member Truong Chinh to Moscow to attend the funeral. Truong Chinh and Gorbachev met "in an atmosphere of fraternal friendship" and had "complete identity of views."[70]

Nevertheless, Hanoi was undoubtedly concerned about several aspects of the new Soviet leader's intentions. For one thing, Gorbachev clearly intended to have his country undertake more initiatives in Southeast Asia on its own. Indeed, in March and April 1985, Soviet Deputy Foreign Minister Mikhail Kapitsa spent a month travelling through East Asia. On numerous occasions, especially in Beijing, he declared that the U.S.S.R. wanted to be a "peacebroker" in Southeast Asia.[71] In early May, the Kremlin also agreed to act as a go-between for ASEAN and Vietnam, carrying ASEAN's proposal for "proximity talks" between Cambodian factions to the Vietnamese and Cambodian governments.[72]

Similarly, Gorbachev intended to improve relations with China. In April 1985, Deng Xiaoping acted to improve Sino-Soviet relations as well by announcing that as far as China was concerned, the U.S.S.R. could keep its military bases in Vietnam if the Vietnamese withdrew from Cambodia.[73] Throughout 1985 and early 1986, the pace of improvement in Sino-Soviet relations quickened as Soviet and Chinese officials continued to meet. The most important meeting took place in December 1985 when Soviet Deputy Foreign Minister Mikhail Kapitsa visited Beijing for 10 days.

Hanoi was also concerned about the impact that improving U.S.-Soviet relations may have had on Moscow's willingness to support Vietnam's Cambodia adventure. In October, U.S. President Ronald Reagan called on the U.S.S.R. publicly to help resolve regional conflicts including Cambodia,[74] and the resolution of regional conflicts was an agenda item on the November 1985 Reagan-Gorbachev Geneva summit meeting.

On the third point, Vietnam's domestic economic and political situations were also critical elements in the equation that led to Vietnam's announcement that it intended to withdraw from Cambodia. Throughout 1985, the Vietnamese Communist Party instituted a series of economic reforms that made it evident the Vietnamese leadership understood how dire their country's economic position was. And politically, 1986 brought major changes to Vietnam's leadership when long-time party leader Le Duan died in July 1986, and when in December, 1986 Nguyen Van Linh, generally viewed as a reformer, was named the new CPV general secretary during the CPV's Sixth Congress. Significantly, at this Congress, delegates agreed unanimously that "renovation" (canh tan) was necessary throughout the Vietnamese economy.

The extent to which the Soviet Union pressured or influenced Vietnamese leaders to move toward economic renovation is not clear, but there were clear manifestations of Soviet desires for Vietnam to institute economic reforms. With both Vietnamese and Soviet sources acknowledging that Vietnam wasted Soviet economic aid,[75] continued Soviet provision of large quantities of economic aid in the absence of changed Vietnamese management practices simply could not have been acceptable to the Kremlin. As if to drive this point home, the Kremlin sent its number-two Politburo member, Igor Ligachev, to Hanoi for the December 1986 CPV Congress, where he offered both additional Soviet aid and warned in no uncertain terms that Soviet aid to Vietnam must not be wasted.[76]

Even so, throughout 1985 and 1986, no significant movement toward negotiations on Cambodia took place. ASEAN and other third countries occasionally proposed discussions, but always, one or another of the primary parties in the Cambodian conflict found problems with the proposed talks. The Soviet Union consistently supported Vietnam's positions on negotiations despite Moscow's growing desire to have the Cambodian conflict end. Meanwhile, the United States retained its low profile in the conflict, although it did begin to provide non-lethal assistance to the non-communist Cambodian insurgents. Even here, however, the low priority that the United States attached to the conflict was evident as the U.S. Congress authorized five million dollars per year in aid, and the executive branch provided only 3.35 million dollars per year. As before, the United States took no active role in efforts to arrange negotiations between the warring Indochinese parties, although American diplomats continued to have occasional conversations on Cambodia with their Soviet, Chinese, and ASEAN counterparts.

As 1987 opened, it was also growing increasingly clear that three specific aspects of New Thinking directly affected Soviet-Vietnamese relations, and raised Hanoi's concerns about the course of future Soviet policy. These three aspects were Gorbachev's accelerated drive to improve relations with China, the implications of New Thinking for Soviet military presence in Southeast Asia, and whether the U.S.S.R. even in the short-term would continue to support Vietnam's military occupation of Cambodia.

Gorbachev's accelerated drive to improve Sino-Soviet relations evoked especially great concern in Hanoi. Gorbachev frequently emphasized that under New Thinking, the Soviet Union intended to pursue friendly relations with China. For example, in his July 1986 Vladivostok speech,

Gorbachev praised the "noticeable improvement in relations" that had taken place between Moscow and Beijing, and called for even closer Sino-Soviet relations in the future.[77] At least in part because of New Thinking, the Soviets and the Chinese solved their border dispute along the Amur River, began building a cross-border railway, and signed a series of new trade agreements. Additionally, the entire political climate of Sino-Soviet relations improved noticeably. Indeed, by the time Chinese and Soviet representatives met in Beijing for the eleventh round of political consultations in October 1987, the Cambodian question was the only apparent major area of disagreement. When in subsequent meetings the Soviets and Chinese narrowed their disagreement over Cambodia,[78] Vietnam's concern that its interests would be jettisoned by the Soviets in favor of improved Moscow-Beijing relations escalated even more. Gorbachev's decision to visit China in May 1989 added to Vietnam's fears.

New Thinking also implied that the Soviet Union should rely less on military parameters of power in its efforts to achieve foreign policy objectives. This clearly had implications for the Soviet Union's military presence at Cam Ranh and Da Nang. In the pre-Gorbachev era, Vietnam recognized that the U.S.S.R.'s desire to retain port and airfield rights at Cam Ranh and Da Nang gave it a certain degree of leverage over the U.S.S.R.

However, as early as July 1986, Gorbachev in his Vladivostok speech implied that he would be willing to end the U.S.S.R.'s military presence in Vietnam if the United States ended its military presence in the Philippines. This caused Vietnam's leaders to wonder if they retained as much leverage as they previously believed they had had. When Gorbachev made an explicit base-trade offer in his September 1988 Krasnoyarsk speech,[79] Hanoi's concerns about its leverage over the U.S.S.R. escalated even more.[80]

As serious as both the Sino-Soviet and access rights issues were, the impact of New Thinking on the Kremlin's willingness to continue supporting Hanoi's military occupation of Cambodia was even more foreboding as seen from Hanoi. Even though the U.S.S.R. had supported Vietnam's policy positions ever since Vietnam invaded Cambodia in 1978, it became gradually clear after Gorbachev's accession to power that the Kremlin preferred that Vietnam withdraw from Cambodia.

There were several reasons for this. First, Vietnam's occupation of Cambodia complicated the Kremlin's efforts to improve relations with China. Second, it also frustrated Soviet efforts to better relations with other Southeast Asian states. Similarly, Soviet support for Vietnam's presence in Cambodia affected adversely Soviet-U.S. relations, Soviet-European relations, and Soviet relations with much of the Third World. With New Thinking insisting that political solutions were preferable to military solutions in resolving regional conflicts, and with so many Soviet foreign policy objectives being complicated by Vietnam's occupation of Cambodia, it was understandable that the Kremlin wanted Vietnam to withdraw.

Perhaps surprisingly, however, the Soviet Union manifested no overt pressure on Vietnam to leave Cambodia. Instead, Moscow preferred to maintain a public posture of solidarity with Vietnam on issues related to Cambodia. Thus, the Soviets supported not only the Vietnamese occupation of Cambodia, but also Vietnam's stated intention to withdraw from Cambodia by 1990 and Vietnam's preference for a postwithdrawal political settlement. Occasionally, the Soviets also observed that a solution to the Cambodian problem depended on "normalization of Sino-Vietnamese relations."[81]

However, in late 1986, the Soviets began to assume a more active posture on Cambodia. At the ninth session of Sino-Soviet political consultations, held in Beijing, October 6–14, 1986, the Soviets for the first time discussed Cambodia with the Chinese. Although the two sides made little progress, the fact that the two sides even discussed Cambodia was a significant step. Six months later, in April 1987, the U.S.S.R. and China again examined Cambodian issues at the tenth session of Sino-Soviet political consultations.[82]

Evidence also began to mount in early 1987 that Vietnam and the Soviet Union did not see eye-to-eye on how the Cambodian conflict should end. This disagreement was apparent during CPV General Secretary Nguyen Van Linh's May 1987 trip to the Soviet Union. While in Moscow, Linh insisted that a political settlement in Cambodia exclude the "Pol Pot clique" from the Khmer Rouge, but Gorbachev in his own speech failed to mention such a condition.[83] Even more telling, the final communiqué for the meeting observed that "an in-depth exchange of views" had taken place "in an atmosphere of traditional friendship and mutual understanding." The final communiqué also offered the curious formula that national reconciliation in Cambodia had to be achieved through "political means" with "the involvement in this or that form of all sides concerned."[84]

Meanwhile, the Soviet Union quietly pursued a series of diplomatic contacts with Thailand, Indonesia, and Malaysia in an effort to impart new momentum to relations between the Soviets and the Association of Southeast Asian Nations (ASEAN) and the Cambodian negotiating process. More proof of the Kremlin's desire to resolve the Cambodian conflict was evident in the Soviet efforts to arrange a meeting between Cambodian Premier Hun Sen and resistance leader Prince Norodom Sihanouk.[85] Eventually, the two Cambodians met in Paris in early December 1987. They agreed that a political solution to the war had to be found involving all parties and guaranteed by an international conference.

The Soviets also tried to influence the Cambodian government to meet with Khieu Samphan, the Khmer Rouge leader, but this time they were not successful.[86] The emerging peace process was further complicated in January, following the second Sihanouk-Hun Sen meeting when Sihanouk refused to continue discussions unless he also met with Vietnamese officials. The Vietnamese refused. For all practical purposes, the process had become deadlocked. What is important here is the fact that the Vietnamese had blocked an initiative launched by the Soviets. Thus, it was evident that Vietnam and the U.S.S.R. disagreed over the urgency of ending the conflict, the way in which the conflict should be ended, or both.

Despite Vietnam's unwillingness to meet with Sihanouk, the Soviets continued to try to find the key to a political settlement. Soviet and U.S. officials met on a number of occasions in the first half of 1988 to discuss Cambodia, and in March, Soviet Deputy Foreign Minister Igor Rogachev met with Indochinese deputy foreign ministers in Phnom Penh. At the meeting, the deputy foreign ministers agreed to speed up efforts to achieve national reconciliation. Following his Phnom Penh visit, Rogachev travelled to the Philippines, Malaysia, Thailand, and Indonesia. Cambodia figured prominently in discussions in all four countries, but the real key to a Cambodian settlement remained Vietnam. Through March, Hanoi had changed its positions little, despite continued Soviet prodding.[87]

This soon changed. In April, Nguyen Van Linh visited Moscow and told the Soviets that Vietnam's withdrawal from Cambodia would be accelerated, and that Hanoi would strengthen its efforts to improve relations with China. The following month, the Vietnamese announced they would withdraw 50,000 troops from Cambodia by the end of 1988 and reaffirmed their intention to complete the withdrawal by 1990. Additionally, Hanoi confirmed that a Vietnamese delegation would attend the resurrected "cocktail party" negotiations, known as the Jakarta Informal Meeting (JIM-I), scheduled to begin in late July 1988. The Soviets profusely praised these Vietnamese positions.

For their part, the Vietnamese remained concerned about the implications of the steady improvement in Sino-Soviet relations for Soviet-Vietnamese relations. Indeed, even though the Kremlin verbally supported Vietnam in March 1988 when the Chinese-Vietnamese dispute over the Spratly Islands escalated once again,[88] the Soviet position had no visible impact on Sino-Soviet relations.

On the eve of the JIM-I, CPV General Secretary Nguyen Van Linh visited the U.S.S.R., ostensibly for a vacation. During his stay in Moscow, he met with Gorbachev, and the two men agreed that their countries were "prepared actively to facilitate the defusing of the situation" in Cambodia. They also noted that China could make a "weighty contribution" to the resolution of the Cambodian problem, and expressed high hopes for the JIM-I.[89]

From JIM-I to Paris: July 1988–August 1989

Despite Linh's and Gorbachev's optimism, the talks produced little other than an agreement to meet again. Nevertheless, that the talks had taken place was significant in itself, since they were the first time that all of the primary parties to the conflict had met together at the same location. The U.S.S.R. had played only a limited role in arranging the talks, by applying pressure to Vietnam. The U.S. had had next to no role.

The Soviet Union made known its position on the JIM-I in an August 3 Ministry of Foreign Affairs statement praising the participants and affirming its own "readiness to contribute . . . to the development of the process of settlement" in Cambodia.[90] Throughout the rest of 1988, the Soviets continued to stress the need for a political settlement, national reconciliation, and their own willingness to help the peace process along. Soviet Deputy Foreign Minister Rogachev, for example, stressed all these points during his November 1988 trip to Hanoi.

Meanwhile, Vietnam had been seeking to initiate a dialogue with China on Cambodia. In November, Vietnam's Foreign Minister Thach told reporters at a Hanoi press conference that Vietnam had offered to hold talks with China on Cambodia, but China had refused. The following month Thach told the 8th Vietnamese National Assembly that Vietnam was prepared for "direct dialogue" with China on bilateral issues.[91] Clearly, Vietnam had felt pressure emanating from Moscow.

The Soviets soon turned up the pressure even more. In early February 1989, Soviet Foreign Minster Shevardnadze traveled to Beijing and reached a nine-point agreement on Cambodia with China. Among other points, the Chinese and the Soviets agreed on the need for a political solution to the conflict, "an effective control mechanism" to supervise Vietnam's withdrawal, an end to foreign military aid, the maintenance of peace in Cambodia, and free elections.[92]

By early 1989, it was clear that the Soviets were intent on a Vietnamese withdrawal from Cambodia. At the same time, they were equally intent on solidifying their emerging relationship with Beijing. New Thinking played a significant role in both of these intentions. The impact of New Thinking should not be overstated, however. Moscow's thinking was not sufficiently new to influence it to jettison its support for Vietnam's occupation of Cambodia, but only to apply pressure through a variety of means to influence Vietnam to adhere to its previously stated withdrawal date. Thus, Moscow was unwilling—or unable—to force Hanoi to withdraw from Cambodia before Hanoi was prepared to withdraw.

Throughout the first half of 1989, events proceeded that had great significance for Cambodia. These events included the JIM-II in February, in which all six ASEAN states and the four Cambodian factions reaffirmed the general framework for a settlement that had been outlined at JIM-I, but moved no further; Vietnam's April declaration that it intended to withdraw its forces from Cambodia by September, which led Prince Sihanouk to ask the French to convene a conference on Cambodia; Mikhail Gorbachev's May 15–18 trip to Beijing, during which the Soviets and Chinese reaffirmed their February foreign ministers' statement; and the June Tianenmen Square massacre in Beijing. Together, these events laid the groundwork for a major international conference on Cambodia, held in Paris, in late July and throughout August 1989.

The conference was in disarray before it started. Before the full conference began, the four Cambodian factions met in an effort to settle some of their many disagreements. They failed. Disagreements over the role of the Khmer Rouge, power sharing formulas, the composition of a transitional government, and other issues were fueled by the personal animosity and mistrust that the four factions had for each other. This virtually guaranteed that no accord could be reached among the Cambodians themselves. Consequently the Paris meeting began with several strikes against it.

Representatives from 18 nations including the United States and the Soviet Union as well as two international organizations attended the Paris Conference. All four Cambodian factions also had representatives in attendance. But in rather short order, it became apparent that the Paris talks could not move the Cambodian peace process forward not only because of continuing disagreements between the four Cambodian camps, but also because of continuing disagreement between other involved actors.[93]

Not surprisingly, one of the major issues was the role that the Khmer Rouge would play both in an interim government and in a future Cambodian government. Vietnam and the PRK (renamed the State of Cambodia, or SOC) opposed their inclusion, as did the Soviet Union. China and Sihanouk argued that the Khmer Rouge had to be included. Meanwhile, the U.S. argued that the Khmer Rouge "should play no role in Cambodia's future" but was prepared to accept their participation in an interim coalition government under Sihanouk's leadership "should he deem it necessary."[94]

An equally large issue was whether the conference should approach only the international dimensions of the Cambodian conflict or seek to achieve a comprehensive solution to the Cambodian problem that included the domestic level of conflict. Vietnam, SOC, and the Soviet Union argued that the Paris Conference should only examine international dimensions of the Cambodian problem, while the CGDK, ASEAN, China, and the United States asserted that the conference should seek a comprehensive settlement.

Another issue that frustrated the conference was the question of Vietnamese "settlers" in Cambodia. The CGDK claimed that 1.25 million Vietnamese had moved to Cambodia during Vietnam's occupation, and demanded that they be repatriated. Vietnam asserted that there were only 80 thousand Vietnamese civilians in all Cambodia, fewer than the number of ethnic Chinese there. Whatever the truth of the matter, this issue became a major sticking point between the CGDK and Vietnam.

In the final analysis, then, the Paris Conference adjourned in late August 1989 in a stalemate. Little progress had been made toward peace in Cambodia, but on the brighter side, none had been lost, either. And it remained evident that despite all the diplomatic activity that had gone on between JIM-I and Paris, the international community including the United States and the Soviet Union remained divided about Cambodia's future.

The U.S.S.R.'s disagreements with Vietnam over Cambodia and the Kremlin's willingness to apply diplomatic and economic pressure to Vietnam to influence Hanoi to adopt more flexible positions on the conflict did not indicate that Moscow was prepared to abandon Hanoi. Moscow remained unwilling or unable to convince Hanoi to accept a role for the Khmer Rouge, and unwilling to use additional tools of influence to try to change Hanoi's outlooks Importantly, the Soviet Union continued to provide Hanoi with large quantities of military assistance that enabled Hanoi to maintain its occupation of Cambodia, and had begun to funnel large quantities of military assistance to the PRK/SOC side as well. One knowledgeable Western source observed that the Soviet Union during the summer of 1989 continued "to pump war material—tanks, howitzers, multi-barrel rockets—through Kompong Som port as if there were no tomorrow."[95]

Importantly for this study, because of domestic politics and humanitarian concerns, the United States for the first time now increased its level of interest in Cambodian affairs once again as well.[96] The U.S.did not want the Khmer Rouge to return to power or the SOC to remain in power without significant alterations. The problem remained finding a formula that was acceptable to the most powerful internal Cambodian factions, the SOC and the Khmer Rouge; the one Cambodian that everyone could agree on, Norodom Sihanouk; and their primary supporters and providers, Vietnam, the Soviet Union, China, and ASEAN.

Resurgent Insurgency or Endgame? August 1989 to Today

Vietnam withdrew it troops from Cambodia on schedule, on September 26, 1989. Most observers expected a test of military strength between the two Cambodian sides to follow, and that was exactly what happened.

CGDK forces led by the Khmer Rouge stepped up their operations at once, especially in western Cambodia, and scored sizeable but not overwhelming gains. The SOC army fought reasonably well, but late in 1989 was sufficiently hard pressed that a limited contingent of Vietnamese troops and advisers returned to Cambodia.

For almost a year after the Vietnamese withdrawal, neither side came near military victory nor military collapse.[97] As it became clear that the Cambodian conflict would continue, the interrupted peace process again began to generate activity. In December 15, 1989, Australian Foreign Minister Gareth Evans proposed a peace plan based on an idea originally put forward by Stephen J. Solarz, Chairman of the U.S. House of Representatives' Subcommittee on Asian and Pacific Affairs, and modeled on the peace settlement in Namibia. According to the Evans Plan, the four Cambodian factions would form an interim coalition council that would temporarily cede political control of Cambodia to the United Nations. The UN Secretary General would then appoint a personal representative to administer the country until an election was held. At the same time, the UN would introduce a large contingent of peacekeeping forces to enforce a ceasefire. During the run-up to the elections, the four Cambodian factions would act as political parties competing for political power rather than as governments or military forces. The Evans Plan also included provisions that external sanctuaries and external military assistance must both end, and that a large-scale international relief and reconstruction program must begin immediately for Cambodia upon conclusion of an agreement.[98]

The Evans Plan generated considerable international interest, at least in part because both Prince Sihanouk and the SOC government had both earlier in December said that under certain conditions, they could accept UN involvement in elections in Cambodia.[99] Also, by placing Cambodia under UN trusteeship, the Evans Plan had potential to artfully defuse the question of whether there were two Cambodian sides—SOC and the CGDK—or four—SOC and the three factions joined together in the CGDK. If the UN became the temporary trustee of Cambodia until a free election were held, then this issue, which had long held up movement toward a political settlement, would become irrelevant—if the four (or was it two?) Cambodian factions agreed to it.

The Evans Plan was the subject of additional discussion at a January 15, 1990, Paris meeting of the five permanent members of the UN Security Council, a discussion forum not before used for Cambodia. Even though they did not specifically approve the Evans Plan, they too responded favorably to the idea of greater UN involvement in Cambodia. Indeed, as 1990 wore on, this "Perm 5" forum met several more times, and although disagreements among the group often appeared, the Perm 5 group steadily moved toward agreement on both the basis for greater UN involvement in Cambodia, and on a concrete operational plan for involvement.

The Evans Plan also served as a primary focus of discussion at three meetings in February related to Cambodia. On February 13–14, the Perm 5 group held its second meeting on Cambodia, this time in New York. On February 21, Sihanouk and Hun Sen met in Bangkok and reached agreement that UN involvement in Cambodian affairs "at an appropriate level" was acceptable to them. And on February 26–28, 1990 another major meeting was held in Jakarta "in the framework" of the suspended August 1989 Paris Conference. Called the Jakarta International Meeting on Cambodia (IMC), the meeting was attended by all four Cambodian factions, the ASEAN states, Vietnam, Laos, Australia, and France. The IMC discussed the Evans Plan, among other things,.but once again, no agreement was reached. Nevertheless, an international consensus appeared to be building around the wisdom of increasing the role of the UN in the Cambodian problem.

Despite continuing diplomatic activity on Cambodia, the next several months saw slow progress toward achieving an acceptable plan for greater UN involvement in Cambodia. No real breakthroughs occured in March, April, May, or June, but continuing diplomatic activity relating to Cambodia during this time showed that a significant portion of the international community was actively seeking to find a way to ameliorate the Cambodian problem. Despite good intentions, however, no one had yet found the proper combination of incentives to accomplish this task. Indeed, some were beginning to doubt whether such a combination of incentives actually existed.

Two related series of events in the summer of 1990, one in Cambodia and the other half a world away, provided renewed momentum to the seemingly stalled peace process. In Cambodia, the Khmer Rouge during the summer of 1990 began to make steady headway in their struggle against the SOC. Although the Phnom Penh government was not about to fall, the specter of a return to power of the Khmer Rouge shook much of the world, the United States included.[100] The Khmer Rouge's military successes led directly to a major American reappraisal of U.S. policy toward Cambodia, and toward Vietnam as well. The results of this reappraisal, based as much and possibly more on American moral and domestic political considerations as anything else, led to a significantly altered equation of forces in Cambodia, and helped move the Cambodian peace process closer to closure than it had ever been before.

The rapid movement toward an agreement on a political solution to the Cambodian problem began at the July 17, 1990 Perm 5 meeting in Paris. A U.S. summary of proceedings stated that significant progress was made toward an agreement on the composition of the Supreme National Council and on peacekeeping issues, and that additional work needed to be done on establishing mechanisms for free, fair elections; safeguarding human rights; and providing international guarantees.[101] The following day, the United States dropped the diplomatic equivalent of a bombshell. After meeting with Soviet Foreign Minister Edward Shevardnadze, U.S. Secretary of State James Baker announced that the U.S. intended to "open a dialogue on Cambodia" with Vietnam, "enhance U.S. humanitarian assistance to Cambodia," and "drop its support of the CGDK for the Cambodian seat at the UN General Assembly."[102]

Events unfolded rapidly in August. On August 6, U. S. and Vietnamese delegates met for three hours in New York at the office of Vietnam's delegation to the United Nations. Both sides were pleased with the meeting. On August 8, Chinese Prime Minister Li Peng declared that China intended to arm the Khmer Rouge as long as the SOC government received external help, but China would not support the Khmer Rouge as the dominant power in Cambodia. On August 22, the three CGDK leaders met in Beijing and agreed to meet in September with SOC representatives in Jakarta to create a Supreme National Council. On August 28, another Perm 5 meeting concluded an agreement on Cambodia that was acceptable to all five countries. The agreement included but was not limited to a ceasefire, a massive UN presence of as many as 10 thousand troops and 10 thousand civilian personnel, UN control and supervision of the Cambodian government, and the end of all external military assistance and sanctuary provision. On August 29, all three elements of the CGDK announced that they supported the plan, while the SOC's response displayed continuing mistrust of the UN. However, the SOC did not reject the plan. Also on August 31, U.S. and Vietnamese delegates to the UN met once again to discuss a Cambodian peace, this time in the American delegation's offices.

If anything, the pace of Cambodian related events accelerated more in the first half of September. On September 5, U.S. Secretary of State Baker said that the United States would meet directly with the SOC government to discuss the Cambodian peace process. Five days later, the four Cambodian factions met in Jakarta as promised and reached general agreement on the Perm 5 peace plan, including a UN peacekeeping force, UN administration of the country, protection of human rights, free and fair elections supervised by the UN, and international guarantees. They also agreed to create a Supreme National Council, possibly chaired by Sihanouk, including six members from the SOC and two each from the three elements of the CGDK. On September 12, the Chinese Foreign Ministry released a statement that said that China was prepared to establish relations with all elements represented on the Cambodian Supreme National Council, which of course included the SOC.

But significant hurdles remained. No agreement had been signed, and significant hatred and mistrust remained between the four Cambodian parties. Thus, it was not surprising that when the Cambodian factions met in Bangkok on September 18–20 to establish the Supreme National Council, they could not agree on its membership. A November Perm 5 meeting produced a draft agreement for a settlement, but even this failed to bring the Cambodian factions closer together. Thus, throughout the rest of 1990, deadlock continued. Indeed, in December, a meeting in Paris to move forward with the Supreme National Council failed amidst accusations from each Cambodian faction that the others sought to gain unfair advantage.[103]

Despite the deadlock, a fundamental change had taken place in the Cambodian conflict during 1990. Between the 1979 Vietnamese invasion and 1990, the Cambodian conflict was the result of many issues including hatred and mistrust between the Cambodian factions; Vietnam's occupation of Cambodia and support for the PRK/SOC; Chinese and Thai support for the CGDK; ASEAN-Vietnamese tension; Sino-Vietnamese hostility; the Sino-Soviet split; and the East-West conflict. During 1990, all but the first of these issues had been removed or had significantly diminished as issues underlying the Cambodian conflict. However, neither the United States nor the Soviet Union—nor any of the other forums and institutions that the international community had in place to address the Cambodian conflict—could exert much influence to resolve this issue.

In addition to diplomatic efforts, the international community including the U.S. and the U.S.S.R. used other pressures to try to bring the internal Cambodian groups into accord. For example, ASEAN, the United States, and other involved states agreed in October 1990 that the annual UN resolution on Cambodia would not be brought up for a General Assembly vote in 1990, and that the question of who occupied Cambodia's UN seat would not be voted, thereby leaving the seat empty.[104] Similarly, also in October, the U.S. Congress ended covert CIA aid to the CGDK, estimated at about ten million dollars per year. Congress approved a 25 million dollar humanitarian aid package for the Cambodian opposition, but specifically prohibited aid to "any Cambodian organization that . . . is cooperating, tactically or strategically, with the Khmer Rouge in their military operations."[105]

Nevertheless, the war in Cambodia continued. Throughout late 1990 and early 1991, the Khmer Rouge gained ground. Throughout much of this period, Chinese weapons continued to reach the Khmer Rouge. Vietnam and the Soviet Union continued to supply the SOC as well. However, in early 1991, the U.S.S.R. declared that it intended to cut its economic aid to Vietnam (but said nothing about its military assistance to either Vietnam or Cambodia), and the U.S. government concluded that China had finally ended weapons shipments to the Khmer Rouge.[106]

These were significant steps forward, but sufficient numbers of weapons were available within Cambodia to guarantee that the conflict would continue. Equally perplexing, the Khmer Rouge by 1991 had begun to grant gem mining and timber cutting concessions to Southeast Asian entrepreneurs. This provided the Khmer Rouge with an independent source of funds with which to purchase weapons in international weapons markets.[107]

Another threat to the stalled peace process was the growth of factional divisions within the SOC, Vietnamese, and Chinese governments. By year's end, the SOC was divided into at least three different factions, with the result that SOC now only wanted a one year UN presence with a yes-no vote on whether SOC should continue to rule. Meanwhile, Vietnam's domestic political battle between hard-liners and reformers spilled over into foreign policy, with the outcome unclear.[108] Much the same situation prevailed in China.

Throughout January 1991, the four Cambodian factions concentrated on blaming each other for the failure of the previous month's Paris talks. In February, diplomats shuttled back and forth between practically every capital involved in the negotiations but achieved no meaningful progress. Also in February, a military coup in Thailand overthrew Prime Minister Chatichai Choonhavan, thereby removing ASEAN's leading proponent for accomodation with Vietnam.

Meanwhile, a Japanese diplomatic delegation traveled to Cambodia to try to achieve a breakthrough on negotiations, but achieved little. Even so, Japan moved increasingly to the front of Asian efforts to arrange a settlement in Cambodia. Thus, in March, Japan suggested a new peace plan based on previous United Nations proposals, but with elections open only to those who accepted a ceasefire. In April, Japanese Prime Minister Toshiki Kaifu traveled throughout Southeast Asia promoting the Japanese plan.

Meanwhile, in late March, the three leaders of the Cambodian opposition met in Beijing, reaffirmed their complete support for the August 1990 Perm 5 Framework Document, and urged all involved parties to implement it. At the end of the month, the French and Indonesian Foreign Ministers acting in their capacity as co-chairmen of the Paris International Conference on Cambodia, in conjunction with UN Secretary General Javier Perez de Cuellar, called on the leaders of the four Cambodian factions to accept a ceasefire to improve the atmosphere for negotiations. Much to everyone's surprise, on April 23, the CGDK accepted the proposal, and the following day, the SOC followed suit. Fighting along the Thai-Cambodian border dropped off, but warfare continued deeper in Cambodia.[109]

Efforts to manage, deescalate, and resolve the conflict continued, but neither the U.S. nor the Soviet Union played a major role. In early June, 1991, all four Cambodian factions met in Jakarta. Hun Sen and Sihanouk reached agreement on the structure of the twelve man Supreme National Council. Under the agreement, Sihanouk would serve as the Council's chairman, and Hun Sen would be vice chairman. However, the Khmer Rouge rejected the Hun Sen-Sihanouk solution. Nevertheless, the meeting was significant since it indicated that Sihanouk and the SOC were moving increasingly close together.[110]

Talks between Cambodia's four warring factions resumed again in late June in Pattaya, Thailand. The Cambodian factions in three days of negotiations reached agreement on a ceasefire, which would be monitored by the Cambodians themselves until all sides accepted the Perm 5 plan; a moratorium on receiving external military assistance; and locating the Supreme National Council in Phnom Penh.[111]

Nevertheless, agreement was far from total. Differences remained over the Perm 5 peace plan, especially the role the United Nations would play in the administration of Cambodia during the period leading to elections. Other issues remained as well. Some of these were resolved at a mid-July 1991 meeting between the four factions in Beijing. By August, the warring factions had finally reached agreement to end the conflict, basing the agreement on the Perm 5 proposal.

The key questions, of course, were whether the ceasefire could hold and whether the final agreement could be implemented. In the absence of an in-place network of international agreements, negotiating processes, external observers, and expectations for peace, this presented a significant challenge. Recognizing this, the Perm 5 group and other members of the international community as well sought to arrange conditions under which UN peace-keeping forces could be introduced to Cambodia. Eventually, these efforts succeeded, and in November 1991, the first UN peace-keeping forces began to arrive. Thus, Cambodia was nearer to peace than it had been at any time since the 1960s.

Conclusions

When all is said and done, then, what may be concluded about U.S. and Soviet peacemaking efforts in Afghanistan and Cambodia? To what extent had the two erstwhile superpowers actually had a "meeting of the minds" on regional conflicts in Asia, and to what extent had they actually contributed to the management, deescalation, and resolution of conflict in Afghanistan and Cambodia? Several distinct conclusions can be reached.

First, international efforts, including those of the United States and the Soviet Union, succeeded in different ways to deescalate both conflicts. The efforts did not resolve the conflicts. Contrary to popular belief, however, it cannot be argued that the U.S. and the U.S.S.R. came to a complete meeting of the minds in either conflict. The Soviet Union, for reasons of its own beyond the conflicts, wanted the conflicts to deescalate. It was and is clear that the U.S.S.R. was prepared to move toward deescalation regardless of the impact that deescalation might have on the course of the conflicts.

Second, the East-West conflict was not sufficient by itself to precipitate direct American involvement in either conflict. In the Afghan case, the U.S. provided substantial military support to the insurgency, but in the case of Cambodia, it ignored the conflict until it appeared that the Khmer Rouge might regain power. Only then did the United States indicate a greater willingness to raise the priority it placed on the Cambodian conflict.

Third, non-combatant regional actors played significant roles in helping establish conditions that were conducive to the withdrawal of external forces from both Afghanistan and Cambodia. In the case of Afghanistan, the primary regional non-combatant was Pakistan. In Cambodia, they were China and the member states of ASEAN. In both cases, it is clear that although the two superpowers played significant roles in the movements toward political solutions to the conflicts, the superpowers did not dominate the negotiating process.

Fourth, it is equally evident that neither the United States nor the Soviet Union was able to "steam-roll" their regional friends and clients, especially in the context of negotiations. In both conflicts, regional friends and clients on both sides identified and sought to defend their own interests, above and beyond what the superpowers desired.

Fifth, in Afghanistan, despite the withdrawal of Soviet combat forces and the deescalation of the East-West conflict, neither the U.S. nor the U.S.S.R. was willing to abandon its erstwhile "ally." Thus, arms continued to flow into Afghanistan long after the U.S.S.R. withdrew its military forces, both to the PDPA government in Kabul from the Soviet Union and to the Mujahadeen from the United States.

Sixth, in Cambodia, despite the withdrawal of Vietnamese combat forces and the deescalation of the East-West conflict, both the U.S. and the U.S.S.R. identified interests in Cambodia and Southeast Asia that in some respects led them to maintain or escalate their interest and involvement in the Cambodian conflict following the Vietnamese withdrawal. In the U.S. case, the specter of the return to power of the Khmer Rouge revitalized American interest in Cambodia, something which even the continuation of the Cold War in earlier years had failed to do. In the Soviet case, at least before the August 1991 coup attempt, the Kremlin was unwilling to abandon its previous positions on Cambodia completely, not only because of its interests in maintaining a certain degree of foreign policy credibility, but also because of domestic political considerations. Even in the "new" Soviet Union, too much could not be abandoned too quickly.

Finally, although this has been a study of only two of the regional conflicts in which the U.S. and the U.S.S.R. were directly or peripherally involved in the 1980s and early 1990s, it is clear that the U.S. and Soviet peacemaking efforts in these two conflicts were not only dissimilar one from another, but also differed significantly between the Afghan and Cambodian conflicts. This, of course, raises questions about the degree to which experiences and lessons learned in one negotiating context may be transferable to other negotiating situations.

There is no single bottom line on U.S. and Soviet peacemaking efforts in Afghanistan and Cambodia. Conflict continues in Afghanistan, and a tenuous ceasefire has been reached in Cambodia. But perhaps most distressingly, this study has also indicated that the degree of U.S. and Soviet cooperation in managing and deescalating those conflicts was much less than is commonly believed. The new-found American and Soviet ability to resolve their own bilateral disagreements has been impressive, but there were clearly limits to the extent to which that ability extended to American and Soviet efforts to resolve the conflicts in Afghanistan and Cambodia.

Notes

1. For a discussion of these anti-Soviet and anti-Soviet client struggles, see for example Mark N. Katz, "Anti-Soviet Insurgencies: Growing Trend or Passing Phase?" *Orbis,* Summer 1986, pp. 365–391.

2. For detailed discussions of how these Reagan administration perspectives fit within the broader context of U.S. policies toward the U.S.S.R. under Reagan, see Daniel S. Papp, "The Changing Face of U.S.-Soviet Relations: An American Perspective," in Hans Gunter Brauch and Robert Kennedy (eds.), *Alternative Conventional Defense Postures in the European Theater: The Military Balance and Domestic Constraints* (New York: Taylor and Francis, 1990), pp. 3–19.

3. Caspar Weinberger, as reported in *The New York Times,* March 5, 1981.

4. Early in his first administration, Reagan sent then-Secretary of State Alexander Haig to the Middle East in an effort to forge an anti-Soviet "strategic consensus" between Israel, Saudi Arabia, Jordan, Egypt, and several other Arab states. The effort failed.

5. This military assistance had been begun by the Carter administration shortly after the December 1979 Soviet invasion of Afghanistan.

6. See Jerry Hough, *The Struggle for the Third World* (Washington: Brookings, 1986); and Daniel S. Papp, *Soviet Perceptions of the Developing World in the 1980s: The Ideological Basis* (Lexington: Lexington Books, 1985).

7. See for example the 1983 statement by Viktor Volsky, the Director of the U.S.S.R.'s Institute of Latin America, as quoted in *The Guardian [London],* April 28, 1983. Volsky declared that "there have been defeats before" for socialism in the Third World, referring specifically to the future of the Sandinistas in Nicaragua.

8. See for example the July 12, 1983 *Pravda* article that argued that progress in Third World states "can only be achieved through the labor of the peoples of these countries and their leaders' correct policies."

9. This theme is developed throughout Daniel S. Papp, *Soviet Policies toward the Developing World During the 1980s: The Dilemmas of Power and Presence* (Montgomery: Air University Press, 1986).

10. For a discussion both of the reasons for Soviet policy change in the Third World and its consolidation options, see again *Ibid,* especially Chapter 12.

11. For different views on the impact of New Thinking on Soviet Third World Policy, see Jiri Valenta and Frank Cibulka (eds.), *Gorbachev's New Thinking and Third World Conflicts* (New Brunswick: Transaction Publishers, 1990). For Gorbachev's own views, see Mikhail Gorbachev, *Perestroika: New Thinking for Our Country and the World* (New York: Harper & Row, 1987), especially pp. 135–254.

12. For the texts of these agreements, see U.S. Department of State, Bureau of Public Affairs, *Agreements on Afghanistan,* Selected Documents No. 26 (April, 1988).

13. For greater details on these events, and indeed on events relating to Afghanistan throughout the proximity talks, see the report submitted to the U.S. Institute of Peace in March 1991 by Daniel S. Papp, "Resolving Regional Conflicts: Comparative Paths to Peace in Afghanistan, Angola, Cambodia, and Nicaragua."

14. This formulation was first put forward by then-U.S. Secretary of State Cyrus Vance on March 27, 1980. See Cyrus Vance, "U.S. Foreign Policy: Our Broader Strategy," *Current Policy No. 153* (Washington: U.S. Department of State, March 27, 1980).

15. The joint Soviet-Afghan communique appears October 1980.

16. For the text of the August 5 Soviet Foreign Ministry statement, see *Pravda,* August, 1981.

17. As reported by a former Afghan diplomat, Abdol Majid Mangal, in *The Sunday Telegraph [London],* June 24, 1984.

18. The four items for discussion included "the withdrawal of foreign troops; non-interference in the internal affairs of states; international guarantees of non-interference; and the voluntary return of the refugees to their homes," as presented in U.S. Department of State, "Afghanistan: Three Years of Occupation," *Special Report No. 106* (Washington: December, 1982), p. 11.

19. *The New York Times,* April 23, 1983.

20. Gorbachev revealed this in a February 1988 speech. See *Pravda,* February 19, 1988.

21. These elements included non-interference in Afghanistan's and Pakistan's internal affairs, arrangements for refugee repatriation, and a declaration of guarantees by the U.S. and U.S.S.R. See Ted Morello, "Ready for the Bear," *Far Eastern Economic Review,* October 24, 1985, p. 41.

22. See for example Richard Evans, "The Battle for Paktia," *Far Eastern Economic Review,* September 12, 1985, pp. 48–49.

23. Views on the impact of New Thinking on Soviet Third World Policy, see Jiri Valenta and Frank Cibulka (eds.), *Gorbachev's New Thinking and Third World Conflicts* (New Brunswick: Transaction Publishers, 1990). For Gorbachev's own

views, see Mikhail Gorbachev, *Perestroika: New Thinking for Our Country and the World* (New York: Harper & Row, 1987), especially pp. 135–254.

24. For the texts of these agreements, see U.S. Department of State, Bureau of Public Affairs, *Agreements on Afghanistan,* Selected Documents No. 26 (April, 1988).

25. For greater details on these events, and indeed on events relating to Afghanistan throughout the proximity talks, see the report submitted to the U.S. Institute of Peace in March 1991 by Daniel S. Papp, "Resolving Regional Conflicts: Comparative Paths to Peace in Afghanistan, Angola, Cambodia, and Nicaragua."

26. This formulation was first put forward by then-U.S. Secretary of State Cyrus Vance on March 27, 1980. See Cyrus Vance, "U.S. Foreign Policy: Our Broader Strategy," *Current Policy No. 153* (Washington: U.S. Department of State, March 27, 1980).

27. The joint Soviet-Afghan communique appears October 1980.

28. For the text of the August 5 Soviet Foreign Ministry statement, see *Pravda,* August, 1981.

29. As reported by a former Afghan diplomat, Abdol Majid Mangal, in *The Sunday Telegraph [London],* June 24, 1984.

30. The four items for discussion included "the withdrawal of foreign troops; non-interference in the internal affairs of states; international guarantees of non-interference; and the voluntary return of the refugees to their homes," as presented in U.S. Department of State, "Afghanistan: Three Years of Occupation," *Special Report No. 106* (Washington: December, 1982), p. 11.

31. *The New York Times,* April 23, 1983.

32. Gorbachev revealed this in a February 1988 speech. See *Pravda,* February 19, 1988.

33. These elements included non-interference in Afghanistan's and Pakistan's internal affairs, arrangements for refugee repatriation, and a declaration of guarantees by the U.S. and U.S.S.R. See Ted Morello, "Ready for the Bear," *Far Eastern Economic Review,* October 24, 1985, p. 41.

34. See for example Richard Evans, "The Battle for Paktia," *Far Eastern Economic Review,* September 12, 1985, pp. 48–49.

35. Richard Nations, "Soviets Looking for Way Out of Afghanistan?" *Far Eastern Economic Review,* December 26, 1985, p. 10.

36. Nayan Chanda, "U.S. Takes New Stance on Afghan Talks," *Far Eastern Economic Review,* January 2, 1986, p. 8. See also *The New York Times,* December 14, 1985.

37. *The New York Times,* February 11, 1988; and March 24, 1988.

38. Nayan Chanda, "Bringing Home the Bear," *Far Eastern Economic Review,* January 23, 1986, pp. 34–35.

39. It must be stressed that the six month timetable was proposed by Cordovez, not the Soviets or the Afghan government.

40. Mikhail Gorbachev, "The Political Report of the CPSU Central Committee," in *Current Soviet Policies IX: The Documentary Record of the 27th Congress of the CPSU* (Columbus: The Current Digest of the Soviet Press, 1986), p. 35. Significantly, in his speech, Babrak Karmal did not mention Soviet plans to withdraw. See *Pravda,* March 1, 1986.

41. See Ted Morello, "It's Now or Never," *Far Eastern Economic Review,* April 17, 1986, p. 22; Rodney Tasker, "Moscow's Withdrawal Ruse," *Far Eastern Economic Review,* June 12, 1986, p. 34; Richard Nations, "Gorbachev's Game Plan," *Far Eastern Economic Review,* July 3, 1986, p. 14; and Anwar Nasir, "New Soviet Gameplan," *Far Eastern Economic Review,* November 17, 1986, pp. 26–27.

42. For the text of the Vladivostok speech, see *Pravda,* July 29, 1986.

43. For the text of Najibullah's New Year's Day 1987 speech, see TASS, January 1, 1987, 1500 GMT, as reported in *FBIS (Soviet Union),* January 2, 1987, pp. D1–D4. The Mujahadeen quickly rejected Najibullah's offer. See Husain Haqqani, "Giving Peace No Chance," *Far Eastern Economic Review,* January 29, 1987, p. 25.

44. *Izvestiya,* January 11, 1987; and TASS, January 12, 1987, 1308 GMT, as reported in *FBIS (Soviet Union),* January 13, 1987, p. D2.

45. *Pravda,* January 7, 1987; and January 8, 1987.

46. Nayan Chanda, "Reading Gorbachev's Mind," *Far Eastern Economic Review,* January 29, 1987, p. 26.

47. *Ibid.*

48. For reportage on Shevardnadze's trip, see TASS, January 6, 1988, 1736 GMT, as reported in *FBIS (Soviet Union),* January 7, 1988, pp. 22–23.

49. For the text of Gorbachev's February 8, 1988 announcement, see Moscow Domestic Service, February 8, 1988, 1600 GMT, as reported in *FBIS (Soviet Union),* February 8, 1988, pp. 34–36.

50. TASS, February 11, 1988, 1107 GMT, as reported in *FBIS (Soviet Union),* February 11, 1988, pp. 24–25.

51. Sophie Quinn-Judge, "Giving Peace a Chance," *Far Eastern Economic Review,* March 3, 1988, pp. 12–13.

52. Ahmed Rashid, "Diplomatic Deadlock," *Far Eastern Economic Review,* March 24, 1988, p. 22.

53. Nayan Chanda, "Peace on Our Terms," *Far Eastern Economic Review,* April 7, 1988.

54. For the text of the declaration, see *Izvestiya,* April 8, 1988.

55. As reported in Ahmed Rashid and Sophie Quinn-Judge, "Patchwork Peace," April 21, 1988, p. 14.

56. *Ibid.*

57. *Pravda,* September 21, 1988.

58. *Pravda,* January 16, 1989.

59. *The New York Times,* November 18, 1988; and TASS, December 2, 1988.

60. *Izvestiya,* December 30, 1988.

61. *The New York Times,* December 8, 1988.

62. *The Washington Post,* September 2, 1989.

63. See Robert M. Kimmitt, "U.S. Policy on Regional Conflicts: Cambodia, Afghanistan," *U.S. Department of State Current Policy No. 1281,* April 18, 1990, p. 2.

64. See Daniel S. Papp, "The Impact of 'Restructuring' and 'New Thinking' on Soviet-Vietnamese Relations," in Charles Bukowski and J. Richard Walsh, (eds.), *Glasnost, Perestroika, and the Socialist Community* (New York: Praeger, 1990), pp. 90–94.

65. See Daniel S. Papp, *Soviet Policies Toward the Developing World During the 1980s: The Dilemmas of Power and Presence* (Montgomery: Air University Press, 1986), especially Chapter 11; and Leszek Buszynski, *Soviet Foreign Policy and Southeast Asia* (London: Croom Helm, 1986).

66. See Nayan Chanda, *Brother Enemy: The War After the War* (New York: Macmillan, 1986), p. 347.

67. See Gareth Porter, "Kampuchea Conference: Cracks in the Coalition," *Indochina Issues*, Number 18 (July 1981).

68. Gerard Hervouet, "The Cambodian Conflict: The Difficulties of Intervention and Compromise," *International Journal.* Volume XLV (Spring 1990), pp. 277–284.

69. For greater details on these points, and on all aspects of U.S. and Soviet efforts at peacemaking in this and later periods relating to Cambodia, see the Papp study submitted to the U.S. Institute of Peace in March 1991.

70. Radio Moscow, March 14, 1985, as reported in *FBIS (Soviet Union)*, March 14, 1985.

71. *Le Monde*, December 20, 1985, as reported in Hervouet, p. 284.

72. BBC, *Summary of world Broadcasts*, FE/.7941/i, May 3, 1985.

73. Deng also stated that the Vietnamese occupation of Cambodia was the easiest of the three major obstacles to overcome in Sino-Soviet relations. The other obstacles were the Soviet build-up on the Sino-Soviet border. For Dent's statement, see Richard Nation's "Great Leap Sideways," *Far Eastern Economic Review*, May 30, 1985, pp. 15–16.

74. See Ronald Reagan's October 24, 1985 speech to the United Nations, in *The New York Times*, October 25, 1985.

75. The November 3, 1986 issue of *Nhan Dan* admitted that Vietnam had wasted "billions of rubles of Soviet aid in recent years." See *Indochina Chronology*, Volume 5, Number 4, October-December, 1986, p. 5.

76. *Pravda*, December 19, 1986, and *Izvestiya*, December 19, 1986.

77. For the complete text of Gorbachev's Vladivostok speech, see Moscow Television Service, July 28, 1986, as reported in *FBIS (Soviet Union)*, July 29, 1986, pp. R1–20.

78. By early February 1989, the USSR and China had reduced their disagreements over Cambodia to the point where they could issue a joint nine-point agreement on Cambodia at the conclusion of Soviet Foreign Minister Shevardnadze's three-day trip to Beijing. This will be discussed in more detail later.

79. For the complete text of Gorbachev's Krasnoyarsk speech, see *Pravda*, September 18, 1988.

80. See Murray Hiebert, "Carping About Cam Ranh: Hanoi Is Unhappy Over Moscow's Offer on the Base," *Far Eastern Economic Review*, October 27, 1988, p. 27.

81. See again Gorbachev's Vladivostok speech, as reported in *FBIS (Soviet Union)*, July 29, 1986, p. R17.

82. See *Bangkok Post*, April 22, 1987.

83. *Pravda*, May 20, 1987.

84. *Pravda*, May 22, 1987.

85. *Washington Post,* May 6, 1988. See also Robert Delfs, "The Sihanouk Card," *Far Eastern Economic Review,* February 11, 1988, p. 35.

86. Nayan Chanda, "Marriage Made in Moscow," *Far Eastern Economic Review,* June 9, 1988, p. 17.

87. See "Moscow's Cambodia Push," *Asiaweek,* May 13, 1988, p. 36.

88. For an example of the Soviet position, see Radio Moscow, April 6, 1988, as reported in *FBIS (Soviet Union),* April 7, 1988, p. 8.

89. TASS, July 20, 1988, as reported in *FBIS (Soviet Union),* August 8, 1988, p. 16.

90. TASS, August 3, 1988, as reported in *FBIS (Soviet Union),* August 3, 1988, p. 15.

91. Nayan Chanda, "Taking the Soft Line: Vietnam Signals China It Wants Improved Relations," *Far Eastern Economic Review,* December 8, 1988, pp. 27–28.

92. For the text of the joint statement, see *Pravda,* February 6, 1989. See also Nayan Chanda, "The Sticking Points," *Far Eastern Economic Review,* February 16, 1989, p. 11.

93. For many different views of the Paris meeting, see a series of articles, reports, and broadcasts in almost every issue of *FBIS* (East Asia) and *Far Eastern Economic Review* in August, 1989.

94. *The New York Times,* October 24, 1990. For a detailed statement of the U.S. government's position on Cambodia at this time, see *Testimony of Assistant Secretary of State Richard Solomon Before the U.S. Congress* (Asian and Pacific Affairs Subcommittee of the House Foreign Affairs Committee), December 10, 1990.

95. See *Indochina Chronology* (October-December, 1990), p. 13.

96. *The Christian Science Monitor,* March 26, 1991.

97. For greater details, see *Indochina Chronology,* p. 15.

98. *The Christian Science Monitor,* May 2, 1991.

99. Ibid.

100. *The Christian Science Monitor,* June 21, 1991, and June 26, 1991.

101. *The Christian Science Monitor,* June 25, 1991, and June 27, 1991.

102. James Baker, July 30, 1989, as reported in U.S. Department of State, "International Efforts for a Peaceful Cambodia," *U.S. Department of State Current Policy No. 1202* (July 1989), p. 2.

103. Douglas Pike, in *Indochina Chronology,* July-September 1989, pp. 14–15.

104. The U.S. was even contemplating sending military aid to the non-communist CGDK forces for the first time. See for example *The Christian Science Monitor,* June 15, 1989; and July 24, 1989.

105. For several of the many discussions of the military situations during this period, see Murray Hiebert, "Going It Alone," *Far Eastern Economic Review,* October 5, 1989, pp. 16–17; Rodney Tasker, "Another Year Zero?" *Far Eastern Economic Review,* November 9, 1989, pp. 12–13; Murray Hiebert, "Hitting the Highways," *Far Eastern Economic Review,* December 14, 1989, p. 33; and Rodney Tasker, "The Endless Struggle," *Far Eastern Economic Review,* May 10, 1990, pp. 10–11.

106. See *The New York Times,* December 3, 1989; and December 14, 1989.

107. For two accounts of the Khmer Rouge's successes and world reaction, see *The Christian Science Monitor,* July 11, 1990; and July 18, 1990.

108. *The New York Times,* July 17, 1990, and July 18, 1990.

109. *The New York Times,* July 19, 1990.

110. Michael Vatikiotis, "Measures of Success: Peace Talks Advance, Though Discord Evident," *Far Eastern Economic Review* (November 22, 1990); Michael Field and Michael Vatikiotis, "Jaw and Peace: Paris Consensus Awaits Verdict of Factions," *Far Eastern Economic Review* (December 6, 1990); Michael Field, "Battle Fatigue: Latest Efforts to Find Peace Formula Founder," *Far Eastern Economic Review* (January 3, 1991); and Rodney Tasker, "Elusive Peace: Gulf Conflict Overshadows Efforts to End Earlier War," *Far Eastern Economic Review* (January 31, 1991).

111. *The New York Times,* December 16, 1990.

6

Security and Uncertainty in the Pacific

Sheldon W. Simon

As the Cold War paradigm begins to fade in Asian international politics, the future of the alliance arrangements created to cope with it are becoming increasingly problematic. These arrangements are being challenged on three fronts: first, the great power confrontations of the post World War II era are dissipating (Soviet-U.S., Sino-Soviet), the need for other Asian states to seek great-power protection has declined accordingly. Second, decades of dependence on external protectors have led to the rise of nationalism within the region. The political legitimacy of new elites, particularly in Korea, depends in part on greater foreign policy and defense autonomy from the guarantors of the recent past. Third, from the perspective of the great powers, the financial burdens of the Cold War have slowed economic growth and undermined their competitive capabilities in the international economic order. The very future of their international status depends on reversing these trends and easing these burdens.

Unlike European security, Asian security has not been organized through opposed multilateral alliances along land boundaries. Rather, Asian alliances are bilateral, essentially unconnected, and scattered along thousands of miles of seaspace. With the exception of Korea, ground forces do not play a significant role in Asian defense agreements. The environment is dominated by navies and air forces.

U.S. Policy in the North Pacific in the 1990s

By the 1990s, Washington's rationale for forward deployment in the North Pacific included elements of the World War II legacy, the Cold War, and the incipient post-Cold War situation. U.S. forces in South Korea were a legacy of that country's division in 1945; U.S. naval and air deployments from Japan were directed against the Soviet Pacific Fleet and air arm to maintain freedom of the seas and intimidate their Cold War adversary;

and, in a post-Cold War explanation, U.S. forces in the region were seen as preempting the need for Japan to become a formidable military power—an outcome desired by no one.

The U.S. forward deployed strategy, particularly as it involves exercises in the northern Seas of Japan and Okhotsk, raised Soviet anxieties. Indeed, there is something of a paradox in current U.S. strategy: for years, Washington urged Soviet leaders to shift their nuclear deterrent to submarines from land-based missiles. Being harder to detect, SSBNs would contribute to strategic stability. However, once the USSR established an SSBN bastion in the Sea of Okhotsk, the U.S. navy began to conduct exercises for the purpose of penetrating that bastion and locating the submarines, undermining the very rationale that had been urged upon the Soviets in the first place. This offensive U.S. strategy is no longer necessary; reducing the risk of inadvertent war should be a priority in the new era.

It appears that the Pacific strategy of the United States is being reconceived. Though it is too early to determine its new parameters, some of its outlines may be discerned. As the Russian threat diminishes, Washington must search for a supplementary rationale for the maintenance of its Asian forces. The strongest candidate appears to be a return to a classical balance of power system. In this arrangement, Russia remains an important player. But the presence of U.S. forces would also serve to offset or preclude additional worrisome buildups by China, India, and Japan. Indeed, in a post-Cold War Asia, a Russian presence might even be welcomed by the United States as part of a multinational constabulary operating throughout the western Pacific to maintain freedom of the seas.[1] Should this prospect occur, what began as a new balance of power could evolve into an Asian collective security system. A continued U.S. presence, even if reduced in size, would reassure the smaller states of the western Pacific that no new hegemon would emerge.

Until radical new dispositions develop, however, U.S. defense doctrine in northeast Asia will probably continue to emphasize burden sharing with both Japan and the Republic of Korea (ROK) as the primary way of maintaining a regional presence at reduced costs. At a *minimum,* U.S. defense estimates for 1995 portend a 10 percent Asian force reduction, and that figure could double.[2] A smaller U.S. air and naval contingent means that collaboration with the services of friendly countries for regional defense becomes ever more important, as is U.S. encouragement of these countries to engage in security cooperation with each other. The inclusion of South Korean forces for the first time in *Rimpac-90* is an example of regional defense exercises that are consciously multinational in planning and execution. *Rimpac* involves amphibious landings, straits blockades, mine-laying and clearing, as well as training for the interoperability of navies, demonstrated by Japanese escorts for U.S. carriers.

While the United States is pressing Japan and the ROK to increase their financial support for U.S. forces in their countries above the current respective 41 percent and 13 percent, Washington seems less willing to acknowledge that Japan had already assisted the arms buildup of the Reagan years by financing much of the 1980s U.S. deficit. Japanese capital inflow to the United States during that decade exceeded U.S. personal savings by a factor of two. Japan's commitment to the maintenance of U.S. forward deployment in the Pacific is based in part on the fear that should the United States withdraw, Japan would have to so greatly expand its own military that its economic preeminence in the region would be undermined.

Russian Policy in the North Pacific in the 1990s

Entering the 1990s, the Russians, too, face even more severe economic constraints on the massive force structure they created in the eastern USSR during the 1970s and 1980s. Emphasizing antisubmarine warfare, the Russian Pacific Fleet currently consists of 80 modern surface combatants, two STOL carriers, 77 attack and cruise missile submarines, 25 SSBNs and one-third of Russia's naval aviation, including 40 nuclear-capable *Backfire* bombers.[3] Yet, the utility of this armada is questionable at a time when Russia is searching more for foreign aid from recent adversaries than the ability to confront them militarily.

Mikhail Gorbachev's goal for the 1990s was to undo the damage done to Asian policy by the confrontational style of the previous two decades. By the time he came to power in 1985, the USSR, through its adventures in Afghanistan, aid to Vietnam in Cambodia, and support for the North Korean military, had created its own worst nightmare: a tacit coalition among China, Japan, the United States, the ROK and ASEAN. The Soviet leader had to demilitarize foreign policy to alleviate the anxieties his predecessors had induced. For the past four years, he repeatedly emphasized the major components of his new policy: (1) security must be mutual; (2) arms control and disarmament negotiations should advantage no single actor; and (3) the Soviets will not interfere in the internal affairs of other countries, socialist or nonsocialist—the repudiation of the Brezhnev Doctrine. In Northeast Asia, the Soviet hope was that by professing mutual security and "defense sufficiency," Japan and the ROK would develop a stake in the USSR's economic modernization by opening their respective aid and investment coffers.

Gorbachev's peace agenda for the Pacific included nuclear free zones, submarine-free encroachment zones, naval arms limitation talks, and the closing of overseas bases.[4] Beginning in 1991, Moscow, in effect, even cut military aid to Vietnam and North Korea by insisting that arms sales be settled in hard currency. The Soviet call for a Helsinki-type regional security conference for Asia was an effort at legitimatizing a permanent Soviet presence and voice in Asian security matters.

The U.S.-Russian-Japan Relationship

Like the United States, Japan is a trading nation dependent upon open sea lanes. The powerful Russian submarine fleet is, therefore, an incipient threat countered currently through an alliance with the United States or perhaps, in the future, through a negotiated reduction in regional arms. For Russia, too, Japan is a potential threat, especially since the world's two largest economies work against Russian interests. If Soviet arms expansion in the 1970s and 1980s triggered Japanese rearmament and Japan and the United States have created a combination of the most modern air and naval forces in the world, then only the prospect of mutual arms reduction can dampen the existing situation.

Arms reductions in the North Pacific are a complex proposition, however. If, for example, the United States unilaterally draws down its forces because of budget constraints, Japan could be faced with a dilemma. If Tokyo were to accelerate its own air and naval expansion to compensate for the U.S. reduction, the Russian threat might be offset, but only at a considerable cost to Tokyo's economic policy toward the rest of Asia. A Japanese military buildup, in conjunction with its economic dominance, would be seen as a move to establish itself as the new Pacific hegemon. From Tokyo's security perspective, then, the status quo or a new arms control regime are both preferable to unilateral arms expansion. Even if Tokyo must pay for an ever-larger proportion of the U.S. military presence in Japan—50 percent by 1993—that cost would be a better policy than moving toward a more independent defense force. As long as Japan's armed forces are seen as adjunct to U.S. deployments, the former will remain politically acceptable in Asia because U.S. forces are acceptable.

The U.S. view of Japan demonstrates an understanding of the relationship's ambivalence. Both U.S. government statements and public opinion polls reveal a bifurcated image: on the one hand, Japan is seen as a reliable defense partner in East Asia and an important contributor to the region's economic development. Alternatively, however, Americans fear Japan as an economic threat and an unfair trader and predator that has been acquiring U.S. companies and real estate at bargain prices. Congress has tried to juxtapose these contradictory views by seeking a voice in Japanese spending decisions. In 1989, the U.S. Senate passed a resolution asking Tokyo to pay for all U.S. forces in Japan, increase its own defense spending and overseas development assistance, and consult closely with Washington on how and where the money should be spent.[5]

Additionally, during the 1991 Persian Gulf war, Congressional pressure for a substantial Japanese financial contribution led the Diet reluctantly to appropriate $13 billion—the largest sum contributed by any country to defray the war's costs. (Germany placed second with a $9 billion contribution.) U.S. policymakers are increasingly asking whether they should pay to protect Japanese trade and investment along the Asian-Pacific rim. Any negative answer to that question, however, comes up against the fact that Japan's *independent* provision for its defense would be unacceptable to Washington's friends and adversaries alike.

A new development in U.S. defense policy may well overcome this inertia in East Asian defense relations. In April of 1990, the Defense Department acknowledged that the U.S. military presence would decline as the Soviet threat diminished. Unilateral Soviet force reductions along the Chinese border, the withdrawal of Soviet forces from Mongolia and Afghanistan, as well as the removal of Soviet air power from Cam Ranh Bay formed the strategic basis for U.S. decision initially to remove up to 15,000 of its 155,000 troops from the region by 1993. Most of these would come from Japan and Korea.[6]

Yet, if Japan agrees to assume the preponderant financial support of U.S. forces on its soil, might it not also insist on the right to determine where and how these forces should be used? This would be *power sharing* growing out of burden sharing. It suggests parallel developments in security policy to Japan's insistence in international financial affairs for greater voting rights in the Asian Development Bank and the International Monetary Fund.[7]

Over the past decade, within a policy designed for the Japan Self Defense Forces (JSDF) to play a subordinate role in Pacific security, a significant air and naval capability has developed. Ten squadrons of F-15s, a destroyer-frigate force of over 60,100 P-3C antisubmarine aircraft, but only approximately a one month supply of ammunition have created a sea control and air screen capability within 1000 miles of the home islands. Japan-U.S. joint exercises emphasize mining of the Japanese straits, defending against amphibious assaults on Hokkaido, and possibly preempting a Russian attack from the northern islands.[8]

By the late 1990s, Japan will add some 100 FSX ground support fighters and possibly new tanker aircraft to increase their effective range. Combined with the acquisition of AWACS early warning aircraft and over-the-horizon radar, Tokyo would be able to discover and respond to potential air and sea threats soon after they appear. Japanese air defense and antisubmarine forces in the 1990s by themselves will provide a significant search and attack capability against Russian bombers and submarines. There are, nevertheless, weaknesses in this buildup, particularly a lack of logistics for sustainability at sea and an insufficient number of attack submarines around the straits to strike at Russian surface vessels and submarines that pass through.[9]

Equally significant is a Japanese agreement to collaborate with the United States on three new critical defense technology projects. One is designed to make submarines less detectible, a second is a radar package for fighter planes better able to discriminate enemy from friendly aircraft, and the third is a highly efficient rocket engine which can be used to increase missile distance and payloads.[10]

Domestically, Japan has opted—with the exception of its air force, which produces most of its inventory under license from the United States—for a self-reliance policy. Though inefficient because of the small domestic market and Tokyo's prohibition on weapons exports, the country produces virtually all of its warships and 80 percent of its army's weapons. Exploiting its electronics advantage, the JSDF is directing considerable effort into developing surface-to-surface missiles, for the protection of its coastlines which can also be used for straits control.[11] Noteworthy, also, is the fact that 240,000 of the 270,000 personnel in the JSDF are officers and noncommissioned officers. In the event of a crisis, the armed forces have the cadres in place for rapid expansion.

Both the RIMPAC and PACEX exercises in recent years reveal that Japan's defense doctrine has been transformed from exclusively the defense of the home islands to one of forward defense by which adversaries would be met on the sea and in the air before reaching Japan. Interestingly, in the PACEX '89 exercise, Korea-based U.S. ground attack aircraft also took part in a simulated defense of Hokkaido, indicating that U.S. forces in the ROK have a regional defense role beyond the peninsula. Nevertheless, PACEX '89 did not include forays into the Sea of Okhotsk and northern Sea of Japan as had previous exercises; and the Soviet naval response to the exercise was correspondingly muted.[12]

Japan's cooperation with other regional defense forces, once anathema, has developed through the Pacific exercises. In March 1990, the Air Self Defense Force approached the South Korean Air Force to discuss personnel exchanges. The navies of the two neighbors are also interested. Both countries seem receptive to some cooperation now because of the U.S. decision to reduce its forces in both Korea and Japan.[13] Perhaps Tokyo and Seoul foresee a situation around the turn of the century when their strategic importance to the United States wanes as the Russian military threat disappears.

For years, the Soviets tried to drive a wedge in the U.S.-Japanese alliance, correctly perceived as a formidable obstacle to their fleet's ability to leave or enter its home waters. During the Brezhnev era, the emphasis was on intimidation: threatening Japan with wholesale destruction in the event of a Soviet-U.S. war in the Pacific. That strategy, however, served only to drive

Washington and Tokyo even closer. Under Gorbachev, with his perestroika approach to Siberian development, there was a strong incentive for a *modus vivendi* with Japan because it could be a source for enormous aid and investment.

Soviet spokespeople noted that the combined Japan-U.S. fleets in the Pacific gave the allies a fourfold superiority in number of surface ships and doubled the number of tactical strike aircraft over Russian regional inventories. They also pointed to a significant reduction in Soviet naval exercises; and Japan's own SDF acknowledges that airspace violations by the USSR in 1989 were the lowest since 1984.[14] Perhaps in recognition of these changes, Tokyo has demonstrated a greater willingness to meet with Russian defense officials and discuss such confidence-building measures (CBMs) as the prevention of accidents at sea.[15] Gorbachev's April 1991 summit with Prime Minister Kaifu resulted in a Soviet pledge to reduce Soviet forces on the disputed northern islands "in the near future" as a CBM. Soviet officials remonstrated that Japan had not reciprocated their east Asian force reductions by either diminishing its defense budget or drawing down its Hokkaido-based forces. The latter are now reportedly equipped with cruise missiles capable of reaching the Russian-occupied islands.[16]

The major impasse to improved Russian-Japan relations on both defense and commercial affairs remains, however, the four northern islands off Hokkaido (the southern Kuriles). Japan will not consider supporting Siberian development projects—estimated to total U.S. $320 billion in investments for copper, nonferrous metals, petroleum, gas, coal and infrastructure—until progress is made toward the return of these territories.[17] Russian sources hinted recently that a negotiated mutual reduction of U.S., Japanese, and Russian forces, including those on the northern islands was possible but only in the context of larger regional arms reduction talks.[18]

The reversion of these islands to Japan seems as improbable as ever. Some Japanese officials believe that patience may pay off since the need for Japanese investment to keep the Russian economy from collapsing could over time render Moscow more accommodating with respect to the islands.[19]

Nevertheless, the Gorbachev-Kaifu 1991 summit proved a singular disappointment. The Soviet President's political authority had become so circumscribed that his delegation to Tokyo included the foreign minister of the Russian Republic as well as that of the Soviet Union. The former insisted that no *Russian* territory could be ceded to another country—the Kuriles are within Russia—without the explicit author1ztion of the republic's parliment. In the event, no progress was made on resolving the territorial dispute; and reciprocally, no Japanese economic aid was proffered.

A case could be made that Japanese officials and the business community are not completely unhappy with the continued stalemate. Japanese business interests are not keen about extensive investments in Russian manufacturing (as distinct from natural resources exploitation where Japanese investment has been considerable for the past 20 years). They dislike Russian bureaucratic controls, do not believe sufficient legal protection exists for foreign ventures, hold a low opinion of Russian labor productivity, and see little incentive to invest in Russia until a market economy is sufficiently developed to insure the ruble's convertibility and repatriation of profits.

From the Japanese government's viewpoint, complete reconciliation with Russia may not be desirable either. Japan's east Asian strategy is premised on the continuation of the U.S.-Japan security treaty. That relationship has legitimized Japan's economic strength and growing political stature throughout the Asia-Pacific rim. The treaty has reassured other Asian states that Tokyo will have no reason to deveop an independent military capacity to augment its dominant economic position. If the Kurile islands are returned and Russian forces in the north Pacfic radically reduced, the rationale for the Japan-U.S. security arrangement may disappear. The treaty's termination could be a disaster for Japan's Asian policy. Therefore, the need for some kind of enduring Russian threat remains—to maintain the viability of the U.S.-Japan security linage even in the post-Cold War era.

Korea's Future

With the prospect of growing stability in Sino-Russian and Russia-U.S.-Japan relations, the importance of Korea's future for East Asian peace assumes even greater significance. For some time the external backers of both Korean regimes have urged restraint and mutual consultation on their partners. Washington, Moscow, and Beijing would all prefer that Seoul and Pyongyang devise a peaceful *modus vivendi,* for the time being as separate political entities.

Even Kim Il Sung in early 1988 stated that North and South must recognize each other's existence, accept each other's systems, and move toward a confederation. Later in the same year, ROK President Roh Tae-woo also announced a willingness to accommodate the North by offering to urge Japan and the United States to improve relations with Pyongyang. In 1989, these encouraging statements were supplemented by announcements from the South that joint ventures were being considered by the two Koreas. Nevertheless, progress on the political-economic front remained fitful as the North severed contacts in protest against the annual *Team*

Spirit ROK-U.S. military exercises and the South's harsh reaction to unauthorized visits to the North by a dissident clergyman and student.[20]

North Korea's ambivalent policy toward the South probably reflects crosspressures within its leadership. On the one hand, Kim Il Sung still views an independent South as anathema and the antithesis of his hopes for Korea's future. Yet, leadership in the North is not unaware of the South's remarkable economic success in the 1980s, the crumbling of communist states' support for Pyongyang's hardline position, and the prospect of aid from the United States and Japan for the DPRK's own faltering economy if normalization with the ROK occurs. Nevertheless, unlike Germany, there is no indication that any confidence-building measures (CBMs) are developing for the Koreas. North Korea still blocks deliveries of mail and telephone calls from the South, has sharply limited family reunions, and has almost no trade with the ROK.[21] Moreover, the bulk of Pyongyang's armed forces remain deployed just north of the DMZ.

While both the North and South now call for a federation as the political form for reunification, there is an important difference in how the process of governance is conceived. For the South, democracy embodied in free elections, political parties, and majority rule is essential. The North, on the other hand, gives no indication that it is prepared to abandon a Leninist single party system. The North also insists that a "just war" may still be warranted to unify the country and drive out imperialism (the United States).[22]

The South sees economic exchange as the most feasible way to improve tense relations on the peninsula. But, Pyongyang is fearful that such exchanges could lead to a loosening of party control over its society, which could result in the kind of pluralism that led to the demise of communist regimes in Eastern Europe. The DPRK recalled its students from Eastern Europe and even from the Soviet Union after Seoul and Moscow established commercial airline arrangements. Instead of viewing reform as the road to economic development, for Kim Il Sung it is the road to the political destruction of the regime he has molded and led for over 40 years.

Each side has developed its own arms reduction proposal. The South's is multistaged: the first emphasizes CBMs—including contacts among military authorities of each side, joint observation and prior notification of exercises, and peaceful use of the DMZ; stage two would engage in reciprocal arms limitations; and stage three would be an arms builddown. Thus, the ROK invited North Korean observers to the 1990 *Team Spirit* exercise—to no avail.[23]

The North Korean proposal calls for a reduction of force by each side to 100,000, ". . . the minimum level for self-defense." Additionally, all foreign troops must be withdrawn.[24] Pyongyang's proposal could form the basis for negotiations in that Northern forces require a considerable numerical advantage to threaten the South. The key issues would be the composition and disposition of the forces permitted for each side.

By 1991, the prospect of international isolation had forced even Kim Il Sung to compromise. After the USSR established diplomatic relations with the ROK (discussed below) and China a trade office, Pyongyang realized tht it would be impossible to keep the ROK out of the United Nations any longer with the argument that only a united Korea should enter. Thus, Pyongyang took a fateful step in agreeing to separate memberships for the two Koreas in the United Nations, in effect accepting South Korean sovereignty even though the two Koreas themselves have not exchanged diplomatic missions.

The DPRK also intiated a dialogue with Japan on prospects for diplomatic relations. Pyongyang has insisted on large scale reparations not only for the period of Japan's occupation from the early 20th century to 1945 but also for the post-1945 period. Although Japan is prepared to compensate the North for the colonial era—as it had the South when diplomatic relations were established in 1965—Tokyo refuses to accept any additional financial responsibility toward Korea after World War II. Given the DPRK's desperate need for hard currency and economic aid as well as its acceptance of both Koreas' UN membership, prospects for Japan-DPRK diplomatic relations seem favorable in the next few years.

The U.S. Role in Korea

The social basis for current tensions in the ROK-U.S. relationship is a function of time, demography, and the politics of alliance. Two-thirds of South Korea's population was born after the Korean War. Its direct experience has not been of U.S. protection from the North but rather that of U.S. support for repressive military governments and, more recently, pressure on Korean farms and industries to open their markets to U.S. products. The advent of a democratic political system in the late 1980s has also made anti-Americanism a useful political rallying cry for dissident groups unhappy with the essentially conservative major opposition party. Even the ruling elites chafe under the current military command arrangement whereby a U.S. general formally commands most of South Korea's forces. Moreover, the U.S. deployment of nuclear weapons in Korea was aimed more at restraining the Soviet military buildup in Northeast Asia than at deterrence on the peninsula.

There is a tension, then, between a growing ROK desire for political independence from the United States versus an ongoing concern about a possible attack from the North. Complicating this strictly national calculation are U.S. pressures for greater South Korean financial support for U.S. forces stationed in the South and increasing moves to incorporate ROK forces in regional security exercises beyond the peninsula. Washington has also urged the ROK to provide economic aid to less fortunate U.S. allies in the Pacific such as the Philippines. In sum, rather than seeing a greater separation between Seoul and Washington in the future, the latter hopes to incorporate the ROK into a broader, regional security relationship that would include Japan. The ROK navy's participation in *Rimpac 90* is an example.[25]

Most military analysts believe that South Korea should be able to deter and defend against the North primarily on its own after the mid-1990s. The North's superiority in numbers of forces and weapons categories, they believe, is offset by the superior quality of the South's weaponry which is newer, more reliable, and more powerful, particularly with respect to aircraft. In the event of an attack from the North the ROK—with U.S. assistance—would quickly establish air superiority and be able to turn tremendous firepower against Korean People's Army troops and supplies being funneled along the only three narrow attack routes available to them. North Korean forces would also encounter the vast array of ROK anti-tank weapons in place along these roads, neutralizing Pyongyang's armor advantage.[26]

A phased U.S. ground force withdrawal from Korea, already initiated by Defense Secretary Cheney's February 1990 announcement that 5000 non-combatants would be removed by 1993, need not undermine stability. The U.S. defense commitment could be demonstrated in a variety of ways, including more frequent exercises with U.S. forces deployed temporarily to the ROK, stepped-up naval maneuvers in South Korean waters, and continued U.S. participation in a joint command, though in a subordinate role. It might even be wise to leave a small Berlin-like contingent of U.S. forces below the DMZ to give an even stronger signal of U.S. involvement in the event of a North Korean attack.[27] Moreover, Japan could also contribute to Korean security through air and maritime patrols and shared intelligence in the Sea of Japan.

As the United States and ROK change the Combined Command structure for Korea, the role of each force in doctrine and exercises should also be altered. At present, as *Team Spirit* reveals, defensive responsibilities are primarily left to the South Koreans. Attacks against the enemy front and beyond are assigned to U.S. units. South Korean forces must begin to take over responsibilities for frontal assaults, particularly through air force training.[28] According to U.S. Undersecretary of Defense Paul Wolfowitz, by the mid-1990s, the U.S. will turn over the lead role for the Combined Command to the ROK as the U.S. 2nd Infantry Division is reduced in size and capability.[29] Korean forces must train, therefore, to assume the leading military role by that time.

Russian Policy Toward Korea

Russian policy toward Korea is part of Gorbachev's larger perestroika framework. The vast changes wrought through commercial, consular, and then in Autumn 1990, diplomatic relations with the ROK, although designed primarily for economic development purposes within the USSR, could yield derivative political benefits as well. They position Russia to assist in the moderation of tensions on the peninsula and to encourage Pyongyang to initiate its own perestroika. At the same time, however, Moscow abandoned neither its military influence nor cooperation with the North. Joint naval and airforce maneuvers have been conducted with the North Koreans annually since 1986, involving 50 or more aircraft and 40 warships. The Soviets also supplied Mig-29s and SU-25 ground support fighters to the KPA.[30] Soviet warships called regularly at two key North Korean ports, Wonsan and Nampo.

Soviet policy toward the Koreas was laced with contradictions. Its military support for the North was extended in hopes of maintaining a modicum of influence so that the DPRK did not move closer toward China's hardline leadership. On the other hand, the economic development of the Russian Far East can only be achieved with the aid of foreign investment from Japan, the ROK, and the United States.

Strains in Moscow's relations with Pyongyang became apparent in 1989. Soviet media complained about the DPRK's waste of resources in hosting the World Federation of Youth and Students and the poor quality of products shipped to the USSR. Even worse, Radio Moscow spoke favorably of South Korea's unification proposal and the admission of both Koreas to the United Nations in conformity with the principle of universality in that body.[31] These strains continued into 1990 as a TASS reporter was asked to leave North Korea following a dispatch complaining about the hardships of life there. The Soviet weekly *Argumenty i fakty,* in early April, published an expose of Kim Il Sung, noting that he was only a captain in the Soviet army during the anti-Japanese war and had turned the North into a "museum" of self-glorification. The crowning blow was an April 22 interview with Soviet historian Mikhail Smironov, who said that the Korean War had, indeed, been initiated by the North with the assistance of arms and supplies from the USSR.

In the two years following the Seoul Olympics, the ROK established full diplomatic relations with socialist bloc nations: Hungary, Czechoslovakia, Mongolia, Poland, Bulgaria, and Romania. Yugoslavia also has diplomatic ties.

Will closer Russian-South Korean relations lead to a North Korean tilt toward China? While this prospect may have produced anxiety in the past, it is less salient for regional stability today. Sino-Russian normalization means that neither Moscow nor Beijing sees a special relationship with North Korea as a form of leverage over the other. Indeed, PRC trade with South Korea far surpassed that of Soviet-South Korean trade—$3 billion versus $600 million for 1989.[32] China stated, in the wake of the Gorbachev-Roh meeting, that it has no plans to establish diplomatic relations with South Korea, though private ties and economic cooperation will continue.[33]

Gorbachev's minisummit meeting with ROK President Roh Tae Woo in April 1991, emphasized the economic dimension of the relationship. The two governments plan to draw up an economic cooperation treaty and increase trade tenfold by the middle of the decade to $10 billion.[34] The ROK may even see Russia as a longterm ally now that both the United States and Russia are reducing their military forces in the region. No longer a direct threat, Moscow could become an additional friend to help Korea avoid being squeezed by China and Japan. The Asia Pacific Economic Cooperation (APEC) forum can be interpreted as part of this same strategy. It helps integrate South Korea into a Pacific rim political and economic consultative forum which includes North America as well as north and southeast Asia.

South Korea's diplomatic victories over the past two years have also led to new initiatives in North Korean diplomacy. In addition to negotiations with Japan on establishing diplomatic relations, the DPRK hosted the Interparliamentary Union on April 1991, and has launched an effort to promote new relations with southeast Asia in hopes of obtaining economic aid from the ASEAN states. Indicative of this redirection of diplomatic effort is Pyongyang's decision to close seven embassies in subsaharan Africa while opening new missions in Thailand and the Philippines.[35]

The Nuclear Issue in Korea

One of the most worrisome features for Korea's future security is the issue of theater nuclear weapons on the peninsula. The North has initiated what may be its own weapons development program, a development that opens up the possibility of nuclear arms control negotiations in Korea for the first time since the Korean War.

According to International Atomic Energy Agency data, North Korea currently operates three nuclear reactors, one developed independently, the others provided by the Soviet Union. Recently released Spot satellite photos reveal both a new nuclear reactor in Yongbyan and a reprocessing facility for nuclear fuel. The latter, alongside what could be a building for testing nuclear detonation devices, have South Korea, the United States, and Russia concerned. The annual amount of plutonium produced by the plants through extraction from spent uranium fuel is six to seven kilograms, enough to produce a single atomic weapon each year.[36]

U.S. anxiety over Pyongyang's nuclear development has several sources: (1) the DPRK would become the first nuclear-armed developing country hostile to the United States. (2) the North has continued to sell missiles and other types of weapons to many countries, including Iraq and Syria. The prospect of nuclear weapons being exported to the Middle East would create a new and even more dangerous security dilemma there; and (3) North Korean acquisition of nuclear weapons could result in a South Korean decision to accelerate its nuclear development, further escalating tension on the peninsula.

Although North Korea signed the Nuclear Nonproliferation Treaty in 1985, it has refused on-site inspections pending a withdrawal of U.S. nuclear arms from the South.[37] Herein lies the possibility for a nuclear arms withdrawal agreement. Given the South's qualitative military superiority, its much larger population, and vastly greater economy, plus the lack of credibility in using nuclear weapons in such a confined location as the Korean peninsula, an agreement on the withdrawal of theater nuclear weapons from the South in exchange for permanent international inspection of Northern atomic facilities seems sensible. Moreover, insofar as Russia fears that some of the Korean-based weapons are really directed against the Russian Far East, Moscow could also be reassured by such an agreement and perhaps even incorporated into it through a broader Northeast Asian arms control regime. Moscow offered to be a guarantor for a nuclear-free Korea.[38]

The United States insists that diplomatic relations with Pyongyang depend not only on IAEA inspection of the Yongbyan complex but also on the destruction of existing facilities which could provide weapons-grade uranium.[39] The South engaged in sabre-rattling over the Northern plant in April 1991. Taking their cue from the Israeli attack on an Iraqi reactor in 1981, the ROK Defense Minister warned that the South might preemptively destroy the DPRK complex if it appeared to be manufacturing atomic bombs within five years. Japan, too, has insisted that diplomatic relations— and by implication economic aid—can only occur after Pyongyang agrees to IAEA inspection and the international agency certifies that no weapons-grade plutonium is being produced or stored.[40] Even the USSR insisted that future cooperation depended on DPRK compliance with IAEA safeguards and inspection.[41]

Responding to pressure from both allies and adversaries Kim Il Sung seemed to relent. In June 1991, North Korea stated it would sign an agreement permitting IAEA inspection of all its nuclear facilities. Pyongyang dropped its demand that inspection in the North be linked to the removal of U.S. nuclear weapons from the South, though DPRK public statements continue to demand their departure.[42]

By September 1991, however, the North had still not arranged an inspection timetable although U.S. theater nuclear weapons have been removed from the South as part of a regional nuclear arms control effort. They were no longer needed as a deterrent to the North as Southern military capabilities increase in the 1990s and Soviet and Chinese guarantees to the North became more circumscribed.[43]

Conclusion: Arms Control Prospects

This discussion of North Pacific security and arms control possibilities breaks logically into two parts: one dealing with the Korean peninsula, where armed forces confront each other along a demarcated land boundary; and the other covering the whole region with its continental, insular, air, and maritime components.

The North Koreans, beginning in 1987, have proposed linking a mutual reduction in the forces of both Koreas with a parallel phased withdrawal of all U.S. forces from the peninsula. Washington and Seoul responded that arms negotiations should be preceded by the development of greater trust between Seoul and Pyongyang, beginning with such CBMs as the mutual notification and observation of military exercises.

Putting the unification issue aside, it seems that the 1990s could provide arms reduction opportunities for the peninsula. U.S. forces are being gradually reduced. Washington and Seoul could negotiate further U.S. force withdrawals in exchange for a pullback of KPA forces from the 38th parallel and their reconfiguration in a less threatening mode.

Interestingly, Russian commentary on the Seoul-Washington proposals for CBMs in Korea has been favorable. Moscow has approved the initial reduction plans for U.S. forces in South Korea as well as the suggestion for mutual notification and observation of North and South Korean military exercises.[44] In its most recent June 1990 proposals, the North reiterated its willingness to accept a neutral nations supervisory presence (NNSC) in the DMZ after the forces of the two sides had been reduced to 100,000 each. Significantly the NNSC proposal seems to include Poland and Czechoslovakia despite their change in political orientation. This should certainly make the concept more agreeable to Seoul and Washington.[45]

While opportunities exist for tension reduction in Korea, the medium-term goals of the two antagonists remain contradictory. The DPRK sees arms control and CBMs as significant only as steps along the path to unification under Pyongyang's terms: the creation of a confederation. For the South, the medium-term goal is cross recognition of two *independent* governments by each side's primary backers—the United States, Japan,

Russia, and China. Although the ROK envisages reunification as a longterm goal, its realization would be based on free elections to form a bicameral legislature whose lower house would be based on population.[46] This arrangement would insure the North's subordination and, therefore, is unacceptable to the DPRK as long as it remains a Leninist regime.

Conclusion

Any *regional* approach to tension reduction must focus particularly on the air and maritime forces of the United States, Japan, the Koreas, and Russia. (Because China's power projection capability in the North Pacific remains limited, its forces are not included in this discussion.) From Tokyo's perspective, the major issues involved in regional security include the reversion of the northern islands and a reduction in threatening Soviet deployments and maneuvers. Washington's defense concerns are the same. The two Koreas would like to lock their major backers into their preferred outcomes on the peninsula and separate their adversary from its mentors. Russia encourages a North Pacific arrangement that would remove the Japanese and U.S. navies from the northern Sea of Japan and Sea of Okhotsk as well as guarantee maritime movement through the Japanese straits. Can any consensus be reached over these seemingly disparate goals?

A first step toward regional negotiations may have been taken in March 1990, when Prime Minister Kaifu suggested a North Pacific conference which would include the actors discussed in this paper plus China. Kaifu proposed the conference focus on Korea. The Soviet response was to welcome the proposal but urge that it be broadened to include Gorbachev's earlier offer to freeze and ultimately reduce the armed forces of all participants in the North Pacific.[47] In his April 1991 Tokyo meeting with the Japanese Prime Minister, the Soviet President tabled another proposal for a five nation regional security conclave consisting of the U.S.S.R., Japan, China, India, and the United States. Mr. Kaifu rejected this idea on two grounds: First, he reiterated that Asian security issues were too diverse to be addressed in a region-wide forum and should be resolved in terms of their individual characteristics. Second, it would be inappropriate for a group of major powers to impose their security views on the smaller states of the region.[48]

It is improbable, moreover, that multilateral talks on regional arms will begin before the middle of the decade for two reasons. First, Japan is involved in a major air and maritime development program to fulfill its commitment to defend the home islands essentially unaided and to monitor the sea and air lanes within 1000 miles of Honshu. Those capabilities will probably not be achieved until the mid-1990s. The United States second major force reduction stage in the Pacific may also occur around that time.

The confluence of these two developments could make regional arms reduction talks more attractive around the middle of the decade. Russia wants to protect its SSBNs and the Russian Far East from the strike power of Seventh Fleet U.S. carrier battle groups. Washington and Tokyo, in turn, seek to reduce the Russian air and naval threat to Japan and would prefer to see Russia commit to keeping most of its Pacific Fleet in home waters.

Some promising signs already exist that Russian deployment trends are declining. In 1989, the Japan Defense Agency reported that 520 Soviet navy ships passed through the Japanese straits, down from a peak of 710 in 1987. Soviet aircraft flying near Japan's airspace declined to 220 in 1989 compared with a high of 395 in 1984. The JDA also predicts that the Russian Pacific Fleet's major surface vessels and submarines will be cut by one-third in the mid-1990s to 81 and 98 respectively.[49]

An important component of arms control discussions in the Pacific should deal with theater nuclear arms at sea. Regional CBMs and crisis management arrangements must cope with the fact that both the Russian and U.S. navies possess nuclear-tipped SLCMs. At the very least, a no-first-use agreement should be considered, for it would reduce the prospect of either side engaging in a preemptive strike during a crisis. Beyond that, more general control of SLCMs is needed. Because they are highly accurate long-range weapons, they could be used for nuclear attack on both sea and land targets. An agreement on the removal of nuclear warheads from sea-based cruise missiles would enhance stability. The problem is verification.

Unsurprisingly, the U.S. Navy adamantly opposes the idea of intrusive verification by monitors visiting U.S. ships at sea to determine whether its cruise missiles are nuclear-tipped. The Navy sees this as a first step toward limiting its ability to ensure freedom of the seas. Other procedures are being developed, however, that may not require the presence of foreigners on board warships. In July 1989, the Soviet Academy of Sciences and the private American Natural Resources Defense Council tested passive radiation detectors that, they claimed, were able to identify missiles with nuclear warheads.[50] Experiments such as these should be continued with official U.S. support rather than rejected peremptorily. Moreover, banning nuclear SLCMs would probably be of greater benefit to the United States than to Russia as short-range SLCMs are the major striking force of the Russian Navy. Banning them would help to insure U.S. fleet survival in a crisis. Moreover, there is a much higher concentration of U.S., Japanese, and Korean populations close to shores than in Russia. Hence, the nuclear SLCM is the greater threat to the United States and its allies. Nuclear SLCMs would also permit Russia to compensate for reduced accuracy.

Additional CBMs for the Russian and U.S. navies could include high-level professional officer discussions of doctrines, deployments, exercise notification, exchange of observers, and an expansion of the incidents at sea agreements.[51] On the Russian side, a cap could be placed on the introduction of new systems for the Pacific Fleet, precluding, for example, the deployment of a fixed-wing aircraft carrier such as the *Tbilisi*. Moscow could also agree to continue to keep the bulk of its fleet within 200 miles of Vladivostok in a defensive configuration. In exchange, Japan and the United States could honor a buffer zone around the Sea of Okhotsk, no longer sending task forces into Russia's SSBN bastion. This agreement could be facilitated if the START treaty leads to an SSBN reduction as one component of a strategic weapons builddown. All three countries could inaugurate reciprocal notification of major exercises while extending invitations to each other as observers. Finally, both the United States and Russia could place limits on the quantity and sophistication of weapons provided to such allies as North Korea, South Korea, Thailand, and Vietnam. Such policy changes would enhance regional stability, reduce the prospect of surprise attack, and lead to a degree of military disengagement.

These alterations in the U.S.-Asian security posture suggested for the 1990s logically grow from the Nixon Doctrine enunciated two decades ago. They presage a region increasingly independent of U.S. military guarantees and responsible for its own security. These changes do not mean the end of U.S. alliance arrangements in the Pacific, but they do portend a reconfiguration as Japan and the ROK take positions on the world political stage commensurate with their economic strength. Washington remains a friend but may no longer be able to serve as mentor. Nevertheless, a continued U.S. military presence in the Pacific remains essential to sustain the balance of power in the area—a balance that will be increasingly multipolar as the 21st Century dawns.

Notes

1. The multinational constabulary concept was presented by Donald Hellmann at the National Defense University's Asian Strategy Conference, May 22, 1990. While it offers an interesting possibility for cooperation with the Soviet navy for SLOC protection, the idea seems less promising with respect to disputed territories such as the Spratly islands in the South China Sea.

2. Susan Rasky, "Administration to Weigh Plan for Military Cut," *The New York Times,* June 7, 1990.

3. These figures are provided by David Anderson, "Asia Needs the Pax Americana," *The Asian Wall Street Journal Weekly,* March 26, 1990.

4. A good review of the Soviet Diplomatic approach to security in Asia may be found in Kenneth G. Weiss, "Throwing Down the Gauntlet: the Soviet Challenge in the Pacific," Comparative Strategy (8) 1989, pp. 149–180.

5. Paul Kreisberg, "The U.S. and Asia in 1989," Asian Survey, January 1990 (30, 1), p. 21.

6. Steven R. Weisman, "Japanese-U.S. Relations Undergoing Redesign," *The New York Times,* June 4, 1990.

7. Larry A. Niksch, Japan-U.S. Relations in the 1990s (Washington, D.C. Congressional Research Service 89–264F, April 7, 1989), pp. 11 and 13.

8. Ibid., pp 8–10.

9. Ibid., p. 6.

10. David E. Sanger, "U.S. and Japan Work Together on Weapons systems Research," *The New York Times,* March 28, 1990.

11. Tai Ming Cheung, "A Yen for Arms," *Far Eastern Economic Review,* February 22, 1990, pp. 58 and 60. Also see Robert L. Rau, "United States-Japan Security Relations: Strategic Issues, Interoperability, Burdensharing, and Powersharing," (a paper presented to the 31st annual meeting of the International Studies Association, Washington, D.C., April 13, 1990), p.6.

12. Robert Y. Horiguchi, "Big U.S. Show of Strength," *Pacific Defence Reporter,* February 1990, p. 43.

13. *The Korean Times* (Seoul) March 13, 1990, in FBIS, *Daily Report East Asia,* March 16, 1990, p. 19.

14. Interview with Pacfic Fleet Commander, Admiral Gennadiy Khvatov, on the Moscow World Service in English, March 6, 1990, in FBIS, *Daily Report Soviet Union,* March 19, 1990, p. 22. The JDSF Stement is reported by *Kyodo,* April 16, 1990, in FBIS, *Daily Report East Asia,* April 12, 1990, pp. 2–3.

15. *Kyodo,* April 14, 1990, in FBIS, *Daily Report East Asia,* April 17, 1990, p. 6.

16. 19. Commentary on Japan's 1991 Defense White Paper carried by Radio Moscow in Japanese, July 30, 1991, in FBIS, *Daily Report Soviet Union,* August 1, 1991, p. 29. Also see *Krasnaya Zvezda,* July 16, 1991.

17. Robert Y. Horiguchi, "Soviets Face Heavy Distrust," *Pacific Defence Reporter,* May 1989, pp.49–50.

18. *Japan Times,* July 22, 1989, *Kyodo,* May 22, 1990, in FBIS, *Daily Report East Asia,* May 23, 1990, p. 8.

19. David E. Sanger, "Japanese Feel Quite Ready For a Visit From Gorbachev," *The New York Times,* June 5, 1990.

20. Cited in Chong-sik Lee, "Political Change, Revolution, and the Dialogue in the Two Koreas," *Asian Survey* (29, 11) November 1989, pp. 1033–1034.

21. James Sterngold, "Sound of Two Hands Shaking Wakes Asia," *The New York Times,* June 10, 1990.

22. This discussion on differing views toward unification is drawn from In-Young Chun, "The Status of Korean Unification Negotiation," (a paper presented to the 31st annual meeting of the International Studies Association, Washington, D.C., April 10–14, 1990) pp. 15–18.

23. *Yonhap* (Seoul) February 24, 1990, in FBIS, *Daily Report East Asia,* February 26, 1990, p. 38.

24. The most recent iteration of Pyongyang's disarmament proposal came in Kim Il Sung's address to the Supreme Peoples Assembly as carried by the Pyongyang Domestic Service in Korean, May 24, 1990, in FBIS, *Daily Report East Asia,* May 24, 1990, especially pp. 17–25. The quotation is drawn from a *Korean Central*

News Agency (KCNA) dispatch, March 21, 1990, in FBIS, *Daily Report East Asia,* March 21, 1990, p. 11.

25. See the reports of March 25, 1990, in *The Korea Times* and *Choson Ilbo,* carried respectively in FBIS, *Daily Report East Asia,* March 26, 1990, p. 47; and March 28, 1990, p. 28.

26. A good military analysis is given by Stephen D. Goose, "U.S. Forces in Korean: Assessing a Reduction," in Ted Galen Carpenter, ed., *Collective Defense or Strategic Independence* (Lexington, Mass.: Lexington Books, 1989)

27. These ideas are explored in Larry Niksch, "South Korea: Should the U.S. Withdraw?" (a paper presented to a conference on *United States Policy Toward the East Asian/Western Pacific Region* (St. John University Institute of Asian Studies, New York, November 17–18, 1989), pp.25–28.

28. See the analysis in *MAL* (Seoul) December 1989, in FBIS, *Daily Report East Asia,* March 1, 1990. pp. 50–52.

29. Susuma Anwanohara, "Flurry of Signals," *Far Wastern Economic Review,* May 3, 1990, pp. 10–11.

30. Stephen Blank, "Violins With a Touch of Brass," pp. 13–14.

31. Cited in Kong-dan Oh, "North Korea in 1989: Touched by the Winds of Change?" *Asian Survey* (30, 1) January 1990, p. 79.

32. Radio Moscow International Service in Korean, April 28, 1990, in FBIS, *Daily Report Soviet Union,* May 1, 1990, p. 24.

33. *Kyodo,* June 7, 1990, in FBIS, *Daily Report East Asia,* June 7, 1990, p.1.

34. James Sterngold, "Gorbachev Reaps Accord in Korea," *The New York Times,* April 21, 1991.

35. *Yonhap* (Seoul) July 22, 1991, in FBIS, *Daily Report East Asia,* July 22, 1991, p. 38.

36. Reports on North Korean nuclear developments were carried by *Chungang Ilbo* May 25, 1990, and *Choson Ilbo,* April 18, 1990, in FBIS, *Daily Report East Asia,* May 25, 1990, pp. 19–20, 37–38; and April 23, 1990, pp.19–20.

37. Press conference in Washington, D.C., given by Choe U-chin, deputy director of North Korea's Institute for Peace and Arms Control in *Hangyore Sinmun* (Seoul) May 22, 1990, carried by FBIS, *Daily Report East Asia,* May 24, 1990, pp. 30–31.

38. *Izvestia,* November 12, 1989, in FBIS, *Daily Report Soviet Union,* November 18, 1989, pp. 26–27.

39. Shim Jae Hoon, "The Pace Quickens," *Far Eastern Economic Review,* August 1, 1991, p. 23.

40. David Sanger, "Furor in Seoul Over North's Atomic Plants," *The New York Times,* April 16, 1991.

41. *Tass,* April 18, 1991, in FBIS, Daily Report Soviet Union, May 2, 1991, p. 6.

42. David Sanger, "North Korea to Allow International Inspection of Its Nuclear Sites," *The New York Times,* June 9, 1991.

43. See, for example, the Rok-U.S. Study Group Report sponsored by the Wast-West Center (Honolulu): *Interests and Opportunities in U.S.-Korea Relations,* February 1991. Especially Chapter Four.

44. *Kraznaya Zvezda,* April 29, 1990, in FBIS, *Daily Report Soviet Union,* May 3, 1990, p. 3.

45. *Yonhap,* June 2, 1990, in FBIS, *Daily Report East Asia,* June 5, 1990, p. 4.

46. *Dialog With North Korea* (Washington, D.C.: The Carnegie Endowment For International Peace, May 30–31, 1989) p. 16.

47. *Pravda,* March 20, 1990, in FBIS, *Daily Report Soviet Union,* March 26, 1990, p. 24.

48. *Kyodo,* April 4, 1990, in FBIS, Daily Report East Asia, June 4, 1990, p. 16.

49. *Kyodo,* June 4, 1990, in FBIS, Daily Report East Asia, June 5, 1990, p. 16.

50. Michael L. Ross, "Disarmament At Sea," *Foreign Policy* (77) Winter 1989–1990, p. 800.

51. Soviet Foreign Minister Edward Shevardnadze proposed these measures at the Internaitonal Open Skies Conference in Ottawa. See *Tass,* February 12, 1990, in FBIS, *Daily Report Soviet Union,* February 13, 1990, pp. 1–3.

7

Conclusion: The End
of Superpower Conflict

Melvin A. Goodman

We've got to stay together on this.
—President Gorbachev to Secretary of
of State Baker during the Persian Gulf crisis in 1990.

A key to the handling of the Iraqi crisis in 1990 was the new Soviet-U.S. relationship, particularly the unprecedented cooperation between the superpowers in response to crises in the Third World. If the United States had not been certain of the Soviet response, it would have been far more hazardous—if not impossible—to transfer its ground forces and modern armor in Europe to the Persian Gulf. If the Soviet Union had lacked confidence about U.S. intentions toward a region so close to its borders, it would have been politically difficult for President Gorbachev to endorse the massive U.S. build-up and join the political and psychological campaign against Saddam Hussein. For the first time since the Suez crisis in 1956, the U.S. and the Soviet Union did not back different clients in a Middle East conflict and, for the first time since the Six-Day War in 1967, Moscow did not offer diplomatic and political protection for an Arab client.

The Soviet Union was unwilling to commit its own forces to the Persian Gulf, but U.S. negotiations with Moscow were central to the series of UN resolutions denouncing Iraq's invasion of Kuwait—particularly the resolution authorizing the use of force—and the exchange of visits between Secretary Baker and Iraqi Foreign Minister Tariq Azziz in December 1990. According to U.S. officials, the Baker mission was in response to Gorbachev's call for one last diplomatic effort to persuade Iraq to withdraw peacefully from Kuwait.[1] In return, the U.S. agreed to give the Soviets advance notice of any use of force and encouraged the conservative Gulf states to provide several billion dollars in aid and loans to the USSR.

Soviet-U.S. cooperation, particularly efforts to resolve differences and work out UN authorization for the use of force, established an important precedent for conflict resolution throughout the Third World. A compromise was arranged in Cambodia, and a settlement in Ethiopia has been achieved. Intensive searches for peace are underway in the Middle East, and Moscow and Washington are cooperating in ending Iraq's strategic capabilities. Improvements have been seen in the conflict between North and South Korea, and progress has been made in Central America. Saddam Hussein failed to understand that Soviet-U.S. security regimes, which once concentrated on arms control, Europe, and nonproliferation, also included Third World issues and could prevent the establishment of regional hegemony.

Conflict Resolution and the Third World

Moscow's interest in resolving regional crises is related directly to Gorbachev's efforts to diminish the Kremlin's world role and chances of military confrontation. Following his accession to power in 1985, the Soviet president conducted a strategic retreat that includes unilateral troop withdrawals from Eastern Europe and the Sino-Soviet border, withdrawal from Afghanistan and Mongolia, reduced military assistance and advisers in the Third World, and a comprehensive arms control agenda. He swept aside Foreign Minister Andrei Gromyko in the summer of 1985 and rapidly changed policies associated with Gromyko. One arms control proposal followed another in the wake of Gorbachev's major disarmament address in 1986. The Soviet grip on Eastern Europe was relaxed after a major statement on the anniversary of the Bolshevik revolution in 1987 and, the following year, the Soviets began to cooperate privately with the United States to reach a cease-fire agreement in Angola that included Cuban withdrawal. Vietnamese withdrawal from Cambodia in 1989 led to a Security Council agreement for monitoring the transition to a national reconciliation government in Phnom Penh. An agreement on conventional forces in Europe in 1990 preceded the dissolution of the Warsaw Pact as a military alliance.

Since 1987, Gorbachev encouraged a role for the United Nations in conflict resolution in the Third World as well as greater use of UN military observers and peacekeeping forces to separate warring parties and mediate disputes. Secretary Baker, during his visit with Gorbachev in November 1990, emphasized the importance of Moscow's approach toward collective security and argued that Saddam Hussein was testing the credibility of the United Nations and the Soviet president's vision of how the world should work. "We cannot have the UN go the way of the League of Nations," said Baker.[2]

Conflict Resolution and Latin America

Over the past two years, Soviet-U.S. cooperation defused several points of conflict in the Caribbean and Central America. The Nicaraguan example was most dramatic, with the Soviets cutting off arms to the Sandinistas in 1989 and pressing for elections in February 1990, then persuading the Nicaraguan government to halt arms shipments to insurgents in El Salvador. Moscow cooperated fully with the UN Observer Group in Central America (ONUCA), which monitors compliance with the Central American agreement prohibiting use of territory to aid guerrilla operations in neighboring states.

Moscow and Washington issued their first joint statement to support a settlement in El Salvador in October 1990, when UN efforts to arrange peace talks reached an impasse.[3] The United States presumably was counting on the Soviets to urge Cuba to support efforts to end the fighting, and Moscow was trying to appeal to those factions in the U.S. Congress that wanted to cut military aid to the government of President Alfredo Cristiani. Moscow's initial efforts on behalf of a peace process led to the reestablishment of diplomatic relations with the government in San Salvador.

A major security agreement was signed in September 1991, when the Salvadoran government and guerrilla representatives agreed on the organization of a new national police force under civilian control and reduction of the armed forces. The government pledged to purge the military of officers who were perceived as corrupt or brutal and to allow the guerrillas to buy and remain on land they have occupied for years. The agreement covers a broad range of security and economic issues that will reintegrate the guerrillas of the Farabundo Marti National Liberation Front into civilian life. For the past several years, the United States and the Soviet Union coaxed and even bullied their clients in El Salvador to negotiate such an agreement.

Conflict Resolution and the Middle East

Moscow has reduced reliance on military influence in the Middle East and the Persian Gulf in order to pursue cooperation with the United States on a broad range of issues. In addition to virtually providing *carte blanche* to Washington in the Gulf, the Soviets endorsed diplomatic solutions to the Arab-Israeli dispute and improved relations with Israel and conservative Arab states. In return for Israeli willingness to attend a peace conference, the Soviets reestablished full diplomatic relations with Israel in October 1991. They urged moderation on all sides in Lebanon; publicly discouraged Libyan, Palestinian, and Syrian use of terrorism; and refused to provide military parity for Syria in its rivalry with Israel.

Soviet condemnation of terrorism in the Middle East and Southwest Asia was a strong indicator of a new policy toward the region. The turning point took place in 1986, when Moscow condemned the Palestinian seizure of a U.S. airliner that resulted in the deaths of more than twenty persons. A TASS statement declared that "there can be no justification for this act, and those who committed the crime, no matter what motives guided them."[4] The Palestinian attack on a Greek cruise ship in 1988 and the bombing of a civilian Israeli bus were described as "terrorist" acts by Foreign Ministry spokesman Gennady Gerasimov.[5] Moscow even cooperated with the Israeli government in 1989, following the hijacking of a Soviet airliner to Tel Aviv, and Deputy Director of the KGB Lt. Gen. Vitaly Ponomarev noted KGB willingness to work with other intelligence services on such matters.[6]

The Soviets reduced their own military activities in the region, particularly military support for clients. There was a decline in the operational tempo and presence of naval forces and aviation in the region: a significant number of military advisers were withdrawn, naval deployments in the Mediterranean were slashed, and joint exercises with Arab navies were reduced. Declining arms sales will mean further cuts in the advisory presence. Gorbachev announced in May 1990 that the USSR would limit arms sales even further if the United States were willing to show restraint in this area. Several months later, a Soviet general officer called for "radical reduction" in arms sales and an "embargo" on dual purpose weapons in order to limit the "threat from the south."[7]

Clearly the Soviets wanted the United Nations to play a central role in conflict resolution in the area. As a result, Moscow paid its assessment for the International Force in Lebanon (UNIFIL) and the peacekeeping forces in the Golan Heights.[8] Gorbachev called for a UN role in verifying regional arms agreements, investigating international terrorism, and establishing standards for human rights. The Soviets endorsed UN Resolution 598 to end the Iran-Iraq war and campaigned for a revival of the Military Staff Committee to implement a series of resolutions dealing with the Iraqi invasion of Kuwait. Moscow's hesitancy in endorsing the use of force against Iraq in 1990 was designed in part to try "new ideas" to obtain a political solution to the crisis.[9]

Conflict Resolution and Africa

Extensive Soviet-U.S. involvement in discussions between the Marxist government in Ethiopia and Eritrean separatists as well as the government and insurgents in Angola led to agreements in both cases. The Soviets reduced military aid and advisors in Ethiopia and Angola and encouraged both states to resume negotiations with the United States. U.S. officials met secretly for the first time with Ethiopian government and separatist officials in October 1990.[10] The Ethiopians were willing to pursue talks with Soviet-U.S. participation, and the Eritrean People's Liberation Front permitted a role for Moscow at the talks that led to a cease fire. Moscow's decision to abandon Mengistu at his point of greatest peril was a strong indicator of Gorbachev's decision to retreat from positions in the Third World and seek accommodation with the United States.

Presidents Bush and Gorbachev agreed at a summit meeting in Washington in June 1990 that they would work together to prevent a new famine in Ethiopia, but the Eritreans blocked progress on that front for several months. Under the Bush-Gorbachev agreement, Soviet transport planes, previously used to ferry Ethiopian military supplies, eventually delivered U.S. food to people living in isolated areas in Eritrea and Ethiopia. Eritrean shelling of Asmara initially prevented the planes from landing. So once again, regional intransigence threatened to prevent the resolution of a regional crisis, but the Soviet-U.S. relationship contributed to an agreement to open the rebel-held port of Massawa on the Red Sea and then transport food to the beseiged Eritrean provincial capital in Asmara.[11] The accord, ending a five-month deadlock that began after the Bush-Gorbachev summit meeting, allowed thousands of tons of food to reach more than four million people threatened by starvation in the Horn of Africa.

Soviet and U.S. intervention also played a role in ending one of Africa's longest-running wars, the sixteen year confrontation between the leftist government of President Jose Eduardo dos Santos in Angola and the American-backed UNITA rebels. Under the terms of the agreement, the rebels put down their arms in May 1991 and dos Santos and UNITA leader Jonas Savimbi signed a peace treaty in Portugal. Angola ended the one-party state and the centrally planned economy that were introduced in 1975, and the Popular Movement for the Liberation of Angola formally abandoned Marxism-Leninism and recast itself as a social democratic party. An accord in 1988, signed by Cuba and South Africa, arranged the departure of more than 50,000 Cuban troops. Soviet-U.S. mediation persuaded the Luanda regime and UNITA officials to reach a compromise on the issue of an election timetable.

In addition to responding to humanitarian emergencies on the Horn and Sudan, Russian-U.S. cooperation could be an important element in resolving numerous food and health problems on the continent. Millions of people are at risk on the Horn of Africa, with the effects of the droughts being aggravated by a civil war that was waged for nearly thirty years. Elsewhere in Africa, the commission which monitored Cuban and South African withdrawal from Angola could be a model for airing and resolving differences in flash point situations. The willingness of Moscow and

Washington to cooperate with various UN institutions was central to the peacekeeping success in Angola, leaving Mozambique as the only country in southern Africa still ravaged by guerrilla warfare. The monitoring of the political process in Namibia could be applied to other areas of democratic reform throughout the continent.

Conflict Resolution and Southwest and Southeast Asia

The Soviet withdrawal from Afghanistan in 1989 acknowledged that Moscow's military presence in Southwest Asia was a major obstacle to its long-term regional objectives in South Asia and could even leave a permanent scar on Soviet relations in the area. Gorbachev presumably believed that complete Soviet withdrawal would not only remove an irritant in Soviet relations with India—the key to Moscow's position in the region—but could open opportunities for improved relations with Pakistan and Iran as well as China and the United States.

The United States and the Soviet Union announced in September 1991 that they would stop all arms sales to combatants in Afghanistan and encourage the United Nations to supervise a transition to free elections for a new government. The two sides agreed not to increase current arms shipments to their respective Afghan allies, thus ending a contentious issue between Moscow and Washington. They finally halted all military supplies by the end of 1991, and the Afghan government collapsed in April 1992.

Soviet pressure on Vietnam to leave Cambodia in 1989 also improved Moscow's regional position. Changes at the global level, particularly the interest of the United States and the Soviet Union in lowering the cost and risk of Third World involvement, produced important steps in creating a Cambodian peace plan. But instability at the regional level, particularly significant differences between the four factions battling for sovereignty, blocked a final settlement.

The breakthrough took place in October 1991, when Cambodia's warring factions signed a peace treaty that produced a cease-fire and called for the repatriation of refugees and elections by 1993. The agreement, brokered by the United States, the Soviet Union, and China, gave the United Nations the central role for insuring that the accord is respected and that Cambodia's Supreme National Council has the power to administer its key ministries, including defense, foreign affairs, finance, and communications. This could become the largest operation that the United Nations has ever administered, including the demobilization of the Cambodian and guerrilla armies, the organization of elections, and the repatriation of more than three hundred thousand refugees.

Although the role of the UN will be crucial, it took close cooperation between Moscow and Washington to arrange such a peace treaty. This agreement came in the wake of Soviet-U.S. success in Namibia, Angola, Afghanistan, and El Salvador. In return for Vietnam's support of the Cambodian agreement, the U.S. agreed to seek a gradual normalization of its relations with Vietnam and to eventually establish full diplomatic relations with Cambodia and Laos. The Russians will gain from the resolution of another difference on regional matters with China.

It will be more difficult for Russians and Americans to mediate the Indian-Pakistani conflict over Kashmir, but Moscow's improved relations with China could encourage the government in New Delhi to pursue its own rapprochement with Beijing. Similarly, any Russian-U.S. agreement on arms transfers to the government in Kabul and the Afghan resistance forces could lessen tensions in South Asia and lead to a dialogue between India and Pakistan. Both Russia and the United States want to limit the transfer of weaponry and technology that benefits nuclear weapons programs in New Delhi and Islamabad. Confidence building measures between Moscow and Washington could serve as a model for observation and verification of military exercises and weapons stockpiles in South Asia.

Conflict Resolution and Asia

Gorbachev's strategy for Asia had been to undo the damage done by the confrontational style of the Brezhnev era, and Yeltsin has continued these policies thus far. The Soviets established diplomatic relations with South Korea, and Gorbachev's trip to Japan, although failing to break the impasse over the issue of the four Soviet-occupied island groups that Japan calls its Northern Territories, marked an improvement in Soviet-Japanese relations. For the first time in twenty years, Russia has admitted that there is a territorial dispute over the islands; an agreement would end Russian-Japanese hostility, still steeped in cold-war bitterness, and improve Moscow's negotiating positions throughout the region.

The Soviets announced a unilateral withdrawal from the islands during the visit to Moscow of Japanese Foreign Minister Taro Nakayama. Moscow did not state when the withdrawal would take place, but indicated that more than 2,000 troops would be involved.[12] The announcement followed Gorbachev's pledge in Tokyo to reduce the Soviet military presence on the islands. The Soviet foreign ministry lifted visa restrictions so that Japanese citizens may travel freely to the islands and stated that free-enterprise zones will be created, giving preference to Japanese firms. Yeltsin will travel to Japan and possibly China in the fall of 1992, and compromises on territorial issues with these former adversaries cannot be ruled out.

Moscow appears to favor a security arrangement for the Pacific that would include naval reductions in return for U.S. and Japanese reductions in the Sea of Japan and the Sea of Okhotsk. In an effort to build confidence in the regime, Moscow has reduced the number of naval ships that pass through the Japanese straits and aircraft that fly near Japanese airspace. Moscow may agree to swap the territories for Japanese cash and credits, which would be similar to the exchange arranged in 1990 for the unification of Germany. Nevertheless, Moscow has applied far less "new thinking" to relations with Japan than to other parts of the world; in 1990, for example, Gorbachev continued to insist that Moscow had "no land to spare" for Japan.[13]

Confidence-building measures for Russian and U.S. navies in the Pacific could include professional military discussion of doctrine and deployment, notification of exercises, exchanges of observers, and expansion of the incidents-at-sea treaty. The Russians could accept a ceiling on the introduction of new systems for the Pacific fleet such as the deployment of a fixed-wing aircraft carrier in return for U.S. acceptance of a buffer zone around the Sea of Okhotsk, Russia's bastion for its SSBNs. Moscow and Washington have ageed to remove all tactical nuclear weapons from surface ships and attack submarines, and could pursue limits on sophisticated weapons provided to such allies as North and South Korea, Thailand, and Vietnam to enhance regional stability and reduce the prospect of surprise attack.

Policy of National Reconciliation

Gorbachev urged a policy of national reconciliation (or power sharing) as an alternative to military confrontation in Afghanistan, Cambodia, Angola, and Nicaragua.[14] Babrak Karmal opposed the policy of national reconciliation in Afghanistan and was replaced by Mohammad Najibullah in 1986, who immediately proclaimed a cease-fire and offered to compromise with opposing Afghan factions. In November 1990, Najibullah met secretly for the first time with leaders of the Afghan opposition in Geneva, seat of UN headquarters in Europe and main site of UN-sponsored talks that led to Soviet withdrawal.[15] Najibullah had long wanted to hold such a meeting as evidence of his growing acceptance in the country and as an indication that Moscow's policy of national reconcilation was beginning to work.

The conciliatory behavior of such Soviet clients as the Afghan government, the MPLA in Angola, the Cambodians, and the Sandinistas was in part a response to Moscow's decision to end the competition with the United States in the Third World. Most recently, Ethiopia's willingness to enter peace talks with Eritrean separatists and allow relief shipment into government-occupied areas marked another success for Soviet-U.S. cooperation.[16] Mozambique has pursued a series of political and economic reforms in the wake of Soviet withdrawal from that country. Angola,

Cambodia, and Mozambique have renounced communism as an official ideology and endorsed mixed or free-market economies.

The deterioration of the Russian economy and Moscow's preoccupation with its internal disarray led to the policy of national reconciliation and the view that Moscow had "no interests justifying the use of military resources outside the socialist community."[17] Andrei Kozyrev, a former high-ranking Soviet foreign ministry official and the current foreign minister of Russia, criticized Soviet policy in the Third World and argued that Moscow's efforts to build an alliance against the West had only aroused distrust of Soviet motives and creation of an anti-Soviet coalition. He acknowledged that the United States had "immeasurably broader and deeper" interests than the USSR in the Third World and made the case for cooperating with Washington in resolving regional conflicts. Following the coup failure in 1991, Kozyrev said that Russian President Boris Yeltsin would move faster than Gorbachev in making unilateral military cuts, including the end of military and economic assistance to Cuba and Afghanistan. Washington had made Soviet aid to Cuba a sticking point in any decision to provide economic assistance to the Soviet Union.

In the past several years, Moscow has moved from trying to be a superpower with global responsibilities to a major power with national interests that emphasize crisis management and prevention in the Third World. A member of the Central Committee's International Department wrote in 1989 that, if the United States wanted to "waste its national resources" in the Third World—that is "its business," but that the Soviets should "exclude themselves" from the struggle in regions that have "no real meaning for our security."[18] As a result, Moscow is pursuing bilateral diplomacy with the United States and multilateral diplomacy at the United Nations to arrange for peacekeeping forces in flash point situations, national reconciliation governments, and mechanisms for preventing the proliferation of dual-purpose weapons.

Policy of Regional Stability

At the 27th party congress in 1986, Gorbachev stressed that the prevention of "international crises" was one of four factors in a "comprehensive system of international security."[19] He then pursued agreements to create a nuclear risk reduction center and prevent "dangerous military activities" between the Soviet Union and the United States. During the Persian Gulf crisis, Gorbachev emphasized the importance of diplomatic and political solutions and, in a conversation with Pope John Paul II, called for increased UN pressure on Saddam Hussein.[20] Soviet officials under Gorbachev stressed the importance of UN peacekeeping efforts, particularly the creation of a multilateral risk-reduction center and revival of the UN Military Staff Committee.

Many of these arrangements would be compatible with areas of conflict in the Third World and the Commonwealth of Independent States, particularly nonproliferation regimes and risk reduction centers. Hotlines would be useful for Indo-Pakistani and Greek-Turkish developments in view of the many military exercises and maneuvers in South Asia and the southern Mediterranean. The Cuban missile crisis teaches that negotiations and agreements can be arranged even in times of greatest peril; in the wake of the crisis, Moscow and Washington concluded a hot line agreement—the first bilateral crisis management measure—and a partial test ban treaty.

Since Gorbachev's call for greater UN participation in resolving crises in the Third World, Moscow has played a role in establishing five peacekeeping operations—in the border area between Iran and Iraq, good offices missions in Afghanistan and Pakistan, monitoring operations in Namibia, verification of Cuban withdrawal from Angola, and an observer force in Central America. In the 1990s, the UN will be playing a bigger role in the Persian Gulf and Southeast Asia, and could become involved in Kashmir and Cyprus as well.

All these actions are consistent with Russian efforts to prevent accidental war, which has been an interest of the Kremlin since the Cuban missile crisis. Russian officials have expressed their concern with the danger of war arising from technical malfunction, human error, political miscalculation, or unauthorized actions. Prior to the opening of strategic arms negotiations with the United States in 1969, foreign minister Andrei Gromyko warned of systems of command and control becoming "more autonomous of the people who create them" and that "governments must do everything in their power to be able to determine the course of events and not become captive to those events."[21]

Growing cooperation between Moscow and Washington is one of the major factors for the success of UN peacekeeping operations, but the two superpowers will ultimately have to turn their attention to resolving the financial and logistical problems associated with peacekeeping. Russian-U.S. cooperation has contributed to enforcing the consensus of the Security Council in the Persian Gulf, facilitating political resolutions in Namibia and Cambodia, monitoring troop withdrawals from Afghanistan and Angola, and returning to the *status quo ante* along the Iran-Iraq border. Without the consent of the parties involved, however, peacekeeping will be a temporary expedient, rather than a permanent solution.

A major test of Russian-U.S. cooperation in the 1990s will be the ability of the two countries to prevent future conflicts or the resumption of old ones. Aerial surveillance is always risky but could be applied when combatants have agreed to maintain a ceasefire or resolve their differences.[22] Russian and U.S. experts could play a role in imagery analysis for peace-keeping operations, with common assessments providing authoritative information in monitoring troop withdrawals and regional arms control measures.

For the first time, a reconnaissance system, a U.S.-piloted U-2, has been placed under full-time UN control to monitor Iraqi production and storage sites for weapons of mass destruction, including chemical and biological arms, nuclear bomb-making equipment, and ballistic missiles. Previously the U.S. had supplied information from its aircraft and satellites in response to Security Council Resolution 687, the cease-fire resolution that ended the gulf war, to ensure Iraqi compliance with the terms of the resolution. The use of the U-2, however, allows for complete photographic and intelligence data by UN inspection teams on a regular basis. The arrangement could not have been made without Russian compliance.

U-2 photography would be useful in monitoring the disposition of government and guerilla forces in Cambodia and Afghanistan, but it is not likely that these governments would agree to intrusive inspection of this type. Formal arrangements for the exchange of surveillance data could lead to discussion of regional risk reduction centers that would encourage Russian and U.S. cooperation in flash point situations. It is far less certain that India and Pakistan would allow monitoring of Kashmir or their ballistic missile programs.

The Russians thus far have not pursued Shevardnadze's call for a risk reduction center in the Middle East, but it could not have escaped Moscow's notice that, only several months after the foreign minister's remarks, India tested its first medium-range ballistic missile, adding a new dimension to a tense security situation in South Asia. The Russians are certain to return to the idea of such centers and presumably try to apply them to discussion of regional conflicts, proliferation, and terrorism. Russian-U.S. success in abolishing intermediate-range missile systems in 1987 and limiting conventional arms in Europe in 1990, along with intrusive on-site verification measures for both agreements, will contribute to the likelihood of a more substantive dialogue on the Third World in the 1990s.

Moscow could return to earlier talks on limiting Russian and U.S. weapons transfers to foreign countries. The Russians have reduced their arms deliveries to all major recipients in the Third World and, prior to Gorbachev's accession to power in 1985, linked the improvement of the "world situation" to the "elimination" of conflict in Asia, Africa, and Latin America.[23] Even Brezhnev acknowledged the need to manage superpower competition in the Third World and discuss international norms with specific application to Third World regions.[24]

Conflict Resolution on the Home Front

In any event, the disastrous Russian economic and ethnic situation assures that Moscow will continue to favor a major U.N. role in conflict resolution in the Third World to avoid friction with the West and demands on scarce resources. On his arrival in Spain in October 1990, Gorbachev described the changes in the USSR as the "beginning of chaos, as irreparable catastrophe."[25] Gross national product continues to decline, and there are shortages of bread, meat, and dairy products in major cities. The description of the economy by a leading Soviet economic expert will suffice: "The market has collapsed, the budget deficit is dreadful . . . monetary circulation and the financial system are on the brink of complete disaster."[26] Even if the agricultural situation improves, poor transportation and inadequate storage and processing facilities will hamper deliveries to urban areas.

The ruble, moreover, has become virtually worthless and, as a result, farmers and industrialists are refusing to sell their output to the central government. Rationed foods and goods are available only to residents, and the country is on the edge of hyperinflation. Scarce resources demand that Moscow continue to flood the international arena with arms control proposals to assure strategic stability between with the United States and regional security measures to avoid flash point situations in the Third World.

At the same time, political rivalries between Russian leaders as well as nationalist and separatist disputes between Russians and non-Slavic minorities demand predictability in the international arena and make large standing armies less relevant. In the wake of the coup attempt, the Yeltsin government is encountering renewed violence between Armenians and Azeris in the Caucasus, and friction between Russian minorities and other ethnic groups in the Ukraine and Kazakhstan. The non-Russian states are demanding their own armies or the establishment of a national guard, and the possibility of violence in several areas is likely in the near term. There was fighting between the Georgian militia and the Georgian national guard during the coup activity in August 1991. China and Iran are particularly concerned with fighting near their own borders in the Caucasus and Central Asia, where Beijing and Tehran have to deal with restive minorities in Sinkjiang and Azeribaijan, respectively.

At the European summit in November 1990, Gorbachev warned that "militant nationalism and mindless separatism can easily bring conflict and enmity, Balkanization and even, what is worse, the Lebanonization of different regions," which could "put a brake on European cooperation and contradict the European process."[27] Numerous republics have passed laws providing for alternative service to the armed forces and restricting draftees' duties to their homelands. Two years earlier at the United Nations, Gorbachev had warned that the "bell of regional conflict tolls for all of us." These statements represent an increasingly apocalypic assessment of Moscow's perception of its geopolitical environment and a reminder of its interest in conflict resolution.

The first major post-Communist attempt at conflict resolution at home took place in September 1991, when Armenia and Azerbaijan signed an agreement that arranged an immediate cease-fire and submitted a territorial dispute to peace negotiations. The agreement was mediated by the leaders of the two largest Soviet republics, Russian President Boris Yeltsin and Kazakhstan President Nursultan Nazarbayev. The dispute centers on a mountainous wedge of territory (Nagorno-Karabakh) in Azerbaijan that is populated by an Armenian majority, and the temporary breakthrough was Armenia's agreement to renounce any territorial claim over the province in return for greater self-rule by the Armenian majority. Similar to Soviet-U.S. efforts in Angola, Cambodia, and El Salvador, the agreement calls for an effort to disarm ethnic militia groups and the resettlement of hundreds of thousands of refugees.

Greater stability at home as well as improved relations with the United States, Western Europe, Japan, and South Korea could lead to the money, credits, and industrial expertise that the Russian economy desperately requires. On the eve of the Conference on Security and Cooperation in Europe in November 1990, Gorbachev travelled in Western Europe and raised several billion dollars in credits from France, German, Italy, and Spain. Following the Soviet support for the use of force in the Persian Gulf against Iraq, Saudi Arabia, Kuwait, and the United Arab Emirates agreed to provide more than three billion dollars in loans, the most dramatic sign of a turnabout in Moscow's relations with the Gulf states that began after Gorbachev's rise to power. In October 1990, Saudi Arabia became the last of the six Gulf states to establish diplomatic relations with Moscow. The Russians now receive more financial assistance from so-called Third World states than they extend to their former clients in the Third World.

Obstacles to Conflict Resolution

Conflict may be the rule in international affairs, but Russian-American cooperation has demonstrated the effectiveness of conflict resolution in Afghanistan, Angola, Cambodia, Nicaragua, and, most recently, the Persian Gulf. Earlier, the United States had demonstrated the effectiveness of negotiations at Camp David, Great Britain had used the Lancaster House talks to resolve the Rhodesian conflict, and Papal mediation solved the Beagle Channel dispute between Chile and Argentina. War weariness contributed to South African withdrawal from Angola, Vietnam from

Cambodia, and the USSR from Afghanistan. Military and political weariness played a role in the U.S. decision to stop funding the Contras in Nicaragua and the Sandinista decision to hold elections in Managua, despite the opposition of hard-liners in both the United States and Nicaragua.

Nevertheless, diplomatic negotiations will not succeed when regional differences persist, witness Israeli and Palestinian opposition to conciliation, and Indian and Pakistani intransigence over the Kashmir dispute. Greece and Turkey have established a diplomatic dialogue in recent years, but a solution to the Cyprus crisis eludes them. Efforts of outsiders have been frustrated in Northern Ireland, Lebanon, and South Africa. Gorbachev won a Nobel peace prize for his "strategic retreat" abroad, but he had to resort to military force in Armenia, Azerbaijan, and Georgia at home.

The greatest threat to Russian cooperation in conflict resolution in the Third World has been internal instability within the Commonwealth of Independent States. The botched coup attempt in August 1991 was the last in a series of events that threatened the pattern of responsible Russian behavior in the global arena since Gorbachev's accession to power in 1985. Foreign Minister Shevardnadze's resignation statement in December 1990 warned that there was opposition to Gorbachev's foreign policy, and Alexander Yakovlev's resignation on the eve of the coup warned of a Stalinist threat to the central leadership. Moscow managed to pursue conciliation in the Third World in the wake of Shevardnadze's resignation but, if the state of emergency that was imposed by the junta had been successful, it is unlikely that the United States would have been willing to continue business as usual with new Soviet government led by the chiefs of the three security services (the defense ministry, the KGB, and the interior ministry).

The coup failed within days, however, and Moscow sent immediate signals that it would continue to cooperate with the United States in the resolution of regional conflict. Moscow cooperated with Washington in establishing a U.N. observer team in El Salvador to monitor the human rights situation, even before the signing of a cease fire between the government and the guerrillas of the Farabundo Marti National Liberation Front. This marks the first time that a UN observer group has been created to verify compliance with a substantive accord, in this case on human rights, instead of a relatively more clear-cut effort such as verifying a cease fire or observing elections. More important, it marked the first time that the UN sent an observer mission into a war-torn country before a cease fire had been established.

The permanent members of the Security Council also moved the Cambodian government and the three resistance groups closer to a peace settlement in the wake of the failure of the coup in Moscow. A cease fire and an arms embargo had been in effect since the summer of 1991 but, following the coup attempt, the Cambodian factions agreed to ask the UN to send an observer group to Phnòm Penh to reinforce the cease fire and monitor the arms embargo. Significant reduction in Russian military assistance to Vietnam and Cambodia persuaded Moscow's two main Southeast Asian allies to support the idea of UN verification and monitoring. Differences remain over the disposition of the armed forces of the four Cambodian factions, including the disarming and demobilization of the armies, but the willingness of Moscow and Beijing to pursue a stable political environment in Southeast Asia bodes well for prospects for a settlement in Cambodia.

One month after the abortive coup, the U.S. and the Soviet Union took steps to resolve three longstanding regional disputes in Afghanistan, Cuba, and El Salvador. Secretary of State Baker and his new counterpart, Foreign Minister Boris Pankin, read a joint statement on September 13, 1991, declaring an end to all arms sales to combatants in Afghanistan and agreeing not to step up current arms shipments to their respective Afghan allies.[28] The two sides had been negotiating such an agreement for more than two years, but there were differences over the nature of elections and a new government in Kabul. Moscow and Washington will turn to the United Nations for resolution of the political issues, particularly the creation of an interim transition commission to manage the electoral process.

Early in September, Gorbachev announced that Moscow would sever its military ties to Cuba, including the withdrawal of a combat brigade and military advisers, approximately 4,000 forces.[29] Moscow already had suspended military shipments to Cuba and significantly reduced economic assistance, including the reduction of oil deliveries. It is not certain that the Russians will evacuate Lourdes, an electronic monitoring facility near Havana that is Moscow's largest and most sophisticated spy station outside its borders. Lourdes is staffed by more than 2,000 technicians and monitors U.S. naval and military maneuvers in the United States as well as U.S. military, space, and domestic communications.

The signing of a major security agreement between the Salvadoran government and guerrilla leaders in late September removed one more source of friction between Moscow and Washington. For the past two years, the U.S. and the Soviets had been pressing the two sides to enter such an agreement, thus ending a war that began in the late 1970s and was responsible for more than 75,000 fatalities. The agreement will reduce the size of the armed forces and allow the guerrillas to buy and remain on land they have occupied for years. Distrust remains between the two sides, and the conflict may be far from over, but the U.S. will no longer have concerns over the smuggling of Soviet arms through Nicaragua to Salvadoran rebels.

Ironically, the Persian Gulf crisis appears to have been the major turning point in the resolution of regional crises. Since the Gulf war, the U.S. and European states have intervened in Iraq to help the Kurds, U.S. diplomats helped to wind up Ethiopia's civil war, Soviet and U.S. officials contributed to diplomatic successes in Cambodia and El Salvador, and European soldiers monitored a tense situation in Zaire. Moscow and Washington also broke a major stalemate in Afghanistan, and the Russians continue their troop withdrawal from Cuba.

Just as the Cuban missile crisis in 1962 convinced the superpowers that it was necessary to get the "nuclear genie back in the bottle," Iraq's invasion of Kuwait may revive the notion of a collective security regime and open a window of opportunity for the United Nations to create such a regime. It is no accident of history that, in the wake of the Cuban missile crisis, the United States and the Soviet Union signed the Partial Test Ban and Hot Line agreements. Soviet political commentator Fyodor Burlatsky remarked that the Cuban missile crisis was a "bad thing with a very good result . . . the first step toward new thinking about each other." The Persian Gulf crisis will mark a contribution toward not only crisis resolution, but crisis prevention, if Third World leaders with global ambitions realize that a new era of Russian-American cooperation will limit the opportunities for threatening regional stability.

Notes

1. Thomas L. Friedman, "How U.S. Won Support to Use Mideast Forces, *The New York Times,* December 2, 1990, p. 1. Soviet Presidential adviser Yevgeny Primakov, an expert on the Middle East, favors a diplomatic solution that includes giving Iraq control over some Kuwaiti oil and territory, an international conference on the Arab-Israeli conflict, Israeli signing of the nonproliferation treaty, and a Soviet-U.S. guarantee of Israeli borders.

2. David Hoffman, "U.S. Carried Out Intense Diplomacy for U.N. Measures," *The Washington Post,* December 2, 1990, p. 1.

3. Clifford Krauss, "U.S. and Soviets Jointly Urge Settlement in Salvador, *The New York Times,* October 19, 1990, p. 3.

4. *Pravda,* September 7, 1986, p. 5.

5. *TASS,* October 31, 1988.

6. *The Washington Post,* March 5, 1989, p. 17.

7. Major General Vadim Makarevsky, "The Threat from the South," *New Times,* August 21–27, 1990, p. 12.

8. Soviet payment of past dues and peacekeeping assessments in 1987 forced the U.S. to begin paying back dues resulting from a partial boycott begun in 1985. The Unites States began payments in 1989, reducing its arrears from almost $1 billion to $300 million by 1991.

9. Clyde Haberman, "Gorbachev is Firm on Gulf Solution," *The New York Times,* Novdember 19, 1990, p. 18.

10. Clifford Krauss, "U.S. Aides Meeting Foes in Ethiopia, *The New York Times,* October 24, 1990, p. 1.

11. Paul Lewis, "Ethiopian Combatants Agree to Open Port to Food, *The New York Times,* November 25, 1990, p. 6.

12. *The Washington Post,* October 15, 1991, p. 11.

13. "When Bears Sniff Chrysantheums," *The Economist,* September 15, 1990, p. 19.

14. W. Raymond Duncan and Carolyn McGiffert Ekedahl, *Moscow and the Third World Under Gorbachev* (Boulder: Westview Press, 1990), pp. 80–81.

15. *The New York Times,* November 21, 1990, p. 3.

16. "Ethiopia Said Willing to Seek Peace," *Washington Post,* November 15, 1990, p. 27.

17. Andrei Kozyrev, "Trust and Balance of Interests," *Mezhdunarodnaya Zhizn,* October, 1988, p. 117. (Kozyrev is director of the Foreign Ministry's international organization division.)

18. Igor Malashenko, *Kommunist,* September 1989, p. 89.

19. ("The Documentary Record of the 27th Congress of the CPSU: Address by General Secretary Gorbachev.") *Current Digest of the Soviet Press,* March 1986.

20. Clyde Haberman, "Gorbachev is Firm on Gulf Solution," *The New York Times,* November 19, 1990, p. 13.

21. "Session of the Supreme Soviet of the USSR: Aspects of the International Situation and the Foreign Policy of the Soviet Union, Report by Deputy A.A. Gromyko, USSR Minister of Foreign Affairs," *Pravda,* July 11, 1969, p. 3.

22. A Syrian anti-aircraft battery shot down a UN plane carrying peacekeepers in 1974. See John Mackinlay, *The Peacekeepers: An Assessment of Peacekeeping Operations at the Arab-Israel Interface*
(London: Unwin Hyman, 1989), p. 143.

23. *Pravda,* January 7, 1983, p. 5. (Political Declaration of the Warsaw Pact.)

24. *Pravda,* April 28, 1981, p. 5. (Brezhnev speech in honor of visiting Libyan leader Qadhafi.)

25. *International Herald Tribue,* October 27, 1990, p. 3.

26. *The New York Times,* November 18, 1990, p. 11.

27. *The New York Times,* November 20, 1990, p. 17.

28. *The Washington Post,* September 14, 1991, p. 1, "U.S., Soviets Agree to Halt Arms to Combatants in Afghanistan" by David Hoffman.

29. *The Washington Post,* September 12, 1991, p. 1.

About the Editor and Contributors

Peter Clement is senior analyst in the Office of Soviet Analysis at the Central Intelligence Agency. He has written several articles on Soviet foreign policy and most recently taught at the University of Maryland. He is currently working on a monograph regarding the politics of political union in the Soviet Union.

W. Raymond Duncan is Distinguished Teaching Professor at the State University of New York–Brockport and previously served as scholar-in-residence at the Central Intelligence Agency. He has written several books and articles on Soviet policy in Latin America. Most recently, he coauthored *Moscow and the Third World Under Gorbachev* (Westview, 1990).

Carolyn McGiffert Ekedahl is diplomatic associate at the Institute for Diplomatic Studies, School of Foreign Service–Georgetown University. She has been senior analyst in Soviet Studies at the Central Intelligence Agency and senior fellow at the Atlantic Council. Most recently, she coauthored *Moscow and the Third World Under Gorbachev* (Westview, 1990).

Melvin A. Goodman is professor of international security studies at the National War College in Washington, D.C. and has served as senior analyst for Soviet affairs for both the Central Intelligence Agency and the Department of State. He has published articles in *Middle East Journal, Journal of Northeast Asian Studies* and *International Journal* and has contributed chapters to several books on the Soviet Union. His most recent book is *Gorbachev's Retreat: The Third World* (1991).

Daniel S. Papp is professor of international affairs and director of the School of Social Sciences at Georgia Tech. He has published over forty articles on various issues concerning U.S. and Soviet foreign and defense policies and is chairperson of the American-Soviet section of the International Studies Association. He edited Dean Rusk's, *As I Saw It* (1990).

Sheldon W. Simon is professor of political science and faculty associate of the Center for Asian Studies at Arizona State University. He is author or editor of six books and seventy research articles and book chapters. His most recent book is *The Future of Asian-Pacific Security Collaboration* (1988).

Index